BLAZING EYE SEES ALL

BLAZING EYE SEES ALL

LOVE HAS WON, FALSE PROPHETS, AND THE FEVER DREAM OF THE AMERICAN NEW AGE

LEAH SOTTILE

GRAND
CENTRAL

NEW YORK BOSTON

Grand Central Publishing
Hachette Book Group
1290 Avenue of the Americas, New York, NY 10104
grandcentralpublishing.com
@grandcentralpub

First Edition: March 2025

Grand Central Publishing is a division of Hachette Book Group, Inc. The Grand Central Publishing name and logo is a registered trademark of Hachette Book Group, Inc.

The publisher is not responsible for websites (or their content) that are not owned by the publisher.

The Hachette Speakers Bureau provides a wide range of authors for speaking events. To find out more, go to hachettespeakersbureau.com or email HachetteSpeakers@hbgusa.com.

Grand Central Publishing books may be purchased in bulk for business, educational, or promotional use. For information, please contact your local bookseller or the Hachette Book Group Special Markets Department at special.markets@hbgusa.com.

Print book interior design by Marie Mundaca

Library of Congress Cataloging-in-Publication Data

Names: Sottile, Leah, author.
Title: Blazing eye sees all : love has won, false prophets and the fever dream of the American new age / Leah Sottile.
Description: New York : Grand Central Publishing, [2025]
Identifiers: LCCN 2024039451 | ISBN 9781538742600 (hardcover) | ISBN 9781538742624 (ebook)
Subjects: LCSH: New Age movement—United States. | Spirituality—United States.
Classification: LCC BP605.N48 S6585 2025 | DDC 299/.930973—dc23/eng/20241210
LC record available at https://lccn.loc.gov/2024039451

ISBNs: 9781538742600 (hardcover), 9781538742624 (ebook)

Printed in the United States of America

LSC-C

Printing 1, 2024

For Joe, who fire walks with me

Any primatologist knows, though, that to decipher a dominance hierarchy, you don't watch for aggression in the dominants. You look for signs of fear in the subordinates.

—Alison Jolly, Lords and Lemurs

As a woman I was taught to always be hungry.
Women are well-acquainted with thirst.
Yeah, we could eat just about anything.
We might even eat your hate up like love.

—Bikini Kill

PART I

THE TEN OF SWORDS

1.

Two hundred million years ago, the Earth was like a house with all of its furniture piled into one corner. The seven continents of our planet were, back then, just one. Australia was shoved into Antarctica; India flopped nearby. South America fit into the elbow crook of Africa, and the land that would one day become the island of Madagascar was trapped in the midst of it all.

The continental plates that act as the foundation of the world began to move, as they are wont to do. As one dragged over another, volcanic magma burbled up from the planet's angry core, rising toward the Earth's surface, searing apart that giant mass of land into jagged new pieces. Those pieces drifted. For eons upon eons upon eons, they kept moving as the planet underwent a great reorganization.

As everything drifted, Madagascar, a wisp of land, spun like a feather in the wind until it settled, finally, 250 miles off the eastern coast of Africa.

Millions more years passed.

In the 1860s a British zoologist named Philip Lutley Sclater sat down at his desk to write an essay about lemurs—those strange, curious-eyed primates. He attempted to explain something that had until that point been a curiosity to men like him: men of answers, men of science.

Sclater was a lawyer and, in the zoological world, an ornithologist mostly—a bird man. But in 1864, he published his essay about lemurs in a small academic journal. At that point, he wrote, the animals primarily lived on the island of Madagascar, but lemur fossils had been unearthed in India as well. India but not Africa. This was a strange mystery: How could the same species be found in two places with a wide, gaping ocean between them, but not across the narrow 250-mile-wide channel that separated the African island from the African continent?

Sclater had a theory. In his essay, he posited that a massive continent had once stretched between Madagascar and India. And that continent had simply vanished. He said lemurs were a relic of this lost world, a living connection to it.

"I should propose the name Lemuria!" Sclater declared.

And with that, a place was born.

In one way, Sclater's story had everything to do with the planet's slow eternal rearrangement. And yet he had no idea that the land had been forever roaming. Scientists had not yet published findings about continental drift, and so Sclater did not know that the Earth was slowly shifting underneath his feet as he came up with this idea of a lost place.

Late in his life, Sclater would hedge on his lost-land theory, characterizing the idea as "hypothetical." But by then, some people had already taken the idea of Lemuria and run with it. An Australian science journal discussed it not as theory but fact. Writers composed speculative stories about Lemurians—what they might have looked like, how they spoke, whether or not they kept pets. When Sclater died in 1913, it was his largest legacy—the story of a place that was never a place called Lemuria.

All the while, the Earth kept moving.

4

2.

From the front window of a yellow house in the remote southern Colorado desert, purple twinkle lights flickered, pulsed, throbbed like tiny sirens in the dark.

It was just before midnight on April 28, 2021, when the sound of tires crunched against the gravel driveway of 4 Alcedo Court as a fleet of law enforcement vehicles pulled in.

The moon was full. A dog barked at their arrival.

The deputies had come to see Mother.

A thin man with a closely trimmed black beard and long straight hair met them at the front door. The Saguache County officers knew by then that people called this man Father, or Father God. His legal name was Jason Castillo. Though it was late, he was dressed in a long-sleeved white shirt tucked into jeans, which were held up on his gaunt frame with a black leather belt. The man greeted them, politely folding his hands in front of his body. One officer asked Jason how many people were inside the house. "Five beings and a child," he said. "And my wife."

The officer said they had a warrant to search the property, and to do a welfare check on the child. And they wanted to see Mother. He nodded.

"Mother is in rest," he said. "She has rested."

Inside, at the center of the house, was a large living room painted yellow, decorated in a style one might encounter at an organic food co-op, or a children's classroom. Mandalas and pink-petaled flowers were drawn on the walls. Across the ceiling, a rainbow arched from one fluffy white cloud to another. A painting depicted the Earth with a pulsing rainbow heart; "Starship," it read.

Twinkle lights blinked from every wall and corner, garlands of pink outlined the room, and strands of purple were laid across the back of a couch. A poster-sized photograph of a thin white woman with her eyes closed and hands clasped in prayer hung on one wall, a contented smile spread across her face. This was the one they called Mother God, and she too was outlined in lights.

The people who lived there were part of a spiritual group Mother deemed "Love Has Won," and they had come from around the world to her side. They believed themselves to be a glowing violet light in a world of darkness, assisting humankind into a higher spiritual dimension. This ascent was imminent. Mother had told them so.

Over time, she had also taught them that she had not only created the Earth and every being on it, but that she *was* the Earth. She was "the Prime Source Creator." She was everything—the feminine life force from which all creation had been birthed, one half of a "twin flame" with a masculine energy called Father God, the man at the door. Mother God—Mom, as her acolytes more often referred to her—was power incarnate. Father acted as a disciplinarian and guard but was otherwise ancillary, a shoulder for Mother God to lean on when the burden of creating everything, and being everything, became too painful to bear alone.

Perhaps more important than any other single idea collectively held by the people of Love Has Won was their belief that Mother God was a reincarnated being who once ruled as queen of a continent called

Lemuria. According to Mother, Lemuria had been a highly advanced ancient fifth-dimensional civilization of twinkling cities and "crystal technology." About 27,000 years ago, the Lemurians had mastered true enlightenment before being destroyed.

Lemuria had defended itself in a great battle with a greedy, violent adversary called Atlantis. During the war, both civilizations had been destroyed and sunk to the bottom of the oceans, never to be seen again. But amid all the chaos, Mother God ascended from the rubble unharmed. Other Lemurians escaped as well but were left in a state of permanent amnesia. "They could no longer remember their true origin, their God selves, or their connection to the Source," a Love Has Won follower named Archeia Aurora wrote in a book about Mother God's teachings.

When Atlantis toppled Lemuria, it was the first shot fired in a thousands-year spiritual battle between the dark and the light.

By 2021, the people who followed Mother believed they were fighting beside her on the front lines of this war. She was battling for the soul of humanity, angling to bring all of humankind toward light and salvation. The enemy now, she told her people, were soulless beings with dark powers called "the Anunnaki." The Anunnaki had shrouded humanity in lies, hypnotizing people into thinking lies were truths and truths were lies. Chief among the Anunnaki's great betrayals had been making humanity believe that Jesus had been a man. By Mother God's teachings, Jesus was a woman.

And she would know. Mother God had actually been Jesus. It was one of her past lives, and she had reincarnated 534 times. She had been the queen of Lemuria, but also said she had lived as Cleopatra and Joan of Arc and Pocahontas and Marilyn Monroe. Among others.

As the centuries passed in this thousands-year war, the Anunnaki had grown and multiplied, breeding new generations of villainous foot soldiers to carry out its dark bidding. The Illuminati, which Mother God said were reptilian hybrid people, and the Cabal—puppet-like minions whose strings were held by the Anunnaki—were all fighting on the side of darkness. Their mission was "domination of the planet and complete enslavement of humanity," Aurora wrote. Mother God was the only thing standing in their way, a bulwark blinding the forces of darkness with her goodness and light, shielding humanity from peril.

According to her followers, just before Mother's final human form manifested on Earth in Kansas in 1975, she had come face-to-face with the leaders of the Cabal and issued them an ultimatum. It was time for her to take her planet back. The Cabal said they would never surrender.

"She told them," Aurora wrote, "to bring it on."

3.

Every year since 2013, California's Chapman University has organized a bizarre but prescient study called the "Survey of American Fears." Over the years, the survey has proved that the things Americans feared most were forces beyond their control. They feared becoming collateral damage in global conflicts, withering from biological weapons, or being reduced to ash by a nuke. They feared their lives being brushed aside like pencil eraser remnants by the hands of the powerful or insane. Maybe Russia would flatten the country in a flash of light and impulse. Or North Korea. Or Iran. People feared world war, even though most living Americans couldn't recall the last one when it had been America that did something powerful and insane by dropping bombs over Hiroshima and Nagasaki, Japan, that killed around 200,000 civilians.

People feared poisoned drinking water. They feared "corrupt government officials." The people who took the Chapman survey seemed to be afraid of everything that was currently happening. They were afraid to die right now and yet also afraid to be alive.

People were also afraid of the Earth itself. Wildfires consumed

California. In Lahaina, Maui, people ran into the ocean to escape
flames. Floodwaters rushed into New York City. Hurricanes pum-
meled; heat waves crushed. Texas got snow and the ocean waters
around Florida felt hot. Ancient glaciers became puddles on mountain-
sides. The climate was warming because of human behavior, and now
we feared what we had done. When we looked into the mirror, the
reflection looking back terrified us.

You couldn't really blame anyone for being afraid. In 2022, in the
midst of the global COVID-19 pandemic, Russia invaded Ukraine at
the orders of President Vladimir Putin, who trafficked disinformation
that the adjacent country needed to be demilitarized and "denazified,"
when it seemed plainly clear he was a conqueror who only wanted
more territory. By October 2023, another violent conflict was raging
around the Gaza Strip. Months later, more than 34,000 Palestinians
were dead. Images of missiles dropping from the sky, bloodied children, and bombed-out hospitals were nightly news. People were dying
everywhere anyway, and still humans found a way to create new ways
to kill each other.

Meanwhile, during the long career of President Donald Trump,
who has had dowsed the darkest undercurrents of Americanism during
two terms, hate crimes and extremism also became a regular feature
of the news cycle. A mob of his supporters stormed the U.S. Capitol
on January 6, 2021, in an attempt to prevent the 2020 presidential election from being certified, sending congressmen fleeing into catacombs.
Women's rights were rolled back when the U.S. Supreme Court over-
turned *Roe v. Wade*, the fifty-two-year-old court decision that allowed
women the constitutional right to seek abortions. "Corrupt government officials top the list of fears once again!" Chapman's 2023 survey
exclaimed.

At times, it felt like if you strained hard enough to hear, you'd catch
a low tone chiming for the death of all hope. The world had become
trapped inside its collective grief, like the only card in humanity's tarot
deck was one of utter vanquishment, the Ten of Swords, where a man

lay dead on the ground with ten blades stabbed through his back. The future has always been unclear, but maybe it was the current inability to tune the horrors of the world out for even a second that kept people suspended in a state of permanent fear.

The Chapman surveys also revealed another part of America's strange psyche: spiritual beliefs that weren't quite fears per se, but also weren't quite *not* fears either. From 2016 to 2018, the university's team released a list of paranormal beliefs that had been expressed by the more than 1,100 adults who were surveyed. Roughly half said they believed houses could be haunted by spiritual entities. About 20 percent believed that Bigfoot invisibly stalked forests, and nearly a third expressed a belief that aliens hovered above, watching us.

More than half of people expressed sincere beliefs that "ancient, advanced civilizations, such as Atlantis, once existed"—a data point that increased over time. More and more, people genuinely believed entire places had simply slipped away.

This belief, though, was not exactly a fear. This one felt more like a hope.

For centuries, humans have woven tales of spectacular and imaginary civilizations: lost golden cities, fabled lands, whole continents displaced by our vast and violent oceans. The seafloor, to those who believe, is pocked like Braille, telling a silent story of everything our world once was. Belief is at the heart of humans' fascination with lost places—in order to see them, you must first believe they are there. Throughout history, people have expressed a feeling of being lost, that we need to search for our real home to better understand ourselves.

Around the year 1136, the cleric Geoffrey of Monmouth wrote about a fabled land called Avalon in his *Historia Regum Brittaniae*. Today, people are drawn to Glastonbury Tor, a rock formation in England, believing it to be the site of the long-lost location of so much heroism.

In 1938, Nazi leader Heinrich Himmler orchestrated an expedition to Tibet in search of a mythical refuge called Shambhala in the Himalayas. Himmler, and other leading Nazis at the time, believed it was where an Aryan master race with magical powers fled after a great catastrophe destroyed their homeland, and where they potentially had secreted away sacred documents and artifacts, like the Ark of the Covenant. They found no mythical Aryans, no prized treasures. However, in the 1980s, this quest was closely tapped for the plot of the first Indiana Jones movie, *Raiders of the Lost Ark*.

And then there's Atlantis, the "mother" of all lost places, as Kenneth Feder, an archaeologist at Central Connecticut State University, called it in his *Frauds, Myths, and Mysteries: Science and Pseudoscience in Archaeology*. Atlantis is a fictional place with an origin story that is "essentially an Ancient Greek version of *Star Wars*," he wrote.

The story is attributed to the Greek philosopher Plato, who in the fourth century BC wrote thirty-five *Dialogues*: stories in which two characters engage in good-spirited argument over big moral questions. In a pair of *Dialogues*, Plato told the tale of a massive island called Atlantis inhabited by "a confederation of kings, of great and marvelous power" that, over time, became driven by avarice and a need for more territory. A great war was sparked by this building greed, with Atlantis attempting to topple the humble but courageous Athens through a naval attack and failing. The war was watched with disbelief by the gods perched atop Mount Olympus, and Poseidon, the god of the sea, was so angered by the Atlanteans' behavior, he shook the continent with an earthquake so powerful, the civilization was subsumed by the ocean.

Because Plato—of all people—birthed the story of Atlantis, it has enjoyed an air of credibility that few other lost place tales can claim. "The idea is that we should use the story to examine our ideas of government and power," wrote Julia Annas, a Plato scholar and professor emeritus in the philosophy department at the University of Arizona, in a 2003 book called *Plato: A Very Short Introduction*. "We have missed the point if instead of thinking about these issues we go off exploring the seabed." But believers in Atlantis who think it is a real place will often cite the fact that Plato, one of history's foremost thinkers, spoke of it as a world that was here, then was not here. For centuries, people have sought to find it.

"If 9,000 years from now people ask whether the *Star Wars* saga is actual history, not fiction, it would not be too different from our suggesting today that Plato's story of Atlantis really happened," Feder wrote. "In trying to convey a rather simple message, one of the great rational minds of the ancient world produced fodder for the fantasies of some of the less-than-great, non-rational minds of the modern world."

Over time, the suggested locations of Atlantis have spanned most of the globe. Sometimes it was near Antarctica, other times the Mediterranean. In 1882, a former member of the U.S. House of Representatives named Ignatius Donnelly wrote a book called *Atlantis: The Antediluvian World*, in which he argued that Atlantis had been located in the Atlantic Ocean and was the place from which modern civilization sprung. He believed that the Garden of Eden had been located there, and that it gave way to the Egyptian civilization. To Donnelly, Atlantis was the embodiment of human perfection, and showed how far we had fallen.

The story has remained a fascination—the subject of animated films, more than one television series, and a continual stream of new books. An Atlantis museum in Greece offers holograms of Plato and a 3D experience of the "earthquake" it says destroyed the place.

In some New Age circles, Atlantis is discussed in cautionary terms: a warning of what will befall those overcome by sin. To some, it is a literal place—flawed, but better than this modern world.

If Atlantis is a morality tale that warns, Lemuria is an allegory that inspires: a sunken not-place that speaks to the act of believing itself.

Like other lost lands, the story of Lemuria has been carried forward in time by believers over multiple generations, handed off like a baton from one runner to the next. Each carrier's motivation to keep Lemuria alive has been slightly different, and with each pass, the tale gains new detail and depth.

When Philip Lutley Sclater published his essay about lemurs, lost continent theories were becoming a fad among biologists and natural-ists to explain species distribution. So common and numerous were lost land theories that a young Charles Darwin penned letters to friends and colleagues about his annoyance with these ideas: "It is really dis-gusting and humiliating to see directly opposite conclusions drawn from the same facts," Darwin wrote in 1855. "My blood gets hot with passion & runs cold alternately at the geological strides which many of your disciples are taking," he complained to a mentor in another letter.

"Why not extend a continent to every island in the Pacific & Atlan-tic oceans!" he continued. "And all this within the existence of recent species!" Darwin joked that there was a region of hell reserved specif-ically for geologists who resorted to such laziness. Others agreed. The naturalist Alfred Russel Wallace lambasted lost continent theories as only interesting to "absolutely unscientific" people.

Even as science progressed in the opposite direction, Sclater's Lemu-ria became a vessel to be filled. By the 1880s, the story was living a life of its own. Lemuria was floated by scientists as a counter-narrative to Darwin's publication of *On the Origin of Species*, seen as radical and out-rageous among polygenists who believed each race had evolved sepa-rately on their own segregated tracks. Darwin, who was a monogenist, theorized that all people had descended from a common ancestor.

In 1868, a white-bearded German zoologist named Ernst Haeckel published his first version of *The History of Creation*, in which he unveiled an elaborate evolutionary counter-theory to Darwin, in which Lemu-ria was believed to be "the possible cradle of the human race" and a "paradise." Haeckel's theory was that there were a dozen separate human races, of which whites were the most superior. "The Caucasian, or Mediterranean man," he wrote, "has from time immemorial been placed at the head of all the races of men, as the most highly developed and perfect." He also advocated for the killing of those with mental ill-ness or physical disabilities. It should come as no surprise that the Nazis were appreciative of Haeckel's theories and later put his ideas of eugen-ics into practice.

Sumathi Ramaswamy, a Duke University historian, argued in her book *The Lost Land of Lemuria: Fabulous Geographies, Catastrophic Histories* that Haeckel exploited Sclater's Lemuria theory as a device to justify his own scientific racism. He "wrests Lemuria from the world of zoo-geography," she wrote, and firmly placed it in the story of mankind's origins, providing a new kind of "missing link" that proved his argument of "how much farther the white European had progressed beyond his less-fortunate Black brethren."

But by 1885, Lemuria was falling apart. That year, the Austrian geologist Eduard Suess published *The Face of the Earth*, which introduced the world to the megacontinents Pangaea and Gondwanaland. In 1915, the German meteorologist Alfred Wegener delivered a crushing blow to Lemuria, Atlantis, and all sunken continents when he published *The Origin of Continents and Oceans*, discussing continental drift. Billions of years ago the supercontinents had slowly split into pieces, which migrated around the surface of the planet and eventually formed the geography we know today.

Continental drift "wipes out straightaway all the mythical lands... that have been conjured up to explain the life-distribution of the earth," wrote geologist Alexander du Toit.

It also gave an answer to the question of why similar rocks or fossils, for example, might be found on distant continents with vast oceans between them. And so a new question formed: How did they drift apart in the first place?

By the 1950s, the answer was becoming clearer. As the seafloors of the planet were mapped using sonar technology developed during World War II, oceanographic cartographers realized they were much more complicated than previously thought. "It was the first time we ever actually saw giant mountain ranges and features on the seafloor," Renee Love, a paleontologist at the University of Idaho, said. "Before then everyone thought the seafloor was basically flat."

The 25,000-mile-long Mid-Atlantic Ridge was mapped in the 1950s, and it affirmed what Wegener had argued with his continental drift theory: the massive ridge marked the edge of several of the world's tectonic plates. "You could think of the Earth as like a broken eggshell," Love said, "and that broken eggshell is moving around and the plates are colliding into each other, pushing into each other."

All that motion is its own kind of havoc, born of convection—the heat at the Earth's center sent plates crashing into each other, or under each other, or lifting high into the air to create mountains. As land lifts, it erodes. Land can drop, too, but not entire continents. The Great Basin of Nevada is an example of a part of a plate that dropped during the process of subsidence, or the Hawaiian island chain, where islands have dropped below sea level.

"I know there's a big conversation of 'will California ever drop into the ocean?' And the answer is definitely not," Love said. Even the most cataclysmic of earthquakes wouldn't make that happen. "Plates will move it around and change it, but something isn't dropped down so far where all of a sudden it's lost, and it disappears."

But by the time plate tectonics came around, the story of Lemuria was too big to put back into the bottle. It was "a place-world that is 'neither entirely "real," nor entirely "unreal,"' but is located somewhere indeterminately between the two," Ramaswamy wrote.

Each time the story was repeated, it was given more detail. Boundaries had been drawn, locations mapped. People mused what Lemurians might have looked like, what their values had been. Some said they had third eyes and blue skin.

On the long-running conspiracy theory radio show *Coast to Coast AM*, one guest told host George Noory that his guardian angels had bestowed upon him the true story of Atlantis, and that it was actually subsumed by the ocean during a volcano eruption. Lemuria, he said, sunk itself with a bomb. During yet another episode, a hypnotherapist said Atlantis and Lemuria actually crumbled because of volcanic gases. An "alternative historian" told the host that Atlantis was not in the Mediterranean or the Atlantic, but Appalachia.

And yet on TikTok a user proclaimed Atlantis had been found in the desert of Africa, in a *no-duh* tone that suggested this was both boring and obvious. A woman with the username goldenheartempress laid out "five signs you've had a past life in Lemuria": (1) You enjoy sustainable living; (2) You don't like technology; (3) You like music; (4) You know how to be in "divine flow"; and (5) "You feel in your bones that new earth can exist." A blonde user called superstarseed with 25,000 followers claimed to speak Lemurian. "I speak this language along with six others and here is what it sounds like . . . *ehn-a-mah-ah, oh-ma-edda-edda-edda. Ah-mah-ah.*"

On her own TikTok account, Holly Madison, the longtime partner of *Playboy*'s Hugh Hefner, held up a long clear crystal to the camera. "This is a Lemurian crystal," she said. "The legend is the ancient people of Lemuria kept records in their crystals, and we just don't know how to access it. Like finding a DVD without a player."

"In what does the peculiar value of religious ideas lie?" the Austrian psychoanalyst Sigmund Freud asked in his 1927 book *The Future of an Illusion*. He wrote that spirituality acts as a salve that can soothe fearful humans in the face of things that "seem to mock at all human control," noting that everywhere—in society and in nature—there seemed to be constant reminders of our mortality. If earthquakes or floods or storms or diseases weren't enough to underscore our helplessness, there was "the painful riddle of death, against which no medicine has yet been found, nor probably will be."

All this roiling chaos, he explained, caused humans to cling to religion, "born from man's need to make his helplessness tolerable."

By 2020, during extended periods of lockdown amid the earliest days of COVID, spirituality seemed to be flourishing and was particularly visible on social media platforms like Facebook, Instagram, and TikTok. People sold tarot cards and crystals; self-help gurus offered coaching and meditation workshops. It seemed like a fresh surge of the New Age—an umbrella term for alternative spiritual ideas and practices popularized in the 1970s and 1980s that focused on self-improvement and healing but were not derived from any single religious tradition. This time, the New Age was online. It was young, but also old. It was a *New* New Age trying to make all our helplessness tolerable.

"New Age gives you this sense of 'I can do something about this,' either by narrowing your view to literally just yourself and your emotional responses, or by giving you this cosmic sense of you've got this higher purpose," said Susannah Crockford, an anthropology lecturer at the University of Exeter. "People got stuck inside for a really long time." The internet offered relief and connection.

The term "New Age" (often used interchangeably with "metaphysical") is literal; historically, New Age seekers share an idea that a new era of human history, and consciousness, is imminent—that if we can just push through the current darkness, there is light ahead. Relief. "There's a belief in progress and that humans, by striving to achieve a higher state of consciousness, are perhaps guided by some higher entity," said Catherine Wessinger, a professor of history of religions at Loyola University New Orleans. But aside from that one belief, the New Age movement is generally "broad and diffuse," Wessinger said. It sprung from many people, many schools of thought, many varying spiritual traditions from around the world.

"It does have its place in American religious history, but it's very different because it's decentralized," said Philip Deslippe, a historian of American religion. "There's no metaphysical church. There's no pope of the New Age."

Whereas in more traditional religious paths, like Catholicism or Islam, where believers take direction from ordained leaders, New Age adherents put stock in their own kinds of leaders: psychics, seers, mediums, spiritual coaches. Beliefs in reincarnation and paranormal phenomena are common, but not required. Nothing is required. There is much talk of science throughout New Age circles, but, simultaneously, just as much pseudoscience masquerading as science. Wisdom can be found in dreams, in stars, in astrological signs, in charts mapping where the sun and moon and stars were at the time of one's birth. Crystals are treated like mystical penicillin, deployed for healing and balance, to de-stress, to calm, to purify. People speak in a language of energy and "vibes": good energy, bad energy, positive energy, energetic vibrations, negative energy to be healed. It's all a part of the wide New Age menu, options from which people can pick and choose to customize their own belief system.

Power is held by those who claim it. In New Age culture, anyone can self-profess their unique abilities. "You can have powers, you can be a healer," said Deslippe. "It really is about specialness." Some declare their ability to access ancient wisdom. Few, if any, give their powers or knowledge away for free.

Scholars differ on who exactly introduced New Age ideas to America. Many agree that its shared ideology of higher consciousness and self-improvement began mainstreaming in America at the moment in 1952 when a preacher named Norman Vincent Peale published a book titled *The Power of Positive Thinking*. Peale, often nicknamed "God's salesman," wrote of vanquishing "inadequacy attitudes" and "fear thoughts." The path to personal success was simple, he explained: picture yourself succeeding and choose positive thoughts over negative ones. This message went viral. The book sold over two million copies in three years and remained on the *New York Times* Best Seller list for 186 weeks. (President Trump has on numerous occasions said that Peale was hugely influential on him.)

In many ways, *The Power of Positive Thinking* was building on a nineteenth-century spiritual movement called "New Thought," which taught adherents that with the adoption of a positive mindset, disease could be cured and material wealth found.

By midcentury, seeking became a counterculture all its own in America. A movement of flower children spouting messages of peace and love flourished among young Americans—a counterpoint to the seemingly never-ending Vietnam War. New Age ideas found a foothold in the wider culture. Sociologists wrote that the phenomenon seemed to provide young people an alternative religious path to the more stringent spiritualities practiced by their parents. And yet, some leaders in New Age culture were simply cherry-picking ideas from world religions, repackaging them and offering them as a buffet of new ideas to eager seekers.

Another offshoot of New Thought, called the "human potential movement," began to thrive, teaching that by simply realizing our fullest potential, we will be happier and thus society will be better off. The ideas were embraced by the writer Aldous Huxley and the Beatles' George Harrison, and seemed to take Peale's ideas to new levels. "I don't know much about that New Age business," Peale remarked to the *Los Angeles Times* in 1988, "but anything that develops legitimate, positive thinking principles, I'm for it."

A series of Gallup surveys found that, by the 1980s, a quarter of Americans believed in both astrology and reincarnation. First Lady Nancy Reagan—well known for courting evangelical Christians with her husband—kept an astrologer named Joan Quigley on retainer for $3,000 a month, and consulted her on the best dates to schedule flights, summits, and debates. Upon this becoming public, Quigley told a *Washington Post* reporter that President Reagan had "the most brilliant horoscope" that she had "ever seen in this country this century."

During the same period, the actress Shirley MacLaine, known for her Oscar-winning role in the film *Terms of Endearment*, published two bestselling books, *Out on a Limb* and *Dancing in the Light*, which revealed her beliefs in UFOs and that she thought herself to be a reincarnated Atlantean from the supposedly lost civilization. Some say this was when the New Age began to find its edges, and the term began to carry a stigma—"Say that someone's a New Ager, and you hear the little cuckoo bird," Deslippe explained. The term "metaphysical" emerged.

In August 1987, a New Age writer named José Argüelles, who wore loose white frocks and colorful silk scarves, predicted that a "harmonic convergence" would soon occur, ushering in a new period of human consciousness. In his estimation, this meant that the planets would align in such a fashion that cleansing energy would wash over all of humanity. "If at least 144,000 people join their minds in harmonic convergence," reported the *New York Times*, "they can set the stage for a new period of peace and hope before the arrival of alien beings by the year 2012." It was like a positive spin on the Bible's Book of Revelation when 144,000 people are chosen by God to survive the horrors of the apocalypse.

Around the world, people held gatherings and rituals, dancing, singing, burning bundles of sage, waiting for this new consciousness to arrive—though no one seemed to know what that would look or feel like. "The old world order is collapsing and disintegrating," one man told the *Albuquerque Journal*.

But not all groups were optimistic about the future. There was something fundamentally "millenarian" about the New Age. Millenarian is often used to describe groups catalyzed by a spiritual, social, or political idea that some event is imminent that will fundamentally change society. Wessinger has studied how millenarian groups can be optimistic, then shift to being pessimistic, or vice versa, based on "events in the believer's context, such as persecution, negative press, or becoming more accepted in mainstream society." In her book *How the Millennium Comes Violently*, she examined millenarian groups whose core belief was that "the human condition will be transcended finally and completely," and by the 1990s, two groups with beliefs that dipped into New Age had turned to violence.

One was the Japanese religious group Aum Shinrikyo, whose members released sarin gas inside packed subway cars in Tokyo in 1995, poisoning more than 5,000 people and killing 13. They were obeying the commands of the group's leader, Shoko Asahara, an unkempt man with long black hair who wore bright pink robes and claimed to be able to levitate. Drawing from Buddhist and Hindu teachings, he taught his followers, often highly educated people, to eschew a life of materialism. He professed himself to be the savior who would create Shambhala. Asahara preached that his followers' salvation from an imminent

Armageddon depended on their devotion to him. Over time, Asahara came to believe that the group must wage a war in order to achieve that goal. (For the sarin gas attacks, he and other leaders of the group were executed in 2018.)

In 1997, another New Age group was in the news. Heaven's Gate, a California-based group whose leaders were interested in astrology, had prepared for years to ascend toward the cosmos, abandoning their "earthly bodies," believing that "they would receive eternal extraterrestrial bodies on a mothership that was following the Hale-Bopp comet," wrote Wessinger. Their ideas weren't entirely fringe: the notion of a spaceship of human-saving aliens was frequently discussed by people who phoned in to *Coast to Coast AM*.

Heaven's Gate members believed a catastrophic, world-ending event would be triggered, and they alone would ascend toward new life.

In 1997, as the Hale-Bopp comet passed by Earth, thirty-nine members of Heaven's Gate were discovered dead in a stately home near San Diego in an act of mass suicide.

The violence at the heart of Heaven's Gate and Aum Shinrikyo cast a pall over the New Age. While the movement appeared grounded in so much optimism, it seemed that those same ideas, in the hands of certain people, could be wielded to control and manipulate and cause irreparable harm.

Later, one of the astronomers who discovered the comet, Alan Hale, gave a speech. "Comets are lovely objects," he said, "but they don't have apocalyptic significance. We must use our minds, our reason."

By the 1990s, much of the New Age had gone mainstream. Conventions showed the movement turning toward health, healing, and environmentalism. Andrew Weil rose to prominence as something of a celebrity doctor within the mainstream by popularizing a combination of holistic healing with traditional medicine. Vegetarianism surged in popularity in the United States, and yoga evolved into a billion-dollar industry—overwhelmingly popular with women.

And the interest in metaphysical ideas continued to extend to America's highest halls of power. In 1994, Democratic president Bill Clinton and his wife, Hillary Rodham Clinton, invited a team of New Age thinkers to Camp David to help dissect the flipping of the House of Representatives from a Democratic majority to Republican. Among them were motivational speaker Tony Robbins, self-help writer Marianne Williamson, and Stephen Covey, the author of *The 7 Habits of Highly Effective People*. A psychotherapist involved in the human potential movement named Jean Houston attended too, according to Bob Woodward's book *The Choice*, and told the First Lady she was "carrying the burden of 5,000 years of history, when women were subservient." Houston said Hillary Clinton was the most scrutinized woman since Joan of Arc, and "she felt that the First Lady was going through a female crucifixion."

This speaks to one of the movement's most undeniable facets: New Age ideas have had a longstanding appeal to women. Dreams and emotions are not discarded, but studied. It is a world where women are not followers but leaders, acting as gurus, mystics, living goddesses. "They're offering a concept of ultimate reality—or God—that is not male," Wessinger said. "It's not an issue of talking about a he or a she. It's just a higher state of awareness, of unity." And this remains starkly at odds with many traditional religions, where women cannot be ordained, and their bodies and sexualities are legislated by men of faith.

But the New Age offered a true spiritual alternative—a path that prized personal insight over the entrenched ideas of spiritual leaders. "A primacy is placed on individual experiences," Deslippe said. "There is an emphasis on anecdotal experience and evidence, rather than science and data." In some circles, that distrust of expertise extended to medicine and technology, politics and government. It made aspects of New Age culture ripe for conspiracies to thrive, and for conspiracism to become valued and seen as its own kind of wisdom. By 2011, this sense of conspiracy was so ubiquitous that a pair of academics dubbed the blending of spiritual belief and conspiracy as "conspirituality." The core belief that humanity is undergoing a drastic consciousness shift remains but is colored by the idea that a secretive elite group—often referred to as a cabal or "New World Order"—is preventing human enlightenment and the dawning of a New Age from happening. People saw evidence of this conspiracy everywhere, even on the American dollar bill, where a blazing eye burns above a pyramid and the words "novus ordo seclorum"—Latin for "new order of ages."

Social media, which prizes personal experience and gives users a sense of exceptionalism, was the perfect space for this New Age to thrive, and as COVID blanketed the world in fear, conspirituality would play out online in wholly new and unprecedented levels. While on one hand, some practitioners of New Age ideas infused fearful people with a surge of love and light, others exploited that fear to sell goods and sow mistrust. One popular "certified juice therapist" donned a T-shirt in posts that read: "VACCINES ARE POISON." Influencers pushed stories in which vaccines contained microchips created by Microsoft founder Bill Gates. The self-centered focus that provided so many with enlightenment, calm, and control in a time of chaos encouraged bucking mask advisories and vaccination despite the fact that doing so could kill immunocompromised people. A 2021 study by the Center for Countering Digital Hate found that one alternative health influencer named Erin Elizabeth—best known for her blog *Health Nut News*—was among the top twelve biggest disseminators of antivaccination rhetoric. On Instagram, she posted about the Gates microchip theory alongside antisemitic memes about a Jewish cabal running the world. (Number two on that list? Robert F. Kennedy Jr.)

Scrambling to respond to the growing hysteria, platforms like Facebook, Twitter, and Instagram automatically placed labels over posts discussing vaccinations in an effort to curb the spread of disinformation that was, in its own way, becoming a new kind of virus.

COVID gave even the most powerful wellness influencers an

opening to make money by sowing doubt. The actress and well-ness tycoon Gwyneth Paltrow, while recovering from long COVID, authored an article on her wellness website Goop, where she suggested supplements and "detoxing superpowder" alongside an $8,600 gold necklace, was helping her recover. One California doctor who sold botox treatments before the pandemic was charged with mail fraud after selling "miracle cure" boxes of medication that he claimed was a "magic bullet" against the virus. Instagram filled with posts about crystals, and cleanses, and essential oils, and drops of colloidal silver as cures, despite no proven evidence any of it would combat the virus, or any ailment.

From the political right and the left, online content around QAnon surged. It was a conspiracy theory that has persisted online during Trump's political career, in which people believe a government insider named "Q" is slowly revealing that the world is controlled by a cabal of Satan-worshipping pedophilic Democrats, who harvest adrenochrome from the blood of children to allow themselves to live longer. It seemed to be a progression of the Patriot movement, which nurtures an anti-government belief that a New World Order of elites are pulling the strings of elected officials.

Many people believe Trump is in fact Q, and on January 6, 2021, the letter was on flags and hats and signs as people stormed inside the Capitol. In ten years, or fifty, or one hundred years, this day might be remembered as an attack, as a committee of the U.S. House of Representatives characterized it. It could be remembered as the "Insurrection," as National Public Radio dubbed it, or it could go down in history as a "protest," as Fox News called it.

If any one person from it is remembered, it will likely be the white shirtless man who entered the Capitol building on that winter day, his face carefully painted red, white, and blue. On his head he wore a hat of coyote fur and wide, pointed horns, like a bull. He carried a six-foot-tall spear with an American flag tied around it. Photographers swarmed him. He could have been going to a football game. He could have been the mascot for this day. He stood like a minotaur atop the vice president's seat in the Senate chamber and flexed his arm muscles, howling into the air.

The man called himself Q Shaman. He was an Arizona resident named Jacob Chansley who believed that occult forces were controlling the country in a battle between dark and light. Later, Chansley told the *Washington Post* that "what we did on Jan. 6 in many ways was an evolution in consciousness, because as we marched down the street along these ley lines, shouting 'USA' or shouting things like 'freedom'... we were actually affecting the quantum realm."

And while the aesthetics and dialects of the Patriot movement, QAnon, and conspirituality influencers couldn't have been more different, the ideas were essentially the same. One researcher dubbed this New Age influencer/vaccine denial space "pastel Q Anon," for the ways the Q aesthetic was softened and feminized for a whole new audience.

For members of the New Age who were certain some societal shift was imminent, COVID and America's political upheaval was a sign. Everything they believed would happen was happening. In Colorado, the loyal followers of a woman who called herself Mother God logged online and told people to leave their lives behind. To join God. The ascension was coming. Soon.

4.

A my Carlson was a daughter of America's heartland, raised in the tornado towns that dot Interstate 35, which runs through the center of the United States from Minnesota all the way to the Mexican border.

Born on November 30, 1975, in the small city of McPherson, Kansas, Amy was the child of a thin blonde woman named Linda Krell and her high school sweetheart, Dennis Carlson. Four years later, the pair had another little girl, named Tara. The family was poor but got by. But things between Linda and Dennis were tense. When one argument finished, another was ahead. By the time Amy was seven, the marriage crumbled. Linda and Dennis divorced and began a contentious custody battle over the girls.

"I wanted them with me," Linda said, "and we spent a lot of money trying to get that."

For a while, the girls split their time between their parents. Both remarried. Linda managed a Holiday Inn, and one morning as she laid out breakfast for guests, members of a seismic oil crew strode into the dining room, and one caught her eye. Later that night, Linda was crawling into bed when a friend called from the bar. "That guy you think is good-looking is here, you need to come up." Linda got dressed. "I went and stood close to him and he said, 'Can I buy you a drink?' And I said, 'Yep,' and there it went."

Linda and that oilman, Reed Haythorne, married and had one more daughter, Chelsea—nine years younger than her eldest sister, Amy. But Reed considered himself a father of three, treating Amy and Tara as his own.

Over time, Linda noticed that when she got Amy and Tara ready to go back to Dennis's house, Tara would throw a tantrum, kicking and screaming. She figured she probably just liked being at home with her better.

But then she found the bruise. One day when she picked Amy and Tara up for her scheduled time with them, she noticed a big purple bruise splashed across Amy's leg. She asked her what happened. Amy was afraid to tell her.

Linda was enraged, and the attorney she had hired for the prolonged custody battle confronted Dennis. "We were gonna call [child protective services] out, and [Dennis] said, 'If you don't call CPS out, you can have the girls. They're yours.'"

From then on, Amy and Tara lived solely with Linda and Reed, and had little to no contact with their father. From time to time, Dennis would mail gifts for their birthdays, but what he sent was never quite right. In his mind, Amy and Tara remained little girls; the toys he sent for their birthdays would consequently end up in their little sister Chelsea's room.

The family eventually moved to Oklahoma City, where they lived until Amy was thirteen, and then they made a permanent move farther south down I-35, to Garland, Texas, a suburb of Dallas. They settled in an upper-middle-class neighborhood called Spring Park. Because of their ages, the three girls were neatly distributed across the area's public schools; Chelsea in elementary, Tara in middle, and Amy at Berkner High School.

It was an American dream kind of life: neighborhood-wide parties and barbecues held in a nearby clubhouse, softball games where the girls played beside their dad. The neighbors next door proved to be life-long friends. There were family dinners around a big round wooden table. Amy's first job was working as a cashier at a local McDonald's; later, as an adult, she became a manager.

Life was comfortable. Amy was given a purple Honda Civic when she turned sixteen, and both of her sisters were handed keys to their own cars when they were old enough. At school, Reed and Linda expected them to bring home good grades, and Amy always did. She thrived being the center of attention. She lived for singing and entered in regional choir competitions. She was the kind of kid who put her entire self into whatever she was doing, committing fully. She loved makeup and fancy clothes, and never walked out of the house unless she looked her absolute best. Hair, perfect; lipstick, flawless. She worried about her weight, which seemed to go up and down. She did a weight loss program with her mother, but would also squirrel away junk food in her upstairs bedroom.

As a teenager, Amy was wildly independent, confident, headstrong. But she could also be impulsive, moody, and self-centered in the way that's typical of so many adolescents. Her bedroom, which had the only entrance to the house's attic, was usually littered with rumpled clothes and cast-aside makeup. When Linda and Reed would ask her to clean up, she'd open the door to the attic, throw the mess inside, and shut the door. Room: clean.

Amy and Tara shared a landline upstairs, and when Linda and Reed grounded them, they unplugged the phone. But the sisters had several extra phones stowed away in their rooms, which they would plug into the line as soon as their parents were out of earshot and resume calls as usual.

Once, in 1992, when Amy was sixteen, after Linda told her she was taking her phone away, Amy screamed that her life was over. She slammed the bathroom door shut and downed an entire bottle of Advil.

Reed rushed Amy to the hospital, where her stomach was pumped; Linda whisked Tara and Chelsea away to the movies to see *The Hand That Rocks the Cradle.*

Linda barely remembers the affair. "I hate to say it," Amy's sister Chelsea said, thinking back, "but she was just being a dramatic teenage girl."

The family wasn't religious in the churchgoing way but considered themselves to be Christians. "We knew about God," Chelsea said. Later, after she'd left the house, Amy started attending services at a nondenominational church.

She also entertained alternative, spiritual-adjacent paths—she was fascinated with zodiac signs and astrology charts, and believed her weekly horoscope to be a factual prediction of her future. More than once, she paid to have her palm read. None of her family members thought it was all that odd. And why would they? Amy was smart, responsible. What harm is there in thinking there might be wisdom in the stars?

Pretty early in Amy's life, her family could tell she had a taste for bad men. Once, when she was seventeen, Reed caught her boyfriend holding a knife to Amy's throat. The police were called, and Amy got a restraining order. Later, someone noticed he had come back around and was parked in his car down the street. Reed grabbed his gun and walked up to the boy's open window and yanked him by the collar. "Don't you ever show up here again," he threatened. That time the kid listened.

"We absolutely would ask her, 'What are you doing? You can do better than this,'" Chelsea remembered.

Amy was thin, blonde, blue-eyed. She had high cheekbones, a tiny mole on the left side of her nose, and her eyes—when a camera shutter caught them—seemed to glitter. She was funny and whip-smart.

When Amy was nineteen, she traded looks with a guy at a party, one thing led to another, and almost nine months later on Christmas Eve, she was in the hospital about to give birth to her first child. Her son Cole was born prematurely, his little body wheeled into a neonatal ICU on Christmas Day, where he would remain for a week. "That's when I started noticing that Amy didn't have the maternal instinct," her mother, Linda, said. "I went up to the hospital and fed Cole more than she did."

Later, she and the boy's father worked out a friendly custody arrangement. But as a mother, Amy seemed irritated by her young son, often arranging for neighbors to watch him when she left for her shifts at McDonald's or when she wanted to go out with friends. Amy didn't seem to like being with Cole. She brought him Happy Meals from work or microwaved him a frozen Kid Cuisine before retreating to the garage to drink beer, smoke cigarettes, and quietly cry. She had aspirations to be a professional singer. Her email was always some incarnation of "Amie Sings"—amiesings2000@yahoo, amiesings2000@hotmail. But as a mother, it seemed the only time she could sing was at sporadic karaoke nights and the rare lullabies for Cole.

She cycled through relationships with other angry men. When her sisters asked her why she stayed with them, Amy always seemed to have a reason. She "defended them a lot of the time," Chelsea remembered. "Like, 'Oh, well, I did something wrong.' Like *she* did wrong and so she deserved it, basically." When a nice guy would come around, Amy would quickly lose interest.

"I think she was always looking for, like, a man to want to be a part of her life. Even though she had my dad, there was something missing there," Chelsea said. "That was the worst part of her life."

At age twenty-four, in 2000, Amy married a man named Matthew Stroud, in a late summer ceremony near Dallas. Her sisters wore violet dresses, and Amy walked down the aisle in a spaghetti-strap gown, carrying pink and white roses. On one arm, she had her mother, Linda, and on the other, her son, Cole; she didn't want to have to choose between her stepfather who raised her or her birth father.

Again, Amy's family was nervous about her choice in men. "I didn't want them to get married," Linda said of the union. "I didn't trust him."

Matthew and Amy bought a stately brick house with shutters on the windows in Rowlett, an upscale suburb east of Dallas. They had a daughter, named Madison, or Maddie for short. But Amy was often leaving the baby and her son with her mother so she could "do her own thing," Linda would later reflect to a documentary filmmaker. "I didn't ask her a lot of questions."

The marriage fell apart quickly. Amy would call her sister Tara crying; Tara told her to bring the kids and move in with her. Her family always made sure she knew she had a lifeline if she needed them—places to stay and feel safe. But Amy never took them up on their offers.

In February 2004, Amy was pulled over for drunk driving by the Royce City police. Afterward, she was ordered to undergo an alcohol education program and pay close to $1,000 in fines and court fees. It was around then that Tara mentioned to her mother that Amy was talking about angels. "Amy was saying things that didn't really make sense," Linda remembers.

Her divorce from Matthew was finalized by 2005. By then Cole was with his father most of the time, and when Madison was young, Matthew's mother began caring for her full-time. That same year, Amy would give birth once more: a boy named Aidan.

Years later, when she no longer thought of herself as Amy, she would relay a story to her followers: that one day, when she put Aidan down for a nap, she saw the Archangel Michael—a figure who battles Satan in the Book of Revelation and is seen as the embodiment of a Christian warrior—hovering over his crib. The archangel whispered to her, "It's time."

"And I was like, 'What?'" she recalled. "Before I could ask him any questions, he just disappeared."

It was during this period that Amy's family noticed she was spending more and more time online. She dropped hints about some of her research—on angels, the fifth dimension or "5D"—but little of it made sense to her mother and sisters. Amy created an account on a website called Lightworkers.org. For her avatar, she uploaded a photo of herself, apple-cheeked, glowing, proudly holding a chubby baby in her arms. "Welcome to the Matrix," the moderator greeted visitors to the site. "It isn't by chance you are reading this page. You know why you have come. You are on a mission yourself, in search of the illusive truth, the meaning of life."

In New Age spaces, the term "lightworkers" can be a catchall to describe people who believe they are from another dimension, or are self-professed psychics and seers. In *The Handbook of UFO Religions*, anthropologist Susannah Crockford described lightworkers as a kind of "starseed"—people who believe they are "an alien or extraterrestrial [who] inhabits a human body."

"At some point the alien consciousness walked into the human body," Crockford wrote. Starseeds and lightworkers were a particular focus of research Crockford conducted in Sedona, Arizona. She wrote that in her interviews and observations, starseeds and lightworkers often talk of a great awakening: a specific moment they became conscious of their "true identity and abilities" and aware that their mission on this planet is to aid in humanity's ascension into the fifth dimension, fleeing the plane of "pain and suffering" that is life in the third dimension. Starseeds tended to be both hyper-positive while also possessing a "thick strain of conspiracism."

"Theories about machinations of the illuminati and the New World Order were common. Starseeds were often working against Reptilians," she wrote. "[They] were the good aliens opposing the bad aliens." Starseeds considered aliens not as hostile intruders, but helpers, shepherds even. An elaborate kind of angel.

The internet was fundamental to the growth of this alien-human hybrid community; how people who believed themselves to be starseeds communed with other starseeds, how they found information confirming their supposed alien existence, how they sold videos and products, and marketed life-coaching services to fund their existence as a starseed.

In a subforum called "Ascension," Amy authored a post titled "mission revealed." She wrote that she had received "a strong urgent message from my guides to leave where I am currently at."

"They are insisting that I move out of 3d completely and begin living fully in 5th dimension ... I have been balancing both," she said, "and my current life situation is living in a world of illusion, which I have stepped away from ... it does not support who I truly am ... and my current life partner is wanting to live in the illusion ..."

But more often than not, Amy's posts to Lightworkers.org were difficult to follow. Sentences were piled upon sentences, like the words came to her in a frantic rush and she attempted to put it all down on paper before the ideas passed. Most of her posts read like they were written by two different Amys. One was a confused person overwhelmed by her own life. "Crying is very cleansing, many moments I just took a shower and just held onto the side for dear life, saying I can't do this anymore," she wrote in one post.

But the other Amy seemed awed by her own complicated ideas and swept up in this sudden spiritual awakening. "I remember standing in my kitchen after I realized I was awake," she wrote in 2007. "I am cleaning the kitchen, baby just down for a nap ... and I feel a tap on my shoulder and a wisk of air in my left ear." A low voice murmured in her ear, "You are going to be President of the United States."

"I am a homemaker, never really got a degree, went to H.U.—Hamburger University—if that counted," she wrote. But a few days later, as she and the father of her youngest son were driving to the movies to see *The Celestine Prophecy*, the idea that she could be important in some way, chosen, was still on her mind. The film was an adaptation of the 1993 James Redfield novel about a man undergoing a spiritual awakening—a book that became wildly popular in New Age circles and sold millions of copies worldwide. In the car, Amy blurted: "I have to be honest with you ... I believe I am a major player in this spiritual upliftment."

In another post, Amy wrote out a decree. "This is a command to the Universe," she said. "'I am' is the most powerful statement we can make."

"'I am' choosing to release all the pain and suffering of illusion and to step into my Magnificence, Beauty, and Greatness I am destined to Be," she wrote. "From this day forth, I release the darkness that society and the status quo have placed on me and choose my Heart, my Truth, my Divine Birthright of Abundance and accept my Royal heritage.

"I am present in the moment of now.

"I am eternal in all ways.

"I am worthy.

"I am closing the door on the old."

Amy was spending more and more time online. Years later, she would refer to the internet rabbit holes she was falling down as "downloads" of information that she was receiving, which all pointed toward her being the living embodiment of Earth.

On Lightworkers.org, she chatted with a man from Mount Shasta, California, named Amerith WhiteEagle—a man she said was her "twin flame." (His legal name, Robert Eugene Saltsgaver, was much more white-bread.) "I feel your heart too is adjusting to this new flow of energy," he told her. "We must be together in the physical."

On December 17, 2007, she posted that she and "Am" would soon be together, reunited after 26,000 years of separation.

Around Thanksgiving, Amy's family had gathered for dinner at a Mexican restaurant in Houston to celebrate her birthday and her sister Tara's. Most of the family was there: her son, Cole. Linda and Reed. Tara. Chelsea.

Midway through dinner, Amy pushed her chair back, stood up from the table, and said she was leaving. No one thought much of it, just that she had to go. "I didn't think she'd just leave and never come back," Chelsea said. No one thought she meant she was leaving all their lives, all her children's lives. No one thought someone could simply walk out of their own life like that.

At first, the family thought Amy had suddenly left town, seeking some kind of spiritual enlightenment. It took years for her mother to fully understand that when Amy left the restaurant that night, she'd quite literally left their lives altogether. "When she left, we thought, 'Okay, she's just going to be finding herself in a hippie-type situation,'" she said. "We had no idea it would turn into what it did."

"I think she wanted to feel special," Linda said. "She wanted to be somebody. She wanted to go somewhere."

Decades later, her family would gather for dinners and birthdays, and the conversation would inevitably turn to Amy—to the person they knew, to all the things that had happened in her early life. The fights over the phone, the bottle of Advil and the hospital trip, that bruise on her little leg. Was there something else they'd missed? Some sign? Added all together, would the sum of those events of Amy's early life indicate that she would one day become unrecognizable? People say hindsight is 20/20. But in Amy's case, hindsight only seemed to give her family less clarity.

"We were raised in what you could say was a normal household," her sister Chelsea said. Linda, too, believed she gave her daughters a normal life. That belief eventually dissolved. Amy's family members tried to maintain their own sense of normalcy while deconstructing the exact moment that illusion broke for them.

PART II
HIGH PRIESTESSES

5.

For centuries, the Catholic Church has battled its own apocryphal tale: a story about a woman named Joan.

The story goes that sometime around the year 860, a young woman disguised herself as a man to get an education. In Rome, she became a scholar and teacher, ascended the ranks of the church, and eventually was so revered, she became the pope of the Roman Catholic Church.

One day, as she rode a horse on a procession through the Vatican, Pope Joan quite suddenly dropped to the ground and gave birth to a child. Onlookers were horrified that their pope could act as a vessel for new life. Joan's feminine secret was revealed. In some accounts, after the child was born, Joan was dragged through the streets behind her own horse, then stoned to death.

"From its first appearance in the late-thirteenth century until the late-sixteenth century, the story was taken to be literally true by virtually everyone," wrote Thomas F. X. Noble, a professor emeritus in the history department at the University of Notre Dame. Pope Joan, he said, has "had almost as many lives as the people who remembered her."

Noble dissects the multitudinous reasons why the story has had such a long life. A woman uses deception to lead a church that prizes men and breaks the vow of chastity while doing it. Her tale is cautionary, as if to say, "Here is what happens when women learn too much." It's transgressive, titillating: if Joan was a gender-fluid pope, then the papacy has been tainted. It's inspiring: that women must take power, not wait for it to be given.

Some scholars of cartomancy see this tale as inspiration for the High Priestess card in the tarot, which in fifteenth-century Italian decks was called "The Popess." It's a card about intuition, the hidden wisdom buried in the subconscious, the strange truth of dreams.

In the book *Radical Tarot*, Charlie Claire Burgess writes about the power of the Pope Joan story. "For a Popess to exist at all was a direct challenge not only to the church but to the nobility, landowners and the entire socioeconomic power structure," they said. The High Priestess card, then, "can indicate a certain anti patriarchal spirit, a kinship of the marginalized."

They continued, "This is a sacred knowledge that is forbidden because it threatens the status quo. This is a radical, self-initiated, experiential theology, a system of belief discovered through listening, ruminating, and feeling, not through dictates and dogma."

When America was colonized by European settlers, their quest was a spiritual one. They believed a promised land awaited them across the raging Atlantic waters. Little heed was paid to the Indigenous people whose land they sought and who had their own spiritual views, many of which were tied to the very place the new arrivals intended to bend into their own kind of Eden.

Two years before the signing of the Declaration of Independence, in 1774, a group from England called the Shaking Quakers landed on the shores of New York, following their leader, Ann Lee. They called her Mother. The Shakers worshipped a God who was both masculine and feminine, and their faith vibrated so strongly inside of them, their bodies would tremble and quake as they worshipped, hence the name.

The Shakers were radical in their dual-gendered view of God, upturning traditional Christian ideas that linked females with temptations of the flesh. This extended to their outlook on society too; correcting the oppressive treatment of women was integral to the faith. In Shaker towns, women governed with an equal hand.

The Shakers' arrival in New York coincided with a surge in a particular flavor of religious fervor, when mystics and clairvoyants emerged at such a rapid pace, it seemed they were rising up from the land itself. From the region emerged the "New Thought" movement, which centered on a philosophy in which God was seen in all things and all people, and reality could be shaped by focusing on positive thoughts. It became particularly popular with women.

Near Palmyra, New York, in 1823, a seventeen-year-old with an affinity for treasure-hunting named Joseph Smith claimed to have been told by an angel where he could find a set of buried golden plates. After unearthing them, Smith deciphered them with "seer stones" placed at the bottom of a hat. The story—which is entirely disputed—is that Smith would peer into the darkness of the hat and read aloud the translated text, which miraculously manifested on the surface of the stones, and that only he could interpret. The transcript he claimed to have deciphered became the Book of Mormon and today is the foundational scripture for the Church of Jesus Christ of Latter-day Saints.

Eight miles away from Palmyra, on a cold evening in March 1848, inside a tall cottage near the sleepy community of Hydesville, the family of John and Margaret Fox crawled into their beds. But soon, the house seemed to rattle and shake underneath them. Knocks and cracks emanated up from the floorboards and out from the walls. The sounds became a nightly occurrence.

"A patter of footsteps was sometimes heard, the bed clothes were pulled off," reported local newspapers.

While John and Margaret felt tyrannized by the unexplained

noises, the couple's daughters, Maggie and Kate, a pair of moon-faced girls who were fourteen and eleven respectively, seemed to be more intrigued than startled. Reportedly when young Kate heard the raps, she responded by snapping her fingers. Once, twice. The invisible tyrant responded: once, twice. Kate did it again. *Knock, knock.* Two knocks came back to her.

"Now, do as I do; count one, two, three, four, five, six," she instructed, clapping along with her words. The sounds, again, came back.

The family, standing in their long nightgowns, called out questions—quizzing the noisy entity on their respective ages as candlelit shadows danced up the walls.

One particular night, when the cracking and clunking began, John Fox ran through the snow and pounded on his neighbors' front door, asking them to come witness the strange sounds. Mary Redfield followed Fox back to his house and peered at the walls alongside the family. She heard it too.

For weeks, the Foxes formed something of a relationship with the knocking spirit, which eventually decided to respond only to the queries of the young sisters and no one else. Over time, the mother, Margaret, became convinced the house was possessed by a demon after the girls told her the noises were coming from the spirit of a man who had been murdered and buried underneath the home. They named him "Mr. Splitfoot"—a nickname for the devil. The girls were sent to live with a sister in Rochester (who would later become a Spiritualist medium). A search party scoured the basement and dug up bone fragments.

Word spread: the Fox sisters were mediums who could talk to the dead. That story grew wings and flew far beyond Hydesville, Rochester, and New York State itself. Soon the girls were performing on stages, conjuring thuds and snaps for crowds of ticketed audiences.

In 1851, New York newspapers wrote skeptically of the Foxes and the belief that they had inspired. Many people thought there must be more to the girls; perhaps these weren't just sounds, but some kind of spiritual message or even a prophecy "redeeming the world from the bondage and corruption of sin," one newspaper reported.

As they got older, Maggie and Kate conducted séances for the purpose of contacting the dead. The events were often attended by male newspaper reporters. One described the girls as "none of your ugly style of modern spiritual women," but petite and pleasing to listen to. During a séance Maggie conducted for three journalists, each was "lost in wonder and speculation." The sisters seemed to have an uncanny ability to convert skeptics into believers.

A tide of Spiritualism had risen up in America, carrying the Fox sisters forward on a wave of belief. Eventually, it would also wash them away. Those first knocks seemed to have shaken something loose in America, revealing a populace eager for a new kind of faith. Spiritualism centered on everyday mystics and mediums, on rituals and ceremonies that played out in parlor rooms, not churches. And death received an overhaul. It was no longer something to be feared—not an end, but merely another state of being.

The girls' abilities seem to have been contagious. One book review published in 1870 claimed that there were eight million Spiritualists in America at the time; it was probably between one to two million, which Emma Hardinge, a British writer and advocate for Spiritualism, estimated in the aftermath of the Civil War. During the war, a chasm had formed in the country, and loss touched nearly every household, crossing class boundaries. Spiritualism was an antidote for a place that felt irreparably broken, and for that reason, people feared what it could do to Christianity in America. "Spiritualism is undermining the authority of the Bible in the minds of what are called the common people faster than all other causes put together," wrote one woman in 1862.

And in a way, that was exactly right. At the time, Spiritualists—who had no organized hierarchy—often rejected Christianity because most churches hadn't taken a stand on slavery. Churches were seen as "enslavers of the human spirit," explained Ann Braude, a scholar from

Harvard Divinity School, in her book *Radical Spirits*. "The religious anarchism of Spiritualism provided a positive religious expression that harmonized with the extreme individualism of radical reform."

By the time the Fox girls were in their thirties, hundreds of Spiritualist lecturers were touring the United States, nearly half women. The *New York Times* predicted Spiritualism would decline, but the opposite seemed to occur. In Chittenden, Vermont, William and Horatio Eddy—known as the Eddy Brothers—held séances in their home, summoning spirits who supposedly inhabited a large cabinet. Victoria Woodhull, who would later become the first woman in America to run for president, marketed herself as a clairvoyant and a "magnetic healer."

Spiritualism became a realm where women could reject the Victorian values that caged them. As Spiritualists, women found a profession they could excel in, and an independence from patriarchy. Mediumship was a world where the feminine qualities that society had deemed feeble and weak were actually seen as a strength. Women spoke about being chosen as mediums by spiritual forces, not earthly ones.

And from its outset, Spiritualism and women's rights were intertwined. Strange rappings marked the proceedings of the Seneca Falls Convention in 1848, the first convention to discuss women's rights in America, jittering the very table where suffragists Lucretia Mott and Elizabeth Cady Stanton wrote the Declaration of Sentiments, which outlined the rights women should be entitled to, including the right to vote. "While not all feminists were Spiritualists, all Spiritualists advocated women's rights," Braude wrote.

The Fox sisters held séances from New York to London, Berlin to Saint Petersburg. Their abilities were sought after by the rich and the powerful. First Lady Jane Pierce, wife of Franklin Pierce, was anguished over the death of her eleven-year-old son, Bennie, who had been killed when a train derailed. In 1854, according to an apocryphal tale, she invited the Fox sisters to the White House to conduct a séance so she might communicate with her son beyond the veil. Afterward, the First Lady wrote to her sister: the boy had come to visit in her dreams. The sisters, it seemed, were mystical high priestesses who could converse in the silent language of the spirit realm.

The Pierces' successors, Abraham and Mary Todd Lincoln, had also lost a son, to typhoid fever. In 1863, the Lincolns hosted a séance in the Crimson Room of the White House to communicate with him, an event attended by two cabinet secretaries, a medium, and a reporter from the *Boston Gazette*. In an illustration of the event, President Lincoln and his wife sit closely together on cushioned chairs with several others; Lincoln leans in, brow furrowed.

In the aftermath of Lincoln's assassination two years later, Mary Todd was beset by grief. She had been holding her husband's hand when he was shot. Around 1870, she visited a Spiritualist photographer, who produced a carte de visite image of the woman. Behind her in the photo, the deceased President Lincoln loomed—there but not there, hands on her shoulders, gazing down on her from above. It popularized the Spiritualist cause: that death was not an end, but a continuum.

Later, the photograph was proven to be a hoax, but people still wanted to believe in a gauzy Lincoln hovering behind his beloved Mary Todd—just out of reach.

As Spiritualism aged and the Fox sisters grew up within it, the public was less dazzled by their abilities, and more interested in their slow decline. Kate Fox became a widow and was arrested for child neglect after she was found to be drunk around her children. Newspapers reported on both Kate's and Maggie's frequent drunkenness (they had begun drinking wine as children during their séances), and their financial hardships. "Margaret Fox," the *New York Times* cruelly reported, "is sick and destitute."

In October 1888, advertisements publicized an event dubbed the "Death Blow of Spiritualism" at the New York Academy of Music, in which the sisters appeared before a full audience. Kate sat in the front row, and Maggie Fox took the stage, nervously reading from a prepared statement. She explained that the rappings of their youth had begun as a prank to spook their mother—an easily frightened woman. Later, the girls got creative, tying a string around an apple, plunking and rolling it against the floor in an upstairs room. They cracked their knuckles and made loud snaps with their toe joints, sounds Maggie demonstrated from the stage. And the bones that had been unearthed under the house had been from a chicken. When the Fox sisters had been sent away to Rochester, their older sister saw a cash cow and taught them how to perform. A newspaper report from the event said that Maggie told the crowd "all mediums are deceivers, and all manifestations can be reduced to sleight of hand or trickery."

After this confession, the newspapers that had spilled so much ink trying to prove the girls as fraudsters questioned if they now had ulterior motives. One reporter at their hometown newspaper later wrote that Kate Fox must have only staged the event because she "wanted money, possibly bread, and that in her weakened condition of mind she had taken this way of getting those essentials."

A year after her confession, Maggie attempted to recant it. The raps *had* been real, but by then the Fox sisters' time to be heard was over. Both died soon thereafter from complications from alcoholism. "The Fox girls were fraudulent, but innocent," wrote historian Whitney Cross, "the victims of an invention begun as a childish prank and perpetuated when adults took it seriously."

But because of these adults, two children had been a vehicle for something miraculous: they had democratized spirituality with a few literal snaps of their fingers. They delivered miracles to the everyday person. They brought God down from the rafters, and within reach.

When the Fox sisters said it was all fake, their message was received less like a mea culpa, and more like the confession of two fallen angels who'd forgotten how to believe.

Later, a sign would be nailed over the door of the Fox home:

MODERN SPIRITUALISM ORIGINATED IN THIS HOUSE MARCH 31, 1848.

6.

After years of posting to the Lightworkers website, Amy and Amerith WhiteEagle decided the time had come to start their own website, one they called the Galactic Free Press. Amy had many ideas to share about UFOs and ascension, about removing oneself from the trappings of mainstream society, and began constantly posting them. It was like her own little newspaper, where the world was seen through the lens of astrological predictions.

The pair lived together in Crestone, Colorado. The small remote town, located in the San Luis Valley, is a place of vast bright skies, low brush, and clouds so massive they cast shadows on the land between the San Juan and Sangre de Cristo mountain ranges, which loom large, a constant reminder of just how small one human really is. The area had long served as a hunting route for several bands of the Ute people, who were forcefully relocated to reservations in the late 1800s by the U.S. government.

The region has long held an appeal for New Age seekers and has been called the "Shambhala of the Rockies." It is home to dozens of retreat centers, Zen centers, meditation centers, yoga centers, temples, ashrams, spiritual institutes, and fellowships. Some people think it's a place of hidden UFO bases and portals to other worlds.

There in that wide land, Amy and Amerith would take videos of the clouds passing over the ragged Sangre de Cristo Mountains that they believed were cloaking alien ships that were surveilling the planet. "Take a long look," Amy said in one video. "Hi guys!" she called to the sky.

With her new partner, Amy revamped herself. No longer was she the woman with the perfect hair, the perfect lipstick. She wore long dresses and scarves, ditched her makeup, smoked joints, let her blonde hair grow long and go back to its natural brown.

In her online posts, Amy started signing off as Mother God, and referred to Amerith as Father God.

In 2011, the pair began wandering around the West. In Eugene, Oregon, Amy and Amerith settled for a time at a commune called Dancing Heart. It looked like any utopian community in the Pacific Northwest: lots of dreadlocks and flowing skirts, green gardens and communal meals. They set up a pyramid, sitting cross-legged under-neath it, lit bonfires, held meditation circles and Earth dances in the rain. There were several children and babies there with their parents, and Amy rocked them on her lap like they were her own. Online, she told her readers to join them in Oregon.

"Our ships are going to de-cloak at any moment, and the focus right now is raising the vibrational frequency on the planet for that to occur," Amy said on a phone call with a young woman from Phoenix, Arizona. "Humanity's graduation date and the end of time is October 28, 2011. We announced that years ago . . . Humanity has until that date to awaken."

Amy talked about how they had started a "family as one" in Eugene, and the woman from Phoenix asked how many people had arrived at Amy's calling. "So far, we've got around ten, eleven," Amy said, laughing at the absurdity of how that sounded. "We're not quite there."

The woman on the phone wanted to come to Oregon, but she was nervous about putting her life behind her. She asked Amy how to help friends and family understand. Amy sighed. She said to start by asking them small questions; she suggested, "What do you think about UFOs?" and "How about starships?"

"You can give them more information if they ask," she said. "We're not here to save anybody."

As time passed, Amy was becoming less Amy and more Mother God—introducing herself as such in a vast number of online videos she would amass during this period. "Greetings, love beings!" she would say to the camera in each video, smiling wide.

"This is Mother and Father God, and the Earth allies," Amy said in a November 2012 recording, Amerith at her side. The pair sat on the stoop of a sage-green house. She wore a cotton-candy-colored fleece headband, her face pink like the air outside was fresh and cold.

"We declare peace on Earth, equal heart," Amy intoned.

Both smiled and held up peace signs.

"Peace on Earth!" Amerith, with a long graying beard, said, waving to the camera.

But Mother God wasn't a large enough title for Amy. "It's Mother God," she said in another video, wearing her long hair in two braids. "Also known as Mother Earth, Divine Mother, Universal Mother, White Buffalo Calf Woman—I've got lots of names." She winked at the camera. She started appearing in videos holding a wooden staff.

While Amy fanned her videos across Facebook and YouTube, Amerith delivered their message prolifically across Twitter, promoting events like a conversation with Amy called "What's Really Going On, On Planet Earth=Heart? Deep Changes." Sometimes he would post more than a hundred tweets a day, peppering in retweets of motivational quotes and mantras. But he broke the Father God illusion often, tweeting a lot about the results of NASCAR races and trading messages with long-haul truckers, bored behind the wheel and looking for a friend.

In some videos, Amy delivered a string of astrological forecasts and cryptic predictions that the end was coming—though it never arrived. Sometimes she was sitting inside at a computer, other times on a patio with trees swaying behind her. For a time, she wore a headset. She spoke with the confidence of a newscaster. "We are not here to start a revolution," she said. "We are here to advance evolution."

Amy traveled the country. But wherever she went, it seemed she always ended up back near Mount Shasta, in California, or in Crestone—like those were the places that tugged her heart the strongest. And no matter where she was, she could always be found online. "We love you. We are here for you," she would promise her viewers. "You are not alone. We love you unconditionally."

After a few years, she and Amerith went their separate ways. She claimed she was fired from the Galactic Free Press. She started a new website: FirstContactGroundCrewTeam.com.

Regardless of venue, her message resonated with people. More and more viewers accepted her invitations to online chat parties and came to her site to read articles that rehashed ideas from New Age thinkers around the planet. There, people could learn about crop circles and goddesses, read messages from Ascended Masters and archangels, scour astrological forecasts and consider what deeper meanings the supermoon might carry. Lemuria, Atlantis, Shambhala—it was all there.

She began to weave in stories that she herself was Mother Earth, and that she had been reincarnated hundreds of times. She said she was the Queen of Lemuria, Cleopatra, Joan of Arc, Pocahontas, Marilyn Monroe.

Once, she said, she had lived as a woman called Madame Blavatsky.

7.

Helena Petrovna von Hahn was born into a life of wealth and privilege on August 12, 1831, in Yeketerinoslav, Russia (now Dnipro, Ukraine). Her mother was a novelist, her father a colonel in the Russian Royal Horse Artillery. Helena lived a life befitting a Victorian-period film. She was educated in the high-class ways of women of the era, learning to speak French and appear attractive to male suitors. As a young girl, she was introduced to Tibetan Buddhism through the Kalmyks, a Mongolian sub-ethnic group that had migrated to Russia, whom her mother visited with often.

Her entire life, however, she was an off-key note in the harmonious world of high society. As a child, she spoke of imaginary friends she called "hunchbacks" and delighted in scaring other children with her stories. Her own sister, Vera, described her as "the strangest girl one has ever seen."

Her mother died from tuberculosis at the age of twenty-eight, and on her deathbed expressed frustration with her daughter Helena's inability to fit in: "Ah well, perhaps it's best that I'm dying," she supposedly conceded, "so at least I shall be spared seeing what befalls Helena. Of one thing I am certain: her life will not be that of other women, and she will have much to suffer."

At seventeen, Helena briefly attempted to conform by marrying a government man three decades her senior and taking his last name, Blavatsky. The newlyweds unhappily honeymooned, and months afterward, Helena disappeared, never to see her husband (whose name she kept) again. She went to great lengths to never be found, hopping steamships and bribing sea captains for safe passage. Her mother's deathbed prediction—that her life would not be like those of other women—was absolutely right. She is said to have learned to be a circus equestrienne in Constantinople. In India, she was accused of being a spy. In Egypt, she dressed as a man so she could roam freely and attempted to start a Spiritualist society.

In July 1873, she stepped off an ocean steamer onto the muddy streets of New York City. She was "penniless," but in awe, like her feet had touched holy ground. To be in America, a place teeming with Spiritualism by then, it felt like she was "a Mohammedan approaching the birthplace of his prophet," she wrote in a letter.

By the time of her arrival, much of the hysteria around Spiritualism had dropped away. The Fox sisters were grown women, and twenty years had passed since they ushered in an era of mysticism. The New York newspapers, once so critical of the sisters, now saw Spiritualism as a uniquely American contribution to religious thought. Mormonism and Spiritualism "have stood serious and testing trials; but they still live and prosper," one writer said. "Why should not American thought have its distinctive and peculiar place in the world's great future?"

Much would be written about Helena Blavatsky during her lifetime; most article writers took great pains to describe her body. All who wrote of her seemed to agree that Helena was a fat chainsmoker with eyes so piercingly blue, they appeared purple. The details varied depending on who was writing. One writer described her as "torpid." Others said she sucked down a pound of tobacco a day, which she toted around her neck in a pouch made from the hollowed-out head of a lemur.

In 1874, while attending one of the Eddy Brothers' famed séances at their Vermont home, she caught the eye of a freelance journalist. Henry Steel Olcott was fascinated the moment Helena walked through the door. In the drab Eddy home, she arrived in a whirl of color, dressed in a scarlet blouse, blonde hair tied up. Her face suggested "power, culture and imperiousness," he wrote.

By the time of their meeting, Olcott was well established in New York City as an attorney and a journalist. He wore a navel-length white beard and sparked conversation in high-society circles with his seriously considered articles on the rise of Spiritualism.

By his telling, the Eddy Brothers were farmers who lived in a nearly empty home and were "poor, ill-educated and prejudiced—sometimes surly to their unbidden guests." At their séances, attendees were asked to gather in an upstairs room where William Eddy would position himself inside a closet behind a thick blanket that covered its opening. After William entered, the blanket would supposedly peel back, and out would emerge the figures of the dead: apparitions that hovered in the air, and then suddenly dissolved.

Olcott wrote that before Helena arrived, the Eddys' apparitions were "Red Indians, or Americans, or Europeans." But when she got there, the spirits who emerged were altogether new: a Georgian servant, a Muslim merchant, a Russian peasant girl, a Kurdish soldier, an African sorcerer. Olcott thought the unworldly Eddy Brothers wouldn't have been able to dream up such characters or afford elaborate theatrics. He concluded that these new apparitions seemed to have followed Helena, spirits she'd amassed from around the world.

That day, when she stepped outside the Eddy home for a smoke, Olcott offered her a light. The rest was history. The pair would be companions for life—never romantically, always spiritually.

In her, Olcott found a globetrotting medium who claimed to be in direct contact with the Mahatmas, or "the Masters"—wise men she claimed lived in the Himalayas and Tibet who achieved enlightenment and were the keepers of ancient knowledge. They could "perform wonders beyond the reach of ordinary man." And only she could communicate with them, "precipitating" letters from these wise men, which she received in her mind and transcribed to paper.

For years, the pair shared an apartment in New York City that was dubbed "the Lamasery" (the word for a Tibetan monastery; more recently it was an Econo-Lodge). It was a bohemian paradise filled with ornate fans and rugs from China and Japan, and a bevy of "odd, elegant, old, beautiful, costly, and, apparently, worthless things," one reporter described. A crystal ball hung from a ceiling. The stuffed head of a lioness was mounted on a wall, frozen with its jaws open wide. There were pipes and ashtrays, paintings, golden statuettes. In Helena's study, a stuffed baboon stood dressed in a dinner jacket, a copy of Darwin's *On the Origin of Species* tucked under one arm.

Each day the duo rose early, ate breakfast together, then retired to their respective studies to write, before gathering again for dinner. Nearly every night, they had guests. There was no butler; when someone came to the door, Olcott answered.

Helena by then had amassed a reputation for mysterious performances. Once, at a picnic, she unearthed a cup and saucer from the garden where she and friends sat. During meetings at the Lamasery, when people would ask Helena for insight from the Masters, letters would be pulled from out of drawers providing answers. Some would miraculously flutter down from the ceiling, as if they'd been mailed from some ethereal realm.

The pair hosted Spiritualist lectures and gatherings to study works of the occult. During one event on the evening of September 7, 1875, after a lecture that discussed the Pyramids of Giza in Egypt, the Theosophical Society formed.

Egypt, by then, had become an obsession of the Western world. In the late eighteenth century, French military commander Napoleon Bonaparte led an invasion of the country, during which a team of soldiers seized the Rosetta Stone, a codebreaker of ancient Egyptian hieroglyphics. The stone acted like a portal to the mysterious civilization, and kick-started a fascination with the culture, dubbed "Egyptomania."

At that evening's lecture, a man theorized whether the pyramids contained secrets that could allow spirits to be summoned, and the room was in awe of such a prospect. Olcott shot to his feet, declaring that a society should be founded to study these sorts of spiritual mysteries. They would call the group the Theosophical Society; they were the Theosophists. The society was "a universal human brotherhood" that would analyze religions, philosophy, and science, and investigate "unexplained laws of nature and the powers latent in man."

In Theosophy, they weren't creating a new religion, but offering access to the ancient wisdom Helena claimed came from the Masters. The group kept its focus primarily on Buddhism, Hinduism, and the occult, abhorring Christianity and expressing little interest in Islam or Judaism. Their motto became "No religion higher than truth." To some extent Theosophy seemed to be born in spite of science—to them, it was like each advancement by thinkers like Darwin was making the world a little less mysterious.

And the idea caught on. Theosophical Societies popped up around America and in London. Even the scientist Thomas Edison joined. A renowned freethinker, Edison was known to dabble in the spiritual. "I do not believe in the God of theologians," he wrote, "but there is a Supreme Intelligence I do not doubt."

Helena, who had no scientific background or higher education, seemed particularly aggrieved by Darwin, and used her position to float her own theories of human development. And they were the exact sort of thing that would have vexed the scientist, who died several years before she would publish *The Secret Doctrine*, in which she wrote about Atlantis and Lemuria—the latter of which she specifically described as a "god-inhabited continent [that] was not altogether a fable."

The Secret Doctrine, a text she said had been revealed to her through "clairvoyant communication" with the unseen Masters, contained her own kind of evolutionary theory: that seven "root-races"—whose homelands were now lost—explained mankind's origins. It was work that masqueraded as science, and that undermined the work of actual scientists.

She wrote that the first root-race were essentially amoebas. The second root-race were a slightly more advanced, yellow-skinned species. But it was Lemuria—home to the third root-race—where humanity began to thrive. According to Helena, Lemurians were the first upright humans, who had "third eyes" in the center of their foreheads and grunted in a language of monosyllables.

Under her direction, Lemuria made a permanent leap from the world of theoretical science to the world of spiritual belief. Before Helena, it was simply an idea "out there in the ocean. It didn't belong to anybody," Sumathi Ramaswamy said. But she made it much more important—a lost place that also happened to contain the origins of humankind. Helena repackaged Sclater's idea, removing any mention of the strange lemurs of Madagascar and relocating it to the Pacific Ocean, closer to the United States.

Helena placed the fourth root-race in the lost civilization of Atlantis, which was also where the fifth race emerged. By her estimation, it was this fifth root-race that was most superior: the Aryan race.

The sixth race, she predicted, would be the product of selective breeding by the Masters themselves (essentially, eugenics), and would reside on a new continent in the Pacific that would rise suddenly out of the ocean. California would eventually break off from America, drifting across the water to join this new land. She didn't say much about the seventh root-race.

Many modern scholars have argued that Helena was not racist because views of white superiority were commonly held by dominant classes and revered Western thinkers at the time. "The charge has been made that she was responsible for many ideas behind Nazism," wrote James Santucci, a professor of comparative religion at California

State University, Fullerton. The intent of her root-race theories were to simply explain "that the movement or the dance of the cosmos was ordered."

"I think that's one of the things that's tricky with Blavatsky," said the historian Philip Deslippe. "Those ideas are problematic, they lend themselves to other things."

Theosophists were pulling from religious ideas that were inherently Eastern, mashing together an amalgam of Hinduism and Buddhism for their central teachings. And there's simply no way to see the idea of Aryans as a superior race as not racist. Her ideas were similar in many ways to the ones pushed by Ernst Haeckel, who would become so revered by the Nazis.

To Ramaswamy, Helena's work read like a nineteenth-century QAnon—prizing spiritual belief as truth and positioning actual science as a kind of religion. "There's anti-intellectualism at play," she said. "And a real resentment of expert knowledge."

In 1878, Helena moved to India, where she and Olcott would publish a magazine and set up new Theosophical Societies. Perhaps one reason for their move was the headlines in American newspapers portraying Helena as a snake-oil peddler and a charlatan. (Her written work didn't fare much better critically. *Isis Unveiled* was called a "dish of hash" by critics; *The Secret Doctrine* was panned, later dubbed a "massive dredging of her psychic swamp.") She was criticized for cultural and religious appropriation, and for plagiarizing her ideas. The British writer Arthur Lillie, who was a Buddhist, wrote that her "Esoteric Buddhism" was "designed to win over the rich Hindoos [*sic*]." She simply unseated Hindu gods and replaced them with what she called Masters. "Her mind, as I have often stated," he wrote, "lacks originality."

But in her new home in India, people saw Theosophy's respect for Buddhism and Hinduism as a refreshing surprise in an environment where so many colonialist Europeans only came with the goal to sway people to Christianity. She and Olcott converted to Buddhism and became vocal supporters of the anticolonialist Indian independence movement. Helena began a friendship with Mohandas Gandhi that would last the rest of her life.

Letters from the Masters continued to miraculously manifest in Helena's presence. In India, they began magically appearing inside a cabinet.

In 1883, controversy found Helena again when two of her trusted employees, Alexis and Emma Coulomb, leaked a set of letters to the *Madras Christian College Magazine* in which Helena acknowledged using fraudulent tricks; soon thereafter the *Times* in London republished the story.

The article caught the attention of the Society for Psychical Research in London, which conducted investigations of paranormal activity and spiritual mediums. The SPR launched its own inquiry of Helena's work and abilities, dispatching to India an investigator named Richard Hodgson to conduct a three-month-long examination. Hodgson gave some of the letters she claimed were from the Masters to hand-writing analysts, who concluded they were actually written by Helena. He inspected the cabinet where messages from the Masters would mysteriously appear, and found it was "elaborately arranged" with "a sliding panel at the back" where Helena or her employees could insert the letters in secret. Hodgson wrote that Helena was masterful at leading people to ask questions that only the prewritten letters—stashed in the cabinet—would answer. "We think she has achieved a title to permanent remembrance as one of the most accomplished, ingenious, and interesting imposters in history," the society wrote.

In his "voluminous and painstaking" report, Hodgson concluded that Helena was a fraudster who performed elaborate tricks and hoaxes in order to garner support for the Theosophical movement and justify its existence. The "marvelous narratives" she put forth were either "spontaneous illusion, or hallucination, or unconscious misrepresentation or invention."

Later, a Russian writer named Vsevolod Solovyov published *A Modern Priestess of Isis*, chronicling his encounters with Helena toward the end of her life. Their first meeting was in Paris, where Solovyov said that as the pair spoke, light, tinkling bells suddenly chimed overhead. Helena explained to him that it meant her Master was present and listening to their conversation.

Each time they met, the sound of astral bells would tinkle above. But during one conversation, the sound was interrupted when Solovyov heard an object *thunk* to the floor. On the ground lay a tiny silver bell, "delicately worked and strangely shaped." He picked it up. Helena snatched it away.

During their time together, Solovyov noticed her slipping objects into his pocket and claiming they were from the Masters. He confronted her. "Surely it is high time now to put an end to all this comedy," he said. "I have been waiting for you to put an end to this ridiculous game." Helena seemed unbothered to have been found out.

"What is one to do when in order to rule men it is necessary to deceive them?" she said.

There's an argument to be made that Blavatsky's declaration—that to rule men one must deceive them—is the clearest bell she ever rang. It's a lasting statement on power, perhaps more universal and true than anything else written in *Isis Unveiled* or *The Secret Doctrine*. In America, she tapped into the frenzy of Spiritualism, where God spoke through children and was heard in knocks. She pushed that world toward a more fantastical place, where any question could be solved by messages sent by unseen faraway wise men living in unreachable places.

Even after she was exposed, her ideas persisted. Theosophy proliferated, and her work bringing the religions of the East to the West laid the foundation for so many New Age practitioners to come.

Helena was hardly the only spiritual charlatan of her time, but she was an effective one, creating an entire worldview where lost places contained the fantastic roots of humanity. But she was also controversial because she was a woman with so much power—a woman who inhabited a body that was not seen as conventionally attractive, a person who played with gender to live the kind of life she wanted to.

She died in London on May 8, 1891, at age fifty-nine, when a flu pandemic swept the world, killing millions. Her death was met with glee by her critics. "After swallowing a neat brandy and rolling her eyes one final time, she fell dead," wrote one paper years later.

At a London séance in which a medium made contact with Helena beyond the veil, a tinkling of bells was reported to have chimed above the heads of the participants.

Even now, her death is celebrated on its anniversary, a day known to Theosophists as "White Lotus Day."

Critics have since written that Helena might have been remembered by historians for her study of esotericism and the occult, but she took things too far—feeling that she had to perform belief in order to gain respect. "Her miracles were not above the average of ordinary conjuring and hypnotic feats," Henry Ridgely Evans, a magician, wrote. But her stories about the Masters were "too absurd to be believed."

Peter Washington, a professor who wrote a biography of Helena, said that there was great folly in her choice to position herself between faith and science. Darwin has become remembered "as a secular saint" and "the same period has relegated Blavatsky to virtual oblivion," he wrote. "In the modern allegory of Wisdom and Folly, she plays the role of the Fool."

But is it so bad to be remembered as a Fool? In the tarot, the Fool card can be seen as a positive one—where a hapless character smiles as he steps off a cliff. The Fool is "the primitive, unshaped energy, where all things emerge from and return," tarot scholar Laetitia Barbier wrote. And this, perhaps, describes Helena exactly: an origin point for the New Age movement to gain popularity, and whose story must be returned to again and again to understand its motivations.

More than a century after her death, the Theosophists received their due when the Society for Paranormal Research distanced itself from the findings of Richard Hodgson's 1884 report about Helena. But they also didn't say she wasn't a charlatan, or retract his findings.

After her life, the mythology of Lemuria continued to build. In 1904, a Theosophical Society member named William Scott-Elliot published a book entitled *The Lost Lemuria*, in which Lemurians were people akin to film director James Cameron's Na'vi in *Avatar*. They lived among pine forests in a place where pterodactyls soared overhead. They were gangly creatures with long limbs and stood "between twelve and fifteen feet" tall. They had wide-set eyes, enabling them to see sideways and in front, as well as one eye on the back of the head. They wore animal skins, and carried spears, and walked hideous reptiles around on leashes, like trained Labrador retrievers. They laid eggs. They created "airships."

The lost land had begun to take on a kind of science-fiction feel. It was only the beginning.

8.

Online, Amy connected with a man with a silvery beard, neatly combed hair, and glasses from New York, named Miguel Lamboy, who she began calling Archangel Michael Silver. He claimed to have done IT work for the United Nations in the past, and wrote online that he had been healed of cancer "through Mother's spiritual teachings." He started posting stories of aliens and energy and astrological predictions to FirstContactGroundCrewTeam.com. Eventually, he flew west to join Amy in Crestone, and became the business manager of her operation. Sometimes Amy referred to him as her "producer." At one point, she called her mother, Linda, back in Texas, and said she and her producer wanted to come visit. The title caught Linda off guard. Producer of... what? "I didn't think it was a good idea," Linda said. "I didn't know who this Miguel was, and I think they probably wanted money."

By the spring of 2014, Amy and Miguel were posting to the website dozens of times per day. Amy continued producing videos where she passionately read excerpts from the work of hypnotists, mediums, and psychics who'd written about starseeds and lightworkers.

One day, Amy posted a list of "divine decrees" in which she called for an end to violence in the world, for corporations to dissolve, and for the Earth's resources to be "returned to the people."

"The Entire [9/11] truth, as well as The UFO Conspiracy Cover~Up, Must Be Revealed immediately," she added. "If these are Not Revealed immediately, WE The People, Will Abolish that illusionary Government."

Amerith WhiteEagle had been the first Father God, and Amy found a succession of new Father Gods, one after the other, to sit beside her and attend to her every need.

One of the earliest was a cosmetics rep in his thirties with piercing brown eyes from New Jersey named Andrew Profaci. He encountered Amy's videos in Facebook groups devoted to lightworkers during a time he had been falling further into conspiracy theories: 9/11, the Rothschilds, Egyptian prophecies, aliens. Her videos, which spoke vaguely about greater forces at play in society, drew him in.

Andrew had been raised in the Catholic Church but could never quite square up the hypocrisies that he saw in the institution. "The pope sits on a throne made of gold and talks about helping the poor," he said. It "just didn't really sit well with me."

Around the time he encountered Amy's videos, Andrew had overcome a painkiller addiction, had been laid off from his cosmetics job, and was getting unemployment checks every month. "Life had opened up to me in a way that was just like, 'I can do whatever I want right now,'" he said. He had time to waste. And though he never considered himself particularly spiritual, after watching hours of Amy speaking about her ideas, he felt for the first time in his life that maybe spirituality was a path he was willing to walk down. In the lightworker groups on Facebook, people were talking about the same concepts he was interested in. In fact, he noticed lots of people like himself in those groups—people who didn't realize they had been seeking something but felt suddenly touched by a greater spiritual hand.

"They felt like they had all this untapped potential in their life that wasn't being used," he said. "And all of a sudden, they come across these spiritual notions that they have a much bigger role to play. It makes them feel special and validated."

Amy's videos often spoke about how the old ways of the world were breaking apart, and a new world was slowly unfolding—like a flower blossom opening. He found himself dreaming about her night after night, her confident voice dictating his dreams. Eventually they traded private messages and Andrew confided in Amy that he was dreaming about her; she surprised him when she said she had been dreaming about him too. For a little while, Andrew really thought she might be God.

Amy urged Andrew to come join her in Colorado and become a part of the group she had dubbed the First Contact Ground Crew Team. It seemed crazy, but then again, he'd never felt so understood and accepted. "It just felt like there was a place for me—somebody who felt like a bit of an outcast and didn't really fit in anywhere. And it felt like maybe this was the place where I could fit in with people who were like-minded," Andrew said. "So I decided to leave everything. I left a fully furnished apartment. I dropped everything...I even left my dog behind at my mom's house."

He arrived in Denver at midnight, then paid a cabdriver to take him the five hours south to Crestone to the remote address Amy had sent him. He got there at five in the morning. The team came out to greet him, shelling out extra cash for the driver's tip, and brought him into the house.

"It was disgusting," he said. Dishes towered in the kitchen sink. Everything was dirty, like no one had ever cleaned. "I immediately sensed that I had made such a big mistake."

That morning, he saw that Amy was not the clear-voiced muse he saw online. "She was in another world," he said. "She had been drinking for almost two days, awake for two days and tripping on mushrooms. So she was like completely nonresponsive, nonverbal when I got there, literally drooling in her chair." Was this what the living God really looked like?

64

"I was looking around the place in disrepair, looking at her and the state that she was in. You know—things you don't see from the other side of the laptop," he said. But he had traveled so far, and by the second day, when Amy was sober, he really did think she was leading something special. He fell into the First Contact Ground Crew Team's rhythm, learned to speak their language of higher meaning. They all had a role; it felt like "this cosmic game of House being played," he said. Before he arrived, he had this nagging sense that he had potential for greatness. With Amy and her team, he felt like he was growing into that special role.

Shortly after his arrival, Amy told Andrew what his path was—that he was Father God. The masculine energy to her feminine. Her long-lost twin flame. At first, the news was jarring—almost too big for him to grasp. "I spent a handful of weeks trying to come to terms with it, giving her the benefit of the doubt," he said.

Amy announced this news online. "Greetings, love beings!" she called in a video, a room full of pink twinkle lights sparkling behind her. "This is Mother God."

"And Father God," Andrew, wearing a baseball shirt, said. "Hello." He held up a peace sign.

"*And* the First Contact Ground Crew Team! At your service," Amy chimed in, looking around the room. The camera didn't move, but cheers and claps echoed around them in response.

In the house, the team would sit around a big wooden table with their laptops, taking turns playing songs, passing a joint around the circle as they amassed the various articles they would post to the website that day. Around five o'clock in the evening, everyone logged on to the First Contact Ground Crew Team chat room, counseling users about their problems, sharing their spiritual ideas about starships and astrology. Meanwhile, Amy would do spiritual healing appointments on the phone for donations. She would tell the team that their mission, first and foremost, was to heal the world with love. And they felt like they were doing that by being there for the people who came into their website's orbit, who they were also tapping for donations.

Andrew told Amy he thought First Contact Ground Crew Team was a mouthful, and for marketing's sake the group played around with new names. The First Contact Ground Crew Team changed to 5D News, briefly. "We are now entering into a New Phase in the Divine Plan," read one post on the new site. "Now is the time for the New Lemuria to rise from the Depths of the Sea, to rise from the Depths of our Unconscious."

On the summer solstice in 2015, during a ceremony Amy dubbed "New Lemuria Activation Portal," the group stood around in the backyard of the house as she read a list of decrees and predictions from her laptop. She promised that humanity was about to embark on a wild ride of changes. Around them, dogs barked and birds chirped. Amy wore an orange dress with bows at the shoulders, and a headband of turquoise beads that dangled down between her eyebrows, like an Egyptian goddess. She held her gnarled wooden staff in one hand as she read, "The last cleansing is occurring. Humanity is in the final stages of the necessary clearing out of all energies that no longer serve the greater good." The decrees felt like commands, but to whom, it wasn't clear. Her followers bowed their heads, listening. Andrew kept his eyes closed and hands folded in prayer. Miguel wore all white.

When Amy finished, she stood and Andrew held out a notebook for her to read from, like an altar boy. Amy cleared her throat, leaned on her staff, and sang "The Rose," a song popularized by Bette Midler. Her cheeks flushed as she sang, like she was a little sheepish. She coughed at the high notes, but otherwise her voice was bright and clear. When she finished singing, she smiled; Andrew placed a hand over his heart.

After several name changes, Amy settled on calling the group Love Has Won, and they relaunched their website and social media pages accordingly. Unlike her first sites, cluttered with posts, Love Has Won's site was cleaner, fresher, and placed Amy at the center. There were photos of her, eyes closed, hands in prayer. "Learn how to live a happy & enlightened life," the homepage promised. Photos showed her gazing toward the stars, with a gleaming amulet around her neck. "The Mother of All Creation is here embodied and in the flesh," the site read. "She has been in service to humanity for the past 13 years...Love Has Won has taken the reigns as the energies are here to bring the New Earth into physical manifestation. It's All in or nothing."

Visitors began streaming toward the site, first thousands, then tens of thousands. Amy's spiritual healing sessions brought in money, but the group also encouraged people to make donations—small or large: $33, $44, $55. Once someone donated $7,777. (Within the New Age economy, these are often called "angel numbers.") The group lived communally, pooling their money. Andrew's unemployment checks were quickly dissolved into the pool of group funds.

Every night, as the crew busily tapped away in the chat room, around dinnertime Andrew would bring Amy her first drink of the night. "I used to say goodbye to her after I'd give her her second drink," he said. "I'd say, 'I'll see you tomorrow.'"

He began to understand that there were two personalities to the woman he'd met online. There was Amy, the person with the sparkling blue eyes and clear voice. She was fun, charismatic, a little blunt. "She definitely had that alpha vibe to her," he said. "That Scorpio vibe that would just...cut you to pieces but do it for your own benefit."

And then there was Mother God. The more Amy drank every night, the more she talked, and the more the stories from her past came tumbling out of her, a deluge of folklore that pooled together with all the teachings of mediums and psychics and starseeds she had been reading for years. She was creating her own Mother God mythology. "Every life story she had was somehow tied to her being God," Andrew said. "You could see how she wove this web of belief systems and convinced herself she was Mother God." She would swing from being wildly angry, to sobbing hysterically, to screaming at the people around her. It was painful to watch.

"Amy was a wonderful person," he said. "Mother God was a delusional alcoholic."

PART III

THE TOWER

9.

It has become commonplace to believe that the current moment is exclusively rife with falsehoods and misinformation—that this age, especially, is the era of the great hoax. But the 1903 publication of *The Protocols of the Elders of Zion* in Russia is perhaps the best evidence to dispel such a notion. This document remains a powerful and catalyzing piece of propaganda, almost biblical in the ways it continues to find new believers.

The Protocols takes the form of meeting minutes. The meeting is fake, and the fictional minutes tell the story of a nonexistent Jewish conclave that supposedly huddled in secret at a summit in the late 1800s to carefully plot a Jewish takeover of the world. People immediately believed it was real and continue to, often referring to this so-called secretive Jewish conclave as "the cabal." In the 1920s, two British newspaper writers penned panicked screeds claiming that *The Protocols* was proof that Jews intended a seizure of Great Britain. Hitler wrote in *Mein Kampf* that even though mainstream media had proved the document to be a fabrication, it was useful in achieving the Nazi Party's genocidal ends.

Just a few months before the publication of *The Protocols*, on April 19 and 20, 1903, forty-nine Jews were murdered in the Kishinev pogrom in a small Russian city by a mob. Hundreds of Jews were raped and injured, and more than a thousand homes vandalized in the riot. The entire affair, according to historian Steven Zipperstein, occurred over rumors that date back as far as the twelfth century, which speculated that Jews harvested the blood of Christians for their rituals (which shows just how unoriginal the QAnon conspiracy is). At the time, the only newspaper in the region had published pieces with titles like "Death to the Jews" and "Crusade Against the Hated Race," and there had been efforts to pin the deaths of at least one Christian child on Jews, based on the idea that they were killed for their blood. And despite so much violence, only months later, *The Protocols* was published.

For generations of antisemites worldwide, *The Protocols* has served as the thing that they could point to in order to justify their hate. In the United States, it was picked up by a man who spoke the language of capitalism: Henry Ford, the founder of the Ford Motor Company. A wiry man with cavernous eyes, Ford attributed "all evil to the Jews or the Jewish capitalists," as one friend described. He even believed jazz music had been created by Jews as a vehicle to covertly sow sinful ideas into wholesome minds. In response, he dumped massive amounts of money into square-dancing education programs in public schools in order to thwart the creep of jazz. Ford was so vociferous in his antisemitism, Hitler reportedly kept a life-sized portrait of him next to his desk.

Ford purchased his hometown newspaper, the *Dearborn Independent*, in Michigan, and through 1922, ran ninety-one installments of *The Protocols*, retitled "The International Jew: The World's Problem." These were eventually collected into a book, and a million copies circulated throughout America.

At the end of World War I, the United States' economy was shattered, and fear was rampant among the population. Jews became a scapegoat for those tensions. The decade, wrote the academic Eckard V.

Toy Jr., revealed that fundamentalists and millenarians often "held ambivalent attitudes toward Jews, and some of their members flirted openly with anti-semitism."

William Dudley Pelley was one person who believed *The Protocols* was real. He enjoyed a successful career as a fiction writer, and for a time traveled to Russia to report as a journalist on the Bolshevik Revolution for *The American Magazine*. There he began to consider notions that maybe Jews were behind a secret Communist plot.

He was a thin man with slick gray hair and a pointed Vandyke beard who stared out sharply from behind octagon-rimmed frames. He was peculiar, eccentric—the sort to cock his head to one side when he spoke, as if confused or deep in thought. A dyed-in-the-wool New Englander, he had a bright and contagious smile. If you knew the ideas that stirred inside him, that smile shifts to appear wildly sinister.

He became a darling writer of the silent film era in Hollywood, when several of his short stories were adapted to fit the big screen. One of the first was called "White Faith"—a tale that laid bare many of Pelley's prejudices through its villain, a Jewish pawnbroker who aimed to destroy the Holy Grail.

Despite the success it brought him, the film industry only seemed to shape Pelley's antisemitism into something more solid. Eventually, he would deem it "Jewish Hollywood" and everyone in it "Flesh Pots," and leave completely, retreating to a secluded bungalow in the brown mountain foothills above Altadena, California, with only his dog.

On the evening of May 28, 1928, Pelley had a sudden, life-altering, and irreversible revelation. By his telling, that night he fell asleep while reading a book, only to be shaken awake by a voice that seemed to be screaming inside his head. "I'm dying!" the voice shrieked. *"I'm dying!"*

It was a feeling he had never experienced before—a mental and physical paralysis, suspended in a strange in-between state, not asleep but not awake. He would later describe the sensation like tumbling through layers of blue mist.

Suddenly, Pelley found himself transported somewhere else

entirely: he awoke lying naked atop a cold marble slab. Two white-uniformed men, who appeared to be hospital workers, comforted him. He was in a spotless white room where an opal light reflected off the gleaming tiles, like the first rays of morning.

"Where am I?" he asked them.

The uniformed men smirked. "Don't try to see everything in the first seven minutes," one responded.

Pelley didn't know what that meant, and he rose slowly from his marble bed and walked across the room, entering a large Roman bath with "clear-as-crystal" waters, where he felt clothed again—unashamed of his earthly nakedness.

As he soaked in this otherworldly baptismal font, crowds of people passed through the white room, all heading toward a staircase leading outside, where he could see that the world beyond was an infinite expanse of turquoise blue. Every person who passed smiled. Eventually Pelley wandered with that crowd, looking for nothing and yet completely content to be walking toward the strange turquoise place.

Then it was over. He was sitting up in bed in Altadena.

"That wasn't a dream!" the real-world Pelley yelled, waking his dog, which was asleep at the foot of his bed.

For days, the feeling that something important and other-dimensional had happened stuck with him. Again, a few nights later as he read a book, he felt "a strange physical sensation at the very top of my head as though a beam of pure white light had poured down from above and bored a shaft into my skull. A veil was torn away."

Later, he wrote, "In all of my life up to that time I had never seen a ghost, never had more than an academic interest in psychic phenomena, and pooh-poohed Spiritualism as a sort of cracked-brain dogma that belonged in some pigeon-hole with palm reading and astrology. I had not invited any of these experiences that I knew of. They had simply come to me."

Pelley was a changed man. "The only term I can employ that comes anywhere near the truth is spirituality," he wrote. "All I can say is, that

I *know* by experience that there is a great, overpowering existence outside of what we call Life."

He claimed to be suddenly healed of lifelong ailments; a nervous stomach that had plagued him since childhood was gone. A voice told him to throw his cigarettes away, and he did. Later, when he instinctually reached for his corncob pipe, it was slapped from his grip by some unseen hand. He lost weight, gained muscle.

In New York, *The American Magazine*, which also published stories by Dashiell Hammett, F. Scott Fitzgerald, and Upton Sinclair, published Pelley's account of what he claimed occurred that night, an essay called "Seven Minutes in Eternity." Pelley said the intent wasn't to convert anyone, but to convey a clear and urgent message he felt was critical to share: there was no death. Life continues. This knowledge was "the touchstone that unlocks many another mystery." In a later book, he wrote further on the experience, saying "it makes life strong and beautiful and fine and true—something to be lived without fear or doubt or unhappiness."

How his "Seven Minutes" experience is interpreted by scholars varies. To Scott Beekman, a professor of history at University of Rio Grande who wrote a biography of Pelley, "Seven Minutes" was a mental breakdown. It later "opened the floodgates" for people with similar ideas to contact Pelley and make him feel special or chosen, like some kind of divine oracle or seer.

To others, it read as a sort of near-death experience, and Jeffrey Kripal, a professor of philosophy and religious thought at Rice University, said that near-death experiences are manifestations of the "religious imagination." However, he doesn't doubt the authenticity of anyone's near-death experience—if they say it occurred, dissecting its veracity is impossible.

After the publication of "Seven Minutes," the offices of *The American Magazine* were supposedly flooded with thousands of letters from readers who had also undergone beyond-the-veil experiences. Some saw his essay as an invitation to double down on their preexisting Christian beliefs. Others wanted more information, more detail. Before "Seven Minutes" Pelley had been a writer; after he was a man of God.

In a follow-up piece, he wrote that his "Seven Minutes" experience switched on a "mental radio" in his head, which allowed him to tune in to "minds and voices of those in another dimension of being." He would write down what he heard. Pelley claimed one message he received came to him in Sanskrit, a language he did not speak, and were the words of "an ancient Atlantean soul who declared he had not incarnated in mortal form for a period of 65,000 years."

Declaring himself a holy man did not cure Pelley of his rampant antisemitism. In 1933, those voices from his mental radio revealed to him that he should start a civilian paramilitary organization, which he called the Silver Shirts. It would become America's first antisemitic "Christian militia." In flyers for the group, Pelley wrote it was a "program for the advent of The Christ Democracy throughout the United States." The Silver Shirts "will not stand for the country being dominated and conducted by alien people whose ideas and ethics are not our ideas and ethics."

Like the Brown Shirts and the Blackshirts, the civilian paramilitary arms of the Nazi and National Fascist parties in Europe, members wore a uniform: blue corduroy knickers, and "shirts of a beautiful Silver-Gray" with an "L" stitched into the left breast in red thread—standing for love, loyalty, and Liberation. Several hundred men applied to be a member, which cost $10 a year, and an additional $6 for the shirt and knickers. Pelley claimed there were forty-eight chapters across the country.

It was the spiritual element of Pelley's group that appealed to people who might otherwise join the Ku Klux Klan.

The formation of the Silver Shirts drew the attention of the FBI, which began assembling a large dossier on the man. Agents researched Pelley, noting that after "Seven Minutes in Eternity" was published, they believed the stir it created allowed Pelley to "establish himself as a leader among people interested in metaphysics" as a kind of spiritual guru.

Pelley's aspirations did not stop there. In the summer of 1935, he announced he was also running for president of the United States as a member of the "Christian Party of America." His candidacy, he hoped, would be a direct attack on Jews in America. In casting a vote for him, he called for "every menaced Gentile in these prostrate United States to form an overwhelming juggernaut that shall launch itself at predatory Jewry and rip loose the smothering clutch which Jewish Communism has steadily perfected on Christian America." He said he would establish a "City of Jews" where all Jewish people would be forced to live.

Pelley set up his campaign headquarters in Seattle—the largest city in the only state where he could get onto the ballot, and where the Silver Shirts had found an enthusiastic membership among doctors, lawyers, and schoolteachers. In Washington State, the group began to spread a message that Pelley was chosen by God as the "white king" who would lead the country.

Scott Beekman estimates that at its height, the Silver Shirts had some 15,000 members across the country, as well as an additional 75,000 sympathizers. One writer deemed the group the "most vocal, most wild-eyed, and in some ways the most dangerous" of all extremist groups in the United States. Pelley, at one point, traveled with an entourage of 40 armed guards.

Under the direction of his deputies, the Washington State Silver Shirts prepared to overthrow the federal government on September 16, 1936, a date that many conspiracy theorists of the era believed had been etched inside the Pyramids of Giza in Egypt, eons prior. Several Silver Shirt leaders in the region sought to acquire high-caliber rifles and ammunition for the planned uprising. They held a belief there would be a Communist takeover in America before ballots were cast in November, which would prevent the election from happening and be their cue to begin their insurrection. The Silver Shirts would then install Pelley as president. But the election did happen: Pelley received only 1,598 votes. No uprising occurred.

Eventually, Pelley would tuck his tail between his legs, cowering before the federal government—which he so deeply criticized, believing it to be covertly run by Jews. He found himself in the center of congressional investigative crosshairs when the House Un-American Activities Committee asked him to explain some of the antisemitic propaganda he published in his magazines and newspapers. Sitting before them, Pelley testified that the Silver Shirts' presence wasn't needed anymore in America, and he would disband them.

But no amount of pandering would help; in 1942, he was arrested and put on trial for sedition charges. The federal government alleged that Pelley was hindering the American war effort with the continued publication of propaganda. After he was convicted by a jury, he was sentenced to fifteen years in prison.

The Silver Shirts fell apart, but Pelley's acolytes went on without him. In Portland, Oregon, a former Silver Shirt named Henry Beach went on to found Posse Comitatus in the 1960s—a group that would slowly evolve into the far-right Patriot movement. Beach spoke of the Silver Shirts' founder like he was a prophet: "He could take your ring and hold it and he could tell you your life's history," Beach said in 1985. "Pelley taught me how to communicate with the spirit world."

From the Los Angeles area, a young Silver Shirt named Richard Butler would go on to form the Aryan Nations. In the 1980s, he grounded it in a rural compound in North Idaho that for decades acted as a hive for Neo-Nazis and members of the KKK to gather. Butler was much like Pelley: a man who blended his faith with his violent antisemitism and preached it as the word of God from the pulpit of his own church.

Nearly a century later, on January 6, 2021, during the storming of the U.S. Capitol, it was Pelley's version of Americanism that was on display. One man wore a shirt cheering the Holocaust. Q signs were everywhere. When the leaders of the attempted insurrection were convicted, they were noted to be members of the Three Percenters, the Oath Keepers, the Proud Boys—groups that were like ideological grandchildren of Pelley's Silver Shirts.

After serving his sentence, according to Beekman, Pelley was banned from writing anything political. But he could write about the mysticism that "Seven Minutes" afforded him, and he created an entire religious system around it called "Soulcraft." In the 1950s alone, Pelley published more than two dozen books devoted to it, three separate magazines, and weekly sermons that were mailed to Soulcraft chapters nationwide. He claimed to be receiving messages directly from "mentors," just like Helena Blavatsky had from her Masters.

The foundation of Soulcraft was a belief that a cataclysm had destroyed two major civilizations: Atlantis and Lemuria. In a new magazine he called *Valor*, Pelley peddled doomsday predictions and stories about Atlantis and Lemuria. He said the Atlanteans migrated to Egypt after their continent was destroyed, that Christianity's religious roots were in Atlantis. None of these ideas were uniquely his, with Helena Blavatsky's "root-races" becoming "pure races" under Pelley's pen.

He preached that within the world population was a small group of humans who had ascended through five planes of dimension and had chosen to come back to Earth to serve as mentors for humanity. He called them the 144,000, referring to the group in the Book of Revelation who would survive the horrors that would befall the planet after Jesus's return. (Decades later, José Argüelles would revive the idea for his "harmonic convergence.")

Pelley also wrote a lot about aliens, integrating UFOs into the Soulcraft belief system. His idea was that extraterrestrials from other galaxies would bestow new wisdom upon humanity and help usher in the New Age. "These are space Aryans that he's talking about: they're blonde, blue-eyed," Beekman clarified.

Some of the Spiritualists who had initially been drawn in by Pelley's "Seven Minutes" essay were eventually turned off by his unavoidable antisemitism, which dripped from his prolific archive of magazines, newspapers, and books. Some Soulcraft followers gravitated toward other Spiritualist-adjacent groups. Some had already started their own. In Chicago, news of a new group led by Guy Ballard, a mining engineer, and his wife, Edna, a concert harpist, began to pop up. Small meetings became large meetings. Large meetings became multiday workshops, then events held in amphitheaters before audiences in the thousands. Some said the Ballards—who had previously dabbled in Christian Science, Rosicrucianism, Theosophy, and the occult—unabashedly stole their spiritual ideas from Pelley's Soulcraft.

But did that matter? By the time the story of Lemuria was in the Ballards' hands, it had already been strained through layers of theft. Helena Blavatsky had twisted Sclater's scientific theory to create an origin story of humanity that made it more spiritual and cosmic, merging it with piecemeal ideas from Eastern religions that were unfamiliar to most Americans. Then Pelley sifted her ideas through an antisemitic filter, distilling Lemuria into an ideology of white Christian supremacy where Masters weren't just faraway people, but space Aryans ruling the skies.

By midcentury, the foundation of the New Age had been built.

"It's a very messy family tree that contemporary seekers might not fully be aware of," said Deslippe. "The same ingredients that allowed for parts of metaphysical spirituality to go fascist a hundred years ago are also the same ingredients that can allow it to go fascist today."

10.

After several months of living in Colorado, Andrew Profaci could tell that Amy was spiraling deeper into her Mother God mythology. "Amy and I were clashing a lot," he said. "Every single night I'm pretty much saying, 'Look, I love you. You're not God, though. There is a flavor of crazy to what we're talking about here. I think we're doing a lot of great things. I think you have a lot of great ideas. You can definitely embody this energy of a goddess. But you are not The One.'"

It wasn't a popular position to take among the members of the Love Has Won team, who'd put their lives on hold to be there with Amy. They wanted to believe she was God, but in order to believe that, "they had to overlook all of their senses. Like, literally, you have to overlook all of your better judgment in order to get past it and believe. And that's what she was so masterful at."

Amy told anyone who aired doubts about her being God that their ego was getting in the way. If Andrew confronted Amy with her own style of blunt honesty, that was ego too. "She was the ultimate salesperson," he said.

She said ego stood for "Edging God Out" and drew up documents about "The EGO Blackhole."

"The EGO represents everything love is not," it read. "It sees everything as negative... The EGO looks at any situation and finds what is 'wrong' with it, rather than seeing everything as a miracle and lesson or blessing, as love does." It can never be satisfied. "The EGO is a parasite that sucks and sucks without any ending." She gave examples: people who eat too much, or sleep too much, are driven by ego. "Seeing God"—meaning Amy—"as evil and a liar" was derived of ego. Eating sugar was ego. Revering animals: ego. She listed a series of "conditionings" that were common traits among people with ego-programmed minds: "princess conditioning, bitch conditioning, asshole conditioning, duesch [sic] bag conditioning, gay conditioning."

When Amy wasn't around, Andrew would discuss his doubt among the other members. "I'm trying to say, 'Here's what we do that's good. The rest of this is delusion. Why don't we just focus on the good?'" he asked.

Andrew realized that members of the team used the Love Has Won chat rooms to boost Amy's feeling that she was actually God and to make the people who followed her feel like they were extensions of her divine energy. One Love Has Won member operated multiple user profiles. In one instance, a woman worried to the chat room that she couldn't find her mother's will and was afraid she would lose the family estate without it. Another user piped up and told the woman her mother's will would be found under the floorboards in the attic. The woman said she would look, and a few minutes later returned to the chat room: the will had been in the attic floor after all.

It was a miraculous moment—one that awed everyone in the chat, both in Colorado and beyond. But Andrew figured out that all the users involved in that conversation—the woman trying to find her mother's will, the person who pointed her toward the attic floorboards—were fake. It was an elaborate performance that played out in front of the entire Love Has Won following, a trick to make the group feel divinely chosen. Andrew pointed this out; some chose to ignore it. Others left the group over the charade.

"It was a revolving door," Andrew said. People were always coming and going from Amy's orbit, but her feeling was that she could always bring in new members.

In 2015, Andrew realized he was being replaced as Father God. A middle-aged man with a gray five o'clock shadow had recently arrived in Colorado, and Amy began sitting in his lap, snuggling up to him. She shot a quick video of this new man dancing in cargo shorts and a sweatshirt, jittering around like he was at a Jimmy Buffett concert. "There's Father God," she announced.

Andrew wasn't entirely surprised and made plans to leave the group while he was still on good terms with everyone. Before he left, he cautioned this new, older Father God not to give all of his money to Amy. "I was like, 'Dude, you're not gonna be Father God. *I'm* not Father God. I'm telling you now, do not do this. Do not liquidate your 401(k), do not give your money to her. It will be gone. You will never see it,'" he said. "He didn't want to listen. He wanted to be Father God so bad, and it came back to bite him in the ass."

"He left the team two months after giving them $400,000," Andrew claimed, "and he had nothing."

Andrew moved in with his father near Fort Lauderdale, Florida, but he continued to log into the Love Has Won chat rooms to talk to his friends each day. One day, Amy told the group she'd received a message from her angels: she was supposed to join Andrew in Florida. The new Father God drove her to Texas and dropped her off, Andrew picked her up, and the pair drove back across the South together.

Back with Andrew, she became Amy again. "She put the Mother God thing aside. She was fun," he said. They would talk about her unresolved trauma from her childhood, about her drinking problem—how she'd been attacking other people's egos, but maybe she could seek therapy and do some work on her own. "I got her to admit she wasn't Mother God on a couple of occasions," Andrew said. "But just as quickly as I got her to admit it, she would snap right back out of it."

Even when Amy was far away from the group in Colorado, she was always close by online, particularly to Miguel Lamboy, Archangel Michael, her longtime collaborator. For him to continue to be an archangel, Amy had to continue to be God.

Andrew knew he was no match for Miguel. He "was always on the other end of the phone, or the other end of an email, reeling her back in. If she was a marionette, he was the guy pulling the strings."

Amy spent two months in Florida, but when it became clear she was unwilling, or unable, to sever Mother God from her personality, Andrew dropped her off at a hotel and told her goodbye. "I had to eventually admit defeat," he said. When he left her, he left Love Has Won entirely too—the team, the chat room, the community he'd found. He knew that would make him an enemy to the group. "Everybody that ever left the team was called the devil, or they had demons in them," he said. But it didn't matter—he knew by then that the entire project was a delusion built to serve Amy and Amy alone. Even so, he still believes his time with Love Has Won actually helped him. "I wouldn't trade it for anything in the world," he said. "I came out of it a way better person."

Sometimes, though, he thinks the day he dropped her off was the day Amy's downfall began. "After dealing with me," he said, "someone who was breaking down the illusion so hard, I think she went hardcore in the other direction... I do believe I was the catalyst that really drove her into this hard-liner, Mother God belief systems. I think she really took root and was like, 'I'm not letting someone else come in here and get me off being Mother God ever again.'"

When Amy went back west to join Miguel and the rest of the team, instead of her meeting them in Colorado, they convened in California, near Mount Shasta: another place that has a long history of people feeling drawn there because of a spiritual calling.

There Amy spoke of a set of Masters who guided her and bestowed ancient knowledge upon her, much like Helena Blavatsky had. Amy deemed them her "Galactic A Team," or simply "the Galactics." At the helm was Saint Germain; in the 1700s, the Count of Saint Germain was a high-society adventurer, philosopher, and alchemist who lived in France. He is considered one of the most famous occultists of the modern era and was written about by Blavatsky often. Now he is revered by many New Age thinkers.

But under Amy's steering, no longer were the Masters faraway gurus living in the Himalayas. She said the singer Prince, who died in 2016, was a Master. Rapper Tupac Shakur and the pop star Whitney Houston were Masters. Aretha Franklin, Walt Disney, Chris Farley, John Lennon, Michael Jackson, Kobe Bryant, Bob Marley, *Superman* actor Christopher Reeve, Gene Wilder, and Texas comedian Bill Hicks were all Amy's Masters. Her stepfather, Reed Haythorne, became one too.

But to Amy, one Master was above them all: Ascended Master Robin Williams, the comedian and beloved actor, who played an alien living on Earth in the 1970s television sitcom *Mork & Mindy* when Amy was a little girl.

"I give eternal gratefulness, and greatness to Master Robin, and Germain. Two masters who have been by my side for many years now as we make our transition through the ascension process," Amy once said. "Robin and Germain, my best friends."

"People choose their own paths in life," Amy's sister Chelsea said. "Were we upset that she left? Yes. Was it hard for her kids? Of course."

Her family had no idea where she was, but for a while they knew they could probably find her online. Before Love Has Won, Linda, Chelsea, and Tara would try to look at Amy's websites to discern some kind of meaning from them, but it never really made sense. "It was obvious that maybe they were smoking weed or something," Chelsea said, "but it didn't seem like there was anything else crazy going on ... besides that they all believed the same craziness."

Sometimes Chelsea, who has several children of her own, would catch herself thinking about her older sister, somewhere out there in the world, believing she was a God or an alien, while her family was back at home picking up the pieces of the life she broke apart. Everyone was so angry at how Amy abandoned her children.

"I fought so hard to get mine," her mother, Linda, said, "and here she leaves hers."

In 2015, Amy's stepfather, Reed, had a brain hemorrhage, then a heart attack, and died.

Linda sent Amy a text message asking to get on the phone quickly. Something had happened. When she didn't answer, Linda texted her that the man who raised her was dead. "Mom, I already knew that," Amy texted back.

It took Linda aback. "I don't know whether she had heard from somebody else. I don't think so," she said. It was just such a strange reaction. Amy seemed to be saying she knew because she was God.

By then, Amy had been calling herself Mother God for years. But there was never a moment when Linda, or any of her family for that matter, considered that to be true. "I said, 'Amy, you're not God,'" Linda said.

Exactly three months after Reed's sudden death, Chelsea delivered a full-term baby boy stillborn. All this sudden devastation was overwhelming, washing over the family like an ocean. And yet all the while, Amy stayed away. She never came home.

"She should have been there," Chelsea said. "Where was she when I lost my son? Where was she when our dad died?"

After the death of her father and her infant son, Chelsea and her husband found a place of comfort in the face of so much pain—the local Methodist church in their town of Brenham, Texas, where the congregation raised money so they could bury their baby boy. "We're a teacher and a fireman with all these kids. We don't have lots of money," she said.

Eventually the couple would find a permanent spiritual community at a local nondenominational church. One year, when Chelsea broke her foot right before Christmas, people from her church brought over pans of lasagna and trays of brownies. They wanted them to know they were taken care of.

For the first time in her life, Chelsea began to call herself religious. "It's the community for us. We always feel like our life goes better and goes easier for us when we are going to church," she said. "I'm religious now. I wouldn't say I'm spiritual. I am, but in a religious way." Not the way her sister Amy was spiritual. "I chose to go towards God because of losing my dad and losing my son, and I didn't know where else to turn. So, my reasoning for choosing is different."

Sometimes Chelsea tried to understand how her older sister took spirituality in a direction that was so unclear, so conspiratorial, so... online. Chelsea has watched hours of Amy's videos, and still can't discern a teaching that makes any sense to her, or that helps people like the churches in Brenham did for her. But in the end, they both chose God. For Chelsea, God was in the people around her.

For Amy, God was in herself.

11.

In the commonly used Rider-Waite-Smith tarot deck, the Tower card is depicted as a gray obelisk set atop a mountain, looming high into a dark night sky. From one corner of the card, a lightning bolt strikes the structure, and the whole thing bursts into flames. People fall from the windows, or leap to their deaths, and a giant crown tumbles from atop the building.

There are no right or wrong ways to interpret a tarot card; intuitive readers will tell you that it's all about feeling. Many, though, see something biblical in that card, specifically the Old Testament story referencing the Tower of Babel. In the Book of Genesis, the story goes that people built a tower high enough to reach the heavens. But God, seeing this act of unity and cooperation as an attempt to subvert his will, decided the people should be divided. To confuse them, he gave them different languages, so they were unable to communicate and finish the tower. In the story, God is a manipulator, and people are slaves to his grand plan.

The Tower can be seen as a card of sudden, powerful changes. It can mean a structure someone has spent so long building—a career, an educational path, a relationship—could fail. It could mean a realization: that building that path may have been wrongheaded all along. "The old way is no longer viable," *The Library of Esoterica* tarot guide explained. "Cracks appear, the sky opens, bricks crumble ... There is no escape. Chaos, disruption."

Over the years, as tarot cards have become more popular, new interpretations of the Tower have given the card deeper meaning. In the Brady Tarot, designed by Denver printmaker Emi Brady, the tower is depicted as a knotty old tree being struck by lightning. Birds' beaks poke from the tree's holes. Some fly away, others stay.

In his Prisma Visions tarot deck, Los Angeles artist James Eads illustrated the Tower not as an obelisk, or a tree, but instead as a tall Victorian mansion at night, lit up from the inside, like a party is underway. A close look at the card shows that the house is built on unstable ground, the ground below eroded away by water and time, leaving it sitting on the edge of a cliff. From inside, it would seem like waterfront property; from outside, gravity is clearly coming.

And yet the house glows. No one flees. One interpretation could be that maybe people are piled inside the house, jumping on a dance floor knowing that their time to go is coming. They are aware cataclysmic change is inevitable. But instead, they've thrown a party for the end of the world. They plan to go down together.

Mount Shasta is a looming 14,162-foot volcano in the Cascade Range that punches suddenly out of the arid Northern California landscape. In comparison to the prettier, more aquiline Cascade beauty queens to its north—Mount Hood and Mount Jefferson with their picture-perfect peaks; the Three Sisters, huddled together like a girl gang—Shasta is wide and unignorable, a chaotic lump of stiff meringue thwacked down from the sky. All alone, it commands attention.

The mountain acts as a territorial boundary for the Modoc, Shasta, Wintu, and Ajumawi/Atsuwegi people. Plate tectonics, the very process that shaped the Earth's geography, formed Shasta and the mountains around it. The land of Northern California sits atop giant plates that are always moving, ever so slightly. Hundreds of thousands of years ago, an entirely different Mount Shasta stood where the current one does; when that mountain's northern flank collapsed, it triggered an enormous landslide that swept across the landscape. As it was reforming the geography around it, the mountain continued to have a succession of "eruptive episodes," which fashioned the rounded mound of Shasta of today—the mountain that compels every eye to see it.

From the time white explorers first laid eyes on that great peak, it seemed to draw people by the heart and pull them closer.

In 1838, the United States Exploring Expedition sent ships packed with hundreds of military personnel and scientists, including naturalists, botanists, mineralogists, and taxidermists to the Pacific Ocean under the direction of Navy lieutenant Charles Wilkes. The Wilkes Expedition, as it would become known, would sail for four straight years in order to map and explore the Pacific Ocean and the Northwest, among many other locations.

One of the expedition's ships, the *Peacock*, was abandoned when it ran aground in the angry, stormy waters of Cape Disappointment, the place where the Pacific Ocean meets the Columbia River. The thirty-nine men aboard were then dispatched on an overland journey hundreds of miles south from what is now Portland, Oregon. Along the way, they would continue to map, survey, and collect zoological specimens. When eventually Mount Shasta came into view, a geologist professed the mountain was "a vision of immensity" that "pertains to the vast universe rather than to our own planet." Later, other white pioneers described the urge "to kneel in worship" before it.

The mountain had a knack for inspiring wonder and speculation—its own kind of Tower, a place of reckoning, a place of ruin. In 1883, a teenaged local named Frederick Spencer Oliver was mapping family property at the base of the peak when suddenly, he claimed, his hand started scribbling words without his control, as if guided by some unseen force.

It was the kind of automatic writing New Age authors like Helena Blavatsky and William Dudley Pelley practiced, and Oliver's scribblings from that day would eventually become a book called *A Dweller on Two Planets*. It is a story presented as a true encounter with a spirit named "Phylos the Thibetan" on the side of Mount Shasta. His mother, so proud of her son's strange writing, published Oliver's work after he died in 1899, at the age of thirty-three.

"Shasta is a true guardian, and silently towers, giving no sign of that within his breast," Oliver wrote. "But there is a key. The one who first conquers self, Shasta will not deny."

During the Gold Rush, Mount Shasta became a place of fascination for miners and treasure hunters. Oliver stoked this fascination in his book, weaving stories about Atlantis and Lemuria and long passageways that snaked into the heart of the great mountain—not just to hidden deposits of gold, but to a sparkling hidden city made of it:

"Tall basalt cliff conceals a doorway. We do not suspect this, nor that a long tunnel stretches away, far into the interior of majestic Shasta," he wrote. He said those tunnels led to the home of a mystic brotherhood. "Does it truly exist?" Oliver wrote. "Seek and ye shall find."

These words would stoke a belief that buried deep in the core of Mount Shasta was the heart of Lemuria.

Sometime during the spring of 1930, Guy Ballard ventured up the side of Shasta to do his own research. He was a pale man with slicked hair and wide eyes that gave him a look of permanent surprise. Like generations of colonizers and treasure seekers before him, Ballard had taken a keen interest in gold prospecting in the West, and on at least one occasion made a trip to search the Sierra Nevadas for that purpose with the assistance of a Spiritualist medium.

But he had come to Shasta looking for something different—not gold, but a mystical brotherhood that was rumored to have dwelled inside the great mountain.

"Most rumors, myths and legends have somewhere as their origin, a deep underlying Truth that usually remains unrecognized," Ballard would later write. If there was truth to the myth, he believed he would be the man to find it.

He rose before the sun and set out up the south side of the mountain to Panther Meadows, where wide green pastures dappled with purple lupine and marmalade-orange poppies give way to a view of the grand, snow-covered peak.

As the weather warmed, Ballard stopped at a spring and kneeled to fill a tin cup with mountain water. As he did so, "an electrical current passed through my body from head to foot," he wrote, and behind him was a man he hadn't noticed before. "He stood there before me—a Magnificent God-like figure—in a white jeweled robe," Ballard would describe, "a Light and Love sparkling in his eyes that revealed and proved the Dominion and Majesty that are his."

"My brother," this strange hiker said to Ballard, "if you will hand me your cup, I will give you a much more refreshing drink than spring water." Ballard, a seeker who had come here seeking, obliged.

"Instantly, the cup was filled." A "creamy" liquid seemed to manifest from the air itself, and Ballard took a sip.

"While the taste was delicious, the electrical vivifying effect in my mind and body made me gasp with surprise," Ballard said. "I wondered what was happening."

The man explained that the liquid came from "the Universal Supply," and that whatever Ballard desired could be produced from that supply: he only had to ask for it.

"If I wish to use gold—gold is here," the man said. A gold disk was suddenly in his palm.

The man introduced himself as an Ascended Master named Saint Germain.

Ballard and Germain spent that entire day wandering the wilderness, and at the end of it, Germain promised he would return again in the morning.

The next day, as instructed, Ballard waited for Saint Germain to return, sitting on a log to pass the time. As he waited, he noticed a black panther slinking silently toward him through the brush, eyes fixed, readying itself to pounce. (While cougars do call the forests around Mount Shasta home, no black panther species lives in the entirety of North America.) He was being hunted. Ballard became frantic, but then remembered something Saint Germain had told him the day prior. "That life, Omnipresent Life, exists everywhere about us, is subject to our conscious control and direction, is willingly obedient when we love enough because, he said, all the universe obeys the behest of love."

Ballard felt like he had God inside of him, and that the panther did too—like they were two appendages of one holy body, and that a creation of God wouldn't harm itself. Ballard stood and walked toward the stalking predator and was filled "with a great feeling of love." As he got closer, the big cat's eyes softened. It rubbed its huge shoulder against his leg, flopped down, and rolled over like a housecat. Ballard stooped to rub the animal's belly, and only then realized Saint Germain had arrived, and was watching.

When Ballard came down from the mountain, he claimed that he had been appointed as Saint Germain's "divine messenger" on Earth, hand-selected to deliver the truth of what he called the Ascended Masters to humanity. For 600 years, Saint Germain had searched for a "human embodiment strong enough and pure enough" to carry his messages. Ballard said his wife, Edna, and his son, Donald, were also elected to be "accredited" messengers. He also claimed that he had attained "self-immortality," which kept him from aging, getting sick, becoming poor, or being generally miserable.

Compared side by side with the account of Phylos the Tibetan relayed by Oliver in *A Dweller on Two Planets*, Ballard's encounter with Saint Germain is nearly identical. Later, the estate of Frederick Spencer Oliver would sue the Ballards' foundation over copyright infringement and lose.

And few cared anyway. Soon, thousands of people would believe the Ballard family were the chosen ones.

His encounter with Saint Germain on the side of a mountain had been serendipitously timed. The law was bearing down on Guy Ballard, who was accused by a Cook County, Illinois, grand jury of "obtaining money and goods by means of a confidence game" after he got people to invest in a venture that promised wealth from a "lake of gold" in California. But when warrants were issued for his arrest, Ballard was long gone.

The Ballard family's appointment as the messengers of the Masters coincided with American Lemuria obsessives moving the fabled land closer to home. In 1931, a book called *Lemuria: The Lost Continent of the Pacific* relocated Helena Blavatsky's Lemuria to the California coast, where the author said Mount Shasta had once been the civilization's tallest peak. When a *Los Angeles Times* reporter visiting the area asked people about lights he saw flashing on the mountain they told him it was Lemurians.

Spiritualists squabbled over the veracity of these supposed Lemuria-in-Shasta accounts, which seemed to threaten the entire New Age community with a label of quackery. "The whole thing is a figment of the imagination of self-seekers who would exploit an honest seeking people and rake in the shekels," wrote one letter writer to *Light: A Journal of Spiritualism, Psychical, Occult and Mystical Research*, notably using an antisemitic term in his criticism.

The Ballards founded a group they called the "I AM" Activity. They derived the name "I AM" from the moment in the Book of Exodus when Moses saw a burning bush. "And God said unto Moses, I AM THAT I AM: and he said, Thus shalt thou say unto the children of Israel, I AM hath sent you." Ballard believed his time on Mount Shasta with Saint Germain had been his burning-bush moment, and that another name for God was simply "I AM."

As the "Accredited Masters" of I AM, the couple took new names: Guy transformed into "Godfre Ray King." Some simply called him "Daddy." The couple founded the Saint Germain Press, which published Ballard's first book, *Unveiled Mysteries*—a suspiciously Blavatskian name. Edna was renamed "Lotus Ray King." They said they had reincarnated several times and lived myriad past lives. Guy had lived as George Washington; Edna, Joan of Arc. They took direction from Ascended Masters.

Catherine Wessinger, from Loyola University New Orleans, pointed out that when Helena Blavatsky first wrote of the Masters, they were described as wise old men living far away in the Himalayas. But after Pelley incorporated UFOs and extraterrestrials into his Soulcraft system, which the Ballards then duplicated, the Masters became *Ascended* Masters. Wessinger suggested that this placed UFOs, and aliens, at the heart of the I AM belief system. And this alien-ness is evident in even a cursory look at I AM's posters and art, where people are portrayed as having large foreheads, massive unblinking eyeballs, and smooth, unmarred skin.

I AM taught that God was inside each person, and that a person's "higher self" was also known as the "I AM" presence. To followers, the words "God" and "I AM" could be used interchangeably, and a practice of repeating positive affirmations of all the things that one *is*, instead of what one is not, was at the heart of their teachings. "Everyone is divine and perfect in essence, and therefore is always in a condition of perfect health," observed Tim Rudbøg, a historian of religions at the University of Copenhagen.

"When one states a simple sentence, such as 'I AM happy,' one makes use of God's name, which is identical to one's own self," Rudbøg explained. "Thus it is highly destructive to make a statement that includes a negative affirmation, such as 'I AM unhappy.'"

Like Pelley's Soulcraft, I AM was, at its heart, Christian; Jesus was one of the Ascended Masters. Death was reframed in the style of Spiritualists: part of a process of rising toward a new plane of existence, not a total end.

The Ballards instructed followers to use "the Violet Consuming Flame of Divine Love." Today, the Saint Germain Foundation describes it as a force that can be summoned with the power of visualization, violet fire that originates at the feet that slowly moves up the body, consuming "every undesirable thing or condition," freeing a person from imperfection. Because of this, to be a part of I AM meant wearing purple or white clothing. Colors were important to the group: it railed against nefarious "black magicians," who would out themselves by wearing black clothing. Red was affiliated with Communism.

The Ballards started by hosting ten-day workshops at their home in Chicago for just a handful of people, who were all sworn to secrecy. Soon they looked farther afield, and brought their message to Philadelphia, then New York City, then Washington, D.C. First a few people came, then 30, then 150. Over time, the audiences would number in the thousands, drawing in "those who were already believers in the occult," wrote one historian, "and 'patriotic' people."

By 1935, the family had permanently relocated to Southern California, where they required ever larger spaces to hold meetings. In August of that year, they booked the Shrine Auditorium in Los Angeles, which held 6,000 people, for a ten-day string of workshops. The Ballards raked in money from ticket sales and "zoomed away in a couple of flashy cream-colored Chryslers," according to one ex-follower. They claimed to heal people by the hundreds with their powers, believing themselves the key in the "salvation of mankind."

When the Ballards took the stage in front of crowds of their fans, they did not disappoint. Edna had pencil-thin eyebrows, dark lipstick, and her blonde hair pinned up in curls. She was "radiant, and sparkling with jewels, dressed as for the opera," wrote one audience member. Guy wore a white tuxedo and his hair slicked. Sometimes a long indigo-blue cape draped from his shoulders, just like Saint Germain on Mount Shasta, as he delivered messages from the Masters.

During J. Edgar Hoover's tenure as FBI director, organizational files made mention of the Ballard group and contained letters sent from concerned Americans. Some called the group "the purple cult," given their affinity for violet-colored clothing and talk of a violet flame. People surmised I AM was a "fifth column" group, much like Pelley's Silver Shirts, only better at masquerading as a religious organization.

And perhaps that wasn't far off base: when the Ballards poached ideas from Pelley, they also lifted his sense of hypernationalism and anti-Communist rhetoric. Messages received by Saint Germain referenced America as a "Christian Democracy."

In 1940, Gerald Bryan, a former follower of the I AM Activity, labeled the group as totalitarian in a book he published, *Psychic Dictatorship in America* (which the Ballards subsequently instructed their followers to buy and burn). He said members were told to sever contact with anyone who wasn't in the group and that spirits living within house pets should be released—which meant killing them. Meat, garlic, onions, alcohol, tobacco, and sex were to be avoided, and procreation was discouraged because the world might soon end.

I AM ceremonies played out like tent revivals. "I AM LOVE GIFT" envelopes were distributed to the audience by white-robed attendants with American flag pins fixed to their lapels. "Love gifts" were I AM–speak for cash, or even jewelry; the more generous the donations, the more the channels to the Ascended Masters would open.

In his book, Bryan reported that discussion of "vicious forces" throughout America dominated the discussion at I AM ceremonies, and that only the power of Saint Germain could obliterate them. "This is not a religion, but a patriotic movement," one of the Ballards' deputies said from the stage at one event.

The Ballards delivered sermons about the five things they believed were a threat to American society: "spies, communism, the labor movement, dope and war." This idea was reinforced by two auxiliary I AM organizations: The Minute Men of Saint Germain, a men's organization that also acted as bodyguards to the Ballards, and the Daughters of Light—the same, but women. Both groups, according to Bryan, were intended to "fly to the rescue of America, as the Minute Men did in 1776."

Both groups also had their own songs: the Daughters sung of "blazing the light of God throughout America," and the Minute Men's "Marching Song" declared that only "through Saint Germain, America is free."

The news that Guy Ballard had become gravely ill in late 1939 was kept closely guarded; when a journalist named Arthur Orrmont knocked on the door of the family's sprawling twenty-room mansion, located in the exclusive Griffith Park section of Los Angeles, he was "knocked down by a brace of hefty bodyguards, shoved into his car and told to scram." This was not atypical; "for some time now I AM Minute Men had been inhospitable to reporters," he wrote. Orrmont said that a last-ditch surgery had been clandestinely performed on the I AM patriarch in an attempt to save his life.

Guy Ballard, a.k.a. Godfre Ray King, the man who claimed he could not die, *did* die at 5:20 a.m. on December 29, 1939, at age sixty-one. His death certificate listed "arterio-sclerotic heart disease" and "cardiac cirrhosis of the liver" as contributing causes.

"Our Blessed Daddy Ballard made his Ascension," Edna Ballard announced to the crowd at the Shrine Auditorium, "and is now an Ascended Master."

Some followers were confused: Hadn't Guy Ballard stood before them all and told them he was immortal? That he could heal the sick? Edna waved that away; this was what they had been instructing all along. Death was not an end, but a continuation. He was simply existing now on another plane. He had ascended.

I AM might have died alongside its founder, but Edna had other plans. She parlayed his death into a new revenue stream: photographs of Guy Ballard were sold for between $2.50 and $25, and recordings of his speeches became available for purchase.

In the year after her husband's death, the United States accused Edna, their son, Donald, and twenty-two other members of the group of using the U.S. Postal Service to defraud unwitting people and sell "a special brand of immortality" through the mail, offering "cures for disease and blindness."

When news of the charges broke, I AM followers flooded the FBI with hundreds of letters: a form letter that had clearly been given to them by leaders, the language identical, and only the shape and style of their looping cursive penmanship differing. It didn't do much to dispel the notion that they were being led.

> *Dear Sir:*
> *The 'I AM' Activity is an educational and intense patriotic activity…*
> *Since 1933, it has been arousing the American people into action*
> *to sweep out of our country Communism, Fascism, Naziism, the Fifth*
> *Column and all subversive activities and to sustain our form of government*
> *in its original form.*

The letters quoted from the *I AM Discourses*, calling America the "Precious jewel in the crown," and a "flower of Ancient Wisdom and Light." The senders were overwhelmingly female.

Nonetheless, the Ballard case reached a Los Angeles courtroom in December 1940 and the proceedings—which only saw nine of the group's high-profile members on trial—attracted crowds of onlookers and journalists from around the country, curious to learn more about the strange group that had set up hundreds of outposts.

At the trial, Edna Ballard appeared as she did on I AM stages: in a white jacket with a white flower brooch over a white blouse, and a white turban on her head. At her request, the judge relinquished his traditional black robe, a color with such negative energy that she claimed it physically sickened her.

Throughout the trial, details about the group's teachings found their way into the proceedings, despite the charges being about mail fraud. "Defense witnesses," read a column in Ohio's *Akron Beacon Journal*, "declare under oath that the 'I AM' teachings lifted them to a state of virtual perfection, mental, moral and spiritual."

By believing, I AM adherents thought themselves to be participating in a kind of spiritual warfare. Prosecutors read from an I AM periodical in which Ballard was said to have destroyed a fleet of Nazi submarines aimed to attack the Panama Canal with his mind. One witness testified that their collective power disintegrated a squadron of German planes headed for America. The group believed it had prevented the entire Atlantic coast from breaking off from the continent and floating away. Edna Ballard didn't deny any of it.

After a month of arguments, in January 1941, prosecutors failed to gain a single conviction for any of the defendants; the jury acquitted three and couldn't reach an agreement on the others, including Edna and Donald. Edna jumped to her feet in the courtroom, sermonizing that they hadn't "broken the law of God or man in carrying on this great work."

But her woes were hardly over. Just a few months later, federal prosecutors re-tried the case against the Ballards and several of their colleagues on a dozen similar mail fraud charges. The government alleged that Guy Ballard had devised the I AM belief system as an elaborate scheme to scam people out of money and property "by means of false or fraudulent pretenses, representations and promises."

At the second trial, which began in December 1941, Judge J. F. T. O'Connor lectured that this trial was not about the validity of the religious belief system. It was about fraud.

"Religion is definitely not an issue in this case. It is a question of sincerity," O'Connor said. "If these defendants were honest in their beliefs, they should be acquitted. If they were not and used the mails for the purposes of getting money, they should be convicted."

Prosecutors read transcripts aloud to the courtroom of supposed conversations with Saint Germain that had been taken down by the Ballards. A widow took the stand, telling the courtroom that Edna ensured the teachings of I AM would heal her husband's blindness. "Mrs. Ballard told me to visualize a ray of light coming straight down to my husband's head and then leaving it at right angles through his eyes," she said. Her husband remained blind.

In his closing statement, the attorney for the Ballards and their codefendants made a dramatic appeal to the jury: "Is it criminal to defraud people of frowns, disharmony, bad habits, fear of the future and lack of faith in a supreme being?" he asked. If so, "You will convict a new type of criminal—highwaymen who teach people to be good."

This time the jury found the Ballards guilty.

The case ping-ponged through the courts like this for years.

In the spring of 1944, the case facing the Ballards arrived in the columned halls of the Supreme Court. After deliberations, the justices reached a 5–4 decision, with Justice William O. Douglas presenting the court's majority opinion, which sent the case back to a lower court to be re-litigated, where the Ballards were victorious.

"The First Amendment has a dual aspect," Douglas wrote. It "embraces two concepts—freedom to believe and freedom to act. The first is absolute but, in the nature of things, the second cannot be."

At the heart of the I AM case, he said, was a protection that was fundamental to American freedoms. "Men may believe what they cannot prove," Douglas said. "Religious experiences which are as real as life to some may be incomprehensible to others."

Douglas pointed out that America's Founding Fathers likely could not have imagined the religious landscape of the future but had created a document that envisioned "the widest possible toleration of conflicting views. Man's relation to his God was made no concern of the state. He was granted the right to worship as he pleased, and to answer to no man for the verity of his religious views."

In one of the court's two dissents, Justice Robert Jackson seemed mystified by the law protecting such obvious grifters: "I can see in their teachings nothing but humbug, untainted by any trace of truth.

"The chief wrong which false prophets do to their following is not financial," he wrote. "But the real harm is on the mental and spiritual plane. There are those who hunger and thirst after higher values which they feel wanting in their humdrum lives. They live in mental confusion or moral anarchy, and seek vaguely for truth and beauty and moral support. When they are deluded and then disillusioned, cynicism and confusion follow. The wrong of these things, as I see it, is not in the money the victims part with half so much as in the mental and spiritual poison they get. But that is precisely the thing the Constitution put beyond the reach of the prosecutor, for the price of freedom of religion or of speech or of the press is that we must put up with, and even pay for, a good deal of rubbish."

The court's ruling created an impenetrable shield around religion in America. The Ballards' remarkable Supreme Court victory was "an American tale of frauds, charlatans, and the long rise of the post-truth era," wrote religious scholar Charles McCrary in his book *Sincerely Held*. And it underscored something significant: you can say you're a person of God, but that doesn't mean you have to act like a good person.

At every level of the courts, prosecutors in the Ballards' trials had assumed that to believe in any God meant to act in good faith, and that by illustrating how someone is acting in *bad* faith would prove their beliefs moot. One prosecutor had homed in on the slate of commercial products offered by I AM: photos, rings, even facial cream. He said they were all instruments used by the Ballards to dupe people and siphon their money.

Ultimately, the Supreme Court decided that it didn't matter if the beliefs of I AM seemed provably false. People can believe in just about anything with their entire being. And if they believe it completely, it's protected.

It's notable that it was I AM that earned so much protection for all religions in America, or ideas people claim are religious. Because at the heart of its ideology is an idea that dissolves something supposedly impenetrable in America: the wall dividing church from state.

I AM combined church and state, weaving together the life of Jesus with the life of America. Their hymns were American songs.

Every summer, they tell the story of America as a Christian nation.

After Edna Ballard was vindicated by the highest court in the country, the group set its collective eye on the volcano looming in the dry country of Northern California, Mount Shasta. A July 1948 article in the *Mount Shasta Herald* announced the group's arrival.

"Mrs. Ballard," it read, "said that in coming to the city of Mount Shasta her group has no desire to disturb the citizens of the town, or to intrude in any way."

But residents remained concerned. At a town hall meeting, some 200 locals crammed into a lodge to hear Edna bemoan how her group had been unfairly maligned. "Those who have sought to tell untruths (about us) have paid the penalty," she said. "The Constitution gives us the right to believe in God. We give freedom, and we shall maintain our own."

Her group intended to stay in Mount Shasta permanently. The Saint Germain Foundation—I AM's umbrella organization—purchased the vast Shasta Springs Resort overlooking the Sacramento River in Dunsmuir, a few minutes south of Mount Shasta, in 1951. For decades, the resort had been open to the public, advertising "superbly-appointed cottages" in "paradise amid the majestic pines and lordly oaks." It was a summer haven where visitors sampled cool clear water from the famed springs (which was also sold in bottles) and sat in rocking chairs in the clubhouse. Guests rode in a cable car into the treetops high above the misty Mossbrae Falls, a series of spindly threads of water that fall gracefully over ancient rocks. When the Ballards bought it, they permanently closed the white wrought iron gates; only their own people were allowed to enter.

The summer the Ballards came to town, the Alpine Lodge located on Mount Shasta experienced its busiest week, with some sixty-three climbers making successful ascents of the mountain. Thirty-three of them were I AM Youth Conclave members.

That same summer, Edna unveiled one of her biggest plans for I AM: an annual theatrical reenactment of the life of Jesus Christ called the "I AM" Come! Pageant that illustrated the group's ideas about ascension, with all the bad parts removed. "Mrs. Ballard wanted it to be a healing, beautiful side of Jesus' life," said Beatrice Rowe, the longtime director of the pageant, in 1990. In other words, the Crucifixion is left out.

"We are not living in a 'Pollyanna' existence," Rowe told a local reporter; Edna intended the event to be a "positive, simple, beautiful portrayal of the life of Jesus," held in a setting of natural beauty. What remains of Jesus's story without the whole sacrificing-for-the-sins-of-mankind part is the Last Supper, the agony in the Garden of Gethsemane, and the Resurrection.

The elaborate production has been performed since 1948 during the second weekend in August. People come from around the world to act in the production each year—an annual tradition that they consider a "lifelong commitment." One man moved from Switzerland to play the part of Jesus, a role he held for more than a decade. A Detroit man, who worked "as a Y2K consultant for General Motors," played John the Baptist for more than twenty-five years. A welder from Portland, Oregon, played Peter.

Audience members travel to Mount Shasta from all over the world, chartering planes and buses to see the pageant. While it is hosted for free to the public, the Saint Germain Foundation does accept "love offerings from anyone wishing to give them." Attendees are encouraged to wear white or pastel clothing.

In 2019, the "I AM" Come! Pageant occurred on a characteristically bright, sunny day. An organist began to play and a female voice provided the disclaimer that they would skip the violent parts of Jesus's life because "that was the action and the viciousness of the sinister force. It did not reveal beloved Jesus's use of his own God power."

At the pageant's conclusion, as hundreds of actors and audience members looked on, the man playing Jesus ascended thirty-four feet into the air. Some years he disappears into a flash of light.

Around him, crowned and winged angels hold large American flags at center stage. After Jesus rises into the air, a chorus sings "America the Beautiful," which the Saint Germain Foundation explained in pamphlets symbolizes "the 'Ascension' of America into her eternal freedom."

Over the years, the Saint Germain Foundation hosted more pageants, one about the signing of the Declaration of Independence in which Saint Germain appears in a violet suit and gives an impassioned speech. Another was titled "The Consecration of George Washington."

In many ways, the elaborate pageants are reminiscent of those of the Church of Jesus Christ of Latter-day Saints. For fifty-two years, eight days of theatrical productions portraying scenes from the Book of Mormon were held in Manti, Utah. Until 2019, the Hill Cumorah Pageant took place on a ten-level stage in Palmyra, New York, near the place where Joseph Smith supposedly unearthed the golden plates that would become the Book of Mormon.

In their flag-waving brand of patriotism, the similarities between the LDS Church and the I AM Activity are many. Throughout much of Utah, books sold in the church-operated bookstores interweave the LDS faith with the U.S. Constitution. In some conservative circles, people think it is the duty of the Mormons to protect the Constitution from falling to pieces.

Edna Ballard even retained a Mormon lawyer, who told reporters that "he'd become its legal defender because he saw a strong resemblance between the federal 'persecution' of the I AM sect and the 19th century persecution of the Mormon Church by the government."

When Edna Ballard died in 1971, at age eighty-four, she had led I AM for three times as long as her husband. In the end, one of her biggest legacies was ensuring that when thousands of people witnessed Jesus's ascension into a burst of light each summer, the hymns they heard were American ones.

Through the 1970s, a string of I AM offshoot groups continued to flock to Mount Shasta: the Blue Flamers, the Ascended Master Teaching Foundation, the Joy Foundation, the Shasta Student League Foundation. The stories of Lemurians grew more complex. "It is said that several hundred direct descendants of the Lemurian race *still live* inside this mountain," David St. Clair wrote in his 1973 book *The Psychic World of California.* "They have buildings of marble and onyx with domes plated in gold." One local channeler named Aurelia Louise Jones claimed to know the name of the Lemurian city within the peak: "Telos."

One group that came to Shasta called itself the Association of Sananda and Sanat Kumara. In Theosophical traditions, Sanat Kumara is an Ascended Master and Sananda is his "twin flame" and a high priestess from Atlantis.

That group was helmed by an Illinois woman named Dorothy Martin. Martin had previously drawn the attention of sociologists in 1954 when she led another group called the Seekers, who became the subject of the book *When Prophecy Fails*. Martin and the Seekers believed that a UFO would rescue them from a world-destroying natural disaster, but when the disaster failed to happen and the UFO never arrived, they assumed the strength of their faith had spared the planet.

The Seekers would later splinter apart. Martin's followers squabbled over the UFO-centric writings of William Dudley Pelley. Eventually Martin found her way to Mount Shasta, where she renamed herself "Sister Thedra" and purported to be in touch with the Ascended Masters. For years, she wrote a newsletter titled *A Call to Arms* that was intended to deliver the Masters' messages, ensuring that "the transition into the consciousness of the new age can be facilitated."

When Martin died in the 1990s, she left behind thousands of pages of messages from the Masters, scrawled in arthritic script, and a library of books, including many on Lemuria.

12.

ount Shasta Boulevard runs parallel to a set of train tracks and
acts as the small city's backbone. Along with snowboard and
mountain bike types, the main drag often sees a fair share of
white- and purple-clad visitors, who browse store windows and dine
on outdoor patios. It's reasonable to assume many have come to visit
the grounds of the Saint Germain Foundation—the old Shasta Springs
Resort—closed off behind wrought iron gates, where signs warn, in
looping cursive, that there is "absolutely" no trespassing.

Many of the businesses that belong to the local chamber of com-
merce are related to esoteric and metaphysical—or New Age—studies;
many are crystal shops. Crystal Matrix, Crystal Keepers, the Crystal
Room, Crystal Tones, and Shasta Rainbow Angels are all located in
town. Glowing crystal sound bowls call from one store's front windows. Inside the Crystal Room, hunks of green fluorite and yellow
tourmaline have lights positioned in their core, like twinkling cosmic
stars for the home or office.

Across the street, at Crystal Keepers, lumps of milky white Mount
Shasta opal are arranged underneath a sign reporting the myriad

supposed benefits of possessing such a stone: "Mount Shasta Opal has the ability to work in and through all of the Chakras to establish a more balanced Mental, Emotional, Physical, Spiritual & Psychological state of being." It also "expands consciousness," is good for people "working through Trauma, Stress, Anxiety, Depression along with other mental and emotional conditions & patterns." It gives confidence, encourages freedom and independence, evokes feelings of sympathy and forgiveness, inspires creativity, and wards off negative energy.

There are times New Ageism feels like an unsolvable Rubik's Cube: a puzzle of never-ending correspondences and synchronicities and unprovable promises. Many people believe a web of "ley lines" encircles the planet, connecting spiritually significant places from Glastonbury to the Pyramids of Giza in Egypt. And where those invisible lines intersect, you find the Earth's chakras, a Sanskrit word that means "cycle" or "wheel"; Mount Shasta is thought to be one of them. In accordance with Hindu tradition, the human body has seven chakras that run from the base of the spine to the top of one's head and can be opened in order to allow energy to flow freely through the body.

The system of Westernized chakras is one facet of Eastern religion that was reinterpreted and repackaged by Helena Blavatsky and subsequent Theosophists. Charles W. Leadbeater, who went on to be a leader of the Theosophical Society, assigned a scheme of colors to the chakras in his 1927 book on the topic. These colors transform the spine into an inner rainbow, and each color of the chakras carries significance to yogis and New Age practitioners.

Situated at the base of the spine is the "root chakra," which is associated with the Earth, and is signified by the color red. Like crystals, people believe each chakra has a list of associated properties. The root chakra establishes how someone interacts with the world, and when that chakra is in balance, a person is said to feel like they have their feet firmly grounded. They are independent, strong.

The color spectrum goes upward from there. The belly button is the glowing orange "sacral chakra," believed to be a center of sexuality and creativity. The yellow "solar plexus" chakra burns like fire at the base of the rib cage—a place of self-esteem, ego, and anger. The heart chakra is green and located over the cardiovascular system, a center of compassion. The blue throat chakra is tied to one's ability to communicate, and the indigo *Ajna* chakra is between the eyebrows, like a wise and blazing Third Eye. And finally, at the top of the head, the crown chakra is violet or white. This is the place of spiritual enlightenment.

People believe the planet has chakras of its own, too, but in town there is some disagreement over which of the Earth's chakras Mount Shasta is. At Crystal Room, an employee said that the mountain is definitely the world's root chakra. But across the street at Crystal Keepers, Indigo Steele thought it was the heart chakra.

"I'm not 100 percent positive which one it is," she said. The mountain is "a vortex. It's a very, very powerful place to be. I've noticed from my years of being here that a lot of people will come here to solve issues that they have internally. They'll come here and they work things out, and then they move along. It's almost a therapeutic town, in a sense."

Her family's store contained piles of Lemurian quartz, which looked like regular clear quartz, just with a tinge of yellow or flecks of brown inside. A sign reading "Legends of Lemuria" told a story that Lemurian shamans, anticipating that their civilization would be destroyed in a natural disaster, stored "knowledge inside of crystals which they buried deep within the Earth, along with the newly awakened psychic children, who were inside of seed pods."

Stories about Lemuria and Lemurians seem common in Mount Shasta. One is that tall Lemurians used to appear in town in sandals and long white robes and purchased things at the local markets with hunks of gold.

Indigo says that Mount Shasta attracts both good people seeking answers and bad actors looking to exploit the mountain's energy. "A lot of people in this town come and they have very spiritual experiences," she said. "But there are some people who come here who want to bring you back down—want to make you a part of the collective, of the sheep, of McDonald's-eating, nine-to-five-working, very corporate America."

During Amy's frequent visits to Mount Shasta over the years, she blended into the landscape of crystals, rejecting her McDonald's past. She and other members of Love Has Won would drive north from Dunsmuir to browse these stores for new hunks of crystal and long dresses that could add to Amy's goddess persona. She'd insist on spending some of the group's money on drinks on the patio of a local restaurant, and to browse Soul Connections, a two-storefront-wide shop that deems itself a "Golden Age Emporium."

Soul Connections has a large selection of items that would appeal to any kind of New Age seeker, the rooms unfolding like the chambers of an Egyptian pharaoh's tomb—each getting progressively more focused, and distilled, and ideological. The first two rooms offer entry-level items like cheap crystals and jewelry, a clothing section of ponchos and scarves and flowy garments free of seams. The deeper you venture, the further into the New Age aesthetic one goes. There are dream catchers, ornate animal figurines, and statuettes of unicorns. Baskets filled with woody palo santo and hunks of frankincense sit near gallon-sized freezer bags packed with dried sage leaves. Crystals glitter in every color and shape imaginable. Some are the size of a thimble, others are pyramids or orbs or obelisks or wands. There is an entire room of wooden flutes, chimes and bells, and massive gongs, which curious customers tap gently with mallets and steer children clear from.

The deepest room in Soul Connections is where the New Age becomes dogmatic. Rack after spinning rack features portraits of saints idolized by I AM, but none is more available and venerated than Saint Germain. In the estimation of artist Marius Michael-George, whose works seemed to be sold in bulk at the store, the saint of I AM and so many other New Age groups had lily-white skin and violet-blue eyes, a curling red mustache, and a purple fleece jacket. He stares at the viewer, a faint violet glow behind his head. The depictions give off a feel of an iconographic collaboration between Lisa Frank and Anne Geddes—cartoonish, over-the-top, precious, white.

There is a large library of books for sale on natural healing, herbal remedies, and tarot cards. Dozens of Aurelia Jones's titles on "Telos" line the shelves, but most of the books are about conspiracy theories. One display is devoted to the COVID-19 pandemic, where the store sells copies of *Plandemic*—a film turned book that the *Los Angeles Times* dubbed "the most notorious piece of coronavirus disinformation yet" for its assertions that a "cabal" was behind the outbreak. Nearby sits *Is COVID-19 A Bioweapon?*, authored by a man who was once convicted of health care fraud.

Interspersed among books about vaccines are titles on "electromagnetic pollution," "geoengineered transhumanism," the "hidden dangers of 5G," GMOs, chemtrails, alien-human hybrids, and predictions for the end of the world. On the next shelf over are the *I AM Discourses*, *A Dweller on Two Planets*, and ten titles about the fabled Lemurian city inside the mountain.

In early 2023, in the very last aisle of Soul Connections, beyond the COVID denial aisle, shelves labeled "Constitution" and "God Government" overflowed with books like *Socialists Don't Sleep, United States of Socialism, The Problem with Socialism*. There were books on media: *Real Fake News, The Liberal Media Industrial Complex*, and titles by defrocked Fox News hosts Bill O'Reilly and Tucker Carlson. There were books by W. Cleon Skousen, a man who infused his religious reading of the Constitution and his fear of Communism into Mormon culture.

This felt like the aisle of lost hope—that even New Ageism, with all its promises of being something different, was in fact just as red-pilled as the rest of the country. This was the aisle where believers became radicals. A series of books called the *Rise of the New World Order* was on display; one yelled from its cover that "the next election could be the last."

A book called *Nazi UFO Time Travelers* asked, "Do we owe the future to the fuhrer?" Books about Hitler and "the Nazis' incredible secret technology" were mixed among books on the "5 Love Languages."

Outside, discounted crystals had been dumped into baskets across a set of tables, and a woman and her child pawed through them, picking up hunks and holding them up to the light. "Are these even real?" the woman asked—to the child, to herself, it wasn't clear. It felt like the more important question seemed to be: Does it matter if it's real if you decide it is?

In the annals of modern American far-right extremism there is a canon that the movement considers holy. The antisemitic *Protocols of the Elders of Zion* is a treasured part of that canon. The 1978 novel *The Turner Diaries* is another, in which a fictional white supremacist terrorist group overthrows the government. It served as inspiration to Timothy McVeigh when he bombed a federal building in Oklahoma City in 1995, and to an actual white supremacist terrorist group called The Order, that robbed and killed across the western United States in the 1980s. The 1984 Patrick Swayze action movie *Red Dawn* is yet another: a film set in a United States that has been invaded by the Soviets and a group of civilian guerrillas fight back.

In recent years, perhaps no work has been embraced by the culture of American conspiracy theorists more than *The Matrix*, the 1999 sci-fi action film starring Keanu Reeves. The plot swirls around Reeves's character, Neo, a brooding computer hacker who is being followed by government agents and is offered a choice of two pills by other hackers. One pill is blue, and if he takes it, he will remain in ignorance of the realities of this world. The other pill is red, and by swallowing that one, he will gain full knowledge of the nefarious forces at work. He will become part of the resistance, never able to un-know true reality: life as we know it is a simulation, and all humans are kept unconscious—perhaps by choice—while machines harvest their bodies for resources. Neo takes the red pill.

In the decades since that movie was released, saying that someone has been "-pilled" by anything has come to mean they are obsessed suddenly with some new reality. The people who see themselves as "red-pilled" think they are awake to true reality, eyes unblinking, always watching for fresh evidence of conspiracy. Often this language is used to describe people on the far right political fringes of America. But it describes Love Has Won too.

By 2018, Amy largely passed her longtime video-making and live-streaming duties to her acolytes. The group offered even more services to visitors of their varying websites, chat rooms, streaming channels, and social media pages: awakening and healing sessions, spiritual "surgeries" that cost $77.77 and were conducted over the phone. They sold Love Has Won alkaline water, sweatpants, T-shirts. The group's livestreams increased to at least twice every day, with each broadcast lasting two to three hours. The broadcasts had evolved considerably from the days when Amy sat with her laptop on a patio with a head-set, talking about the stars. The streams were typically hosted by pairs of members who held sprawling, marathonic televangelist-style con-versations that often plummeted downward into a bottomless pit of conspiracy.

These members of the group had chosen to go "on mission" with Mother God, meaning they had left their lives behind in some capacity to sit at Amy's feet. They came from around the world. They called her "Mom." The group had settled into a 3,500-square-foot log-cabin-style vacation rental house with tall ceilings, rustic chandeliers, and a mas-sive stone fireplace in the town of Dunsmuir, California, a short drive down the road from Mount Shasta, where Amy believed she had pre-viously opened portals to the Lemurians who lived inside the volcano. The language of I AM had long been a part of Amy's world—whether she knew it or not. It had been on Lightworkers.org: "You created God by who you are. After all...I AM what I AM," wrote the moderator. Amy's early posts read like I AM decrees. It was no wonder Mount Shasta appealed to her.

Avigail Lowes, a thin young woman with long blonde hair and a British accent, joined Amy and the team in California. At the time, she called herself a "chakra healer," and began taking over the healing sessions for Amy. Amy renamed her "Archeia Faith." It was clear the healing sessions were a channel for recruiting, and Faith was effective in bringing in some of the most devout members of the group.

Oftentimes after healing sessions, clients would receive a copy of the Love Has Won "Ascension Guide" in their email. The document laid out their belief in Amy as Mother God, and the ills of "ego-programmed minds." It listed the chakra colors to wear and their associated days of the week. It suggested a menu of "grounding tools" that could be employed to aid in ascension: smoking hand-rolled cigarettes, doing regular garlic cleanses, drinking organic coffee, eating red meat, and consuming cannabis.

The group advised apple cider vinegar and turmeric as a kind of medicine, but also encouraged people to purchase some of Love Has Won's products, like colloidal gold and colloidal silver. "Ours is obviously the highest vibration being in god's field. Colloidal silver is one of the highest medicines on the planet," the guide read. "The four things that Mom recommends daily is coconut oil, turmeric, colloidal gold and colloidal silver." Each day, the guide recommended members spend ten minutes "completing 'I AM,' affirmations in the mirror, whilst looking into your own eyes."

Among the Ascension Guide's dubious claims, the ability to reconfigure water molecules with one's thoughts and the benefits of staring at the sun seemed to be at the top of the list. "The Sun will not blind you," the guide said. "This is a myth to STOP people looking at the Sun because it is one of Our most powerful healing tools. The Sun contains important activation codes that cause us to rise to the frequency of love."

After a session, Faith invited a young man from Pennsylvania named Ryan Kramer to join the group. He'd recently lost his father to an opioid addiction. He arrived in Dunsmuir on a night when the group had a fire blazing in the fireplace and were dancing around to music. Amy gave him a new name too: "El Morya." The members practically tackled him when he arrived, embracing him like he was a long-lost friend. "Come home!" Ryan called to the camera, which was livestreaming when he walked in. "Come home, everyone! Why aren't you here already?"

Faith also invited a Florida attorney named Lauryn Suarez, who found Love Has Won around the time she lost her law license and began to dive deeper into astrology. When she met the group in California, she became known as "Archeia Aurora."

From Massachusetts came an aimless college graduate who'd recently gone through a breakup named Ashley Peluso. She was deemed to be "Archeia Hope." These three women—Faith, Aurora, and Hope—became like Amy's handmaidens. They combed her hair when it was wet, brushed makeup onto her cheeks, served her platters of food, and cleaned around her.

One blue-skied afternoon in Dunsmuir, Walter "Riccey" Paschal was outside attaching a motor to his bicycle. "And I see this guy I've never seen. Dunsmuir's a small town. You know everybody, and everybody knows you," he said. The new guy looked like he was carrying a beer in a paper bag, but when he got closer, Riccey said it was clear he was huffing from a can of compressed air.

Along with him were several other men, and a little boy. Riccey, who is Black, said he took notice because several of them were also men of color, and so he said hello. The group stopped and they struck up a conversation. As they spoke, one of the men—white, with shaggy hair, who he would later learn was Ryan Kramer—turned to Riccey and asked, "What would you say if I told you God is right here in Dunsmuir?" Riccey wasn't sure what to say. Ryan told him it was true, that God was a woman, and the other men nodded as he spoke.

"I'm not stupid. My cult radar went straight up," Riccey said. "I've got these three men telling me that god is a broad and she's up there in a house?"

Riccey was amused, a little intrigued, and also saw potential opportunity: he was selling weed at the time—"I'm trying to sling a little dope and pay the power bill." He said it was not rare for New Age groups to come to Dunsmuir, what with Mount Shasta so close by, and in many ways he shared a lot of their ideas: a sense of oneness, a belief in one's own divine power.

"You can't tell me you've got God in your back pocket," he said, "without me coming and knocking." Riccey followed the men back to the house, and they told him to wait outside.

Once inside, Riccey was surprised to see children and adults of all ages—between fifteen and twenty people altogether. When he entered, a woman in her sixties approached him and said she'd seen him in a dream.

And then there was Amy, the one they called Mother God.

"They said you're God," he offered. Amy said nothing, only raising her eyebrows in response.

"That's kind of odd," Riccey said.

"Why?" Amy asked.

"Because I'm God," Riccey replied.

"We're all God," she said.

Riccey hung around for a while after that. He sold them weed, and if they wanted anything more powerful, he told them he could get it. He would gather along with the other members of the group in Amy's bedroom, where she would smoke weed and preach and direct the disciples at her feet without even getting out of bed. Riccey brushed off some things Amy said. Amy talked about her dislike for Jews, though, and that caught Riccey's attention: he also took pride in nurturing his own antisemitism. His spiritual ideas were similar to those on display on the shelves of Soul Connections: a New Age sense of oneness and personal power with a heavy embrace of bigotry. "Her antisemitism wasn't as deep as mine, it was more blaming the media and the cabal," he said.

Riccey found most of the people in Love Has Won to be irritating, but he liked Amy, a woman preaching about love who could find room inside of that love for antisemitism. She thought about the world a lot like he did. She gave him the name Muhammed.

Amy continued to cast new Father Gods. One was a man named John Robertson, a young military veteran. Robertson had been playing the Father God role when one day in 2018, a new follower showed up: a sinewy, long-haired man from Las Vegas, who'd formerly managed a Blockbuster video store. His name was Jason Castillo.

"I was already aware that the Matrix was real," Jason would later tell a documentary filmmaker, "and that everyone was being enslaved."

According to some former members, John was forcefully unseated from the role of Father God when Jason punched him, which impressed Amy.

One day, Amy sat in bed, wearing all green and a Santa hat on her head, next to Jason—cross-legged, hands resting on his knees with palms upturned. All around the bed sat her followers.

"Love Has Won. Father and Mother of all creation are here on the planet," she announced. "Guess who's the master of atoms with me?"

She pointed to Jason. Everyone clapped. In him she believed she had finally found her twin flame. The divine masculine to her divine feminine. "A fuckin' ancient energy," Jason would say.

During their thousands of hours of livestreams, the members of Love Has Won sat in front of a large photograph of Amy: her eyes closed, cheeks glowing, hands in prayer, head bowed, smile content. They wore matching colors, corresponding to the chakras that they associated with each specific day.

In 2018, people tuned in to watch from around the world. They, too, were welcomed as members of the Love Has Won team, even if they weren't physically with the group. In Florida, a twenty-nine-year-old mother and Starbucks employee named Ashley McCoy had joined several spiritual groups on Facebook in a search for "peace, harmony, everybody getting along," and in one of them she found the Love Has Won livestream.

"It was Amy's picture in the background that kind of jarred my attention because it was this big tapestry," she recalled. "And I was like, 'What is this? Did this person die?' Like it just kind of sparked my attention. And then from there, they started talking and they were speaking about a lot of the things I was coming across at that time."

The livestreams were upbeat and seemed to function to solicit donations, garner likes and reposts on Facebook, and discuss the group's beliefs: from shedding the ego and overcoming trauma, to their labyrinthine beliefs about UFOs, conspiracy theories, the cabal and Illuminati, Atlantis and Lemuria, to their ever-growing love for Donald Trump, who was serving his first term as president. In the summer of 2018, members of the group hinted on the streams that Amy was in declining health, and donations were solicited for an ATV to help her get around. Donations were also gathered for the expressed purpose of buying Amy mobile phone games, which they explained was one tool she had, as God, to attack the cabal.

To a passing listener who might not understand the rhetoric and vocabulary of the truly red-pilled, the livestreams would seem incoherent. But to other seekers, these people were talking in a way that clicked. They promised that they knew the truth about the world, about God.

For a group that was supposedly based in love, the hosts would more than occasionally lash out at Facebook users who came into the livestream's comments to call them a cult. Those commenters were mocked and belittled and told that they were asleep in the face of the realities of the world that had been laid out so clearly by Mom. In one video, Jason Castillo repeatedly used a racial slur for Black people, saying the word also meant "cockroach. It's the fucking lowest form that hates God." As he said this, Hope giggled beside him. The hosts constantly called back to their beliefs in "the cabal," which was by then well-known shorthand for antisemitic ideas about Jews conspiring to control the world and popular among QAnon believers. But they said everything with a smile, as if this was the true language of enlightenment.

During one four-hour livestream on Sunday, August 12, 2018, nine of Amy's followers sat cross-legged on a colorful carpet fit for a pre-school classroom, looking toward the camera. No photo of Amy was there, but a tapestry decorated with a mandala hung behind them, and twinkle lights flashed overhead. Most of the people were young and white. None wore shoes. For hours, they barely shifted.

Nearest to the camera, at the front, were Aurora and Faith, who acted as the show's hosts, talking while also monitoring the stream of Facebook comments on their phones and laptops. Perhaps most important, they read out messages from Amy, who was monitoring from another room. It was unclear why the rest of them were there.

"She *is* the physical embodiment of the planet," Faith said. "That's gonna be really hard for 99.9 percent of the planet to digest. It doesn't matter; it is the truth."

Around her, everyone sat still.

"Mom feels everything on the planet," she continued. "The BP oil spill happened, and she had to process that through her body. She gets boils. But now she's pushing the energy out the other way. Her sneezes and coughs are causing volcanic eruptions, earthquakes."

She was also causing the planet's vibrations to rise, Faith said. Low vibrations were a sign of darkness and evil.

"Low vibration," Faith said, was "getting really challenged right now. This is why everything is coming to light: the Clintons, all of the pedophilia rings, all of the cabal control is completely breaking away. And yes, Donald Trump is a massive part of this plan, he's a part of the divine mission. You can love him or like him, whatever personal 'ego' judgments you have. There is a truth in terms of vibration, and the truth is that he is completely leading this entire ascension process alongside Mother and Father."

Around her, people nodded and smiled.

The cabal, Faith explained, doesn't want humanity to ascend—it keeps power when humans are in fear. But Trump, she argued, was exposing the cabal's lies.

"All the corruption, the false flag attacks, 9/11—all of it was bullshit, all of it was false. You can't even comprehend how many of these things have been done. It's all to create fear," Faith said. "Everything has been to keep us in the illusion. And it's over. It's done. New Earth is coming."

Faith and Aurora traded duties talking about control, touching lighters to the ends of joints as they spoke. They lectured on the ways people control others, the ways society controls people, the ways we insert ourselves into controlling situations. School is control, work is control. But Mom? Not control. This group? Not control.

"Mom embodies all the divine qualities: courage, consistency, strength, compassion, love, nurturing, childlike wonder," Aurora said. "Mom has always been her whole life in perfect balance."

At one point, Hope carried several bowls of food into the room, setting them in front of the group, and people perked up, thanking her. The bowls sat untouched for seventeen minutes, followers staring at them. One man swatted flies away from the food, eventually asking someone offscreen if it was okay for them to eat. The person said yes.

Faith continued to speak to the camera. When Mom was a teenager, she was rushed to the hospital after taking too much Advil. (Whether or not this was a suicide attempt was not addressed.) At the hospital, Faith said, she was tested by doctors: "She had to take this test that basically tests the balance inside of you, and the doctor was just like, 'You're perfectly balanced! That doesn't exist! No one has ever scored that before.'"

The doctor phoned his colleagues in the medical field around the world to share the discovery that a perfectly balanced person had been found.

At that moment Amy sent Faith and Aurora a message, which they read from their laptops: "AB test, balanced zero. Perfect."

It was hard to believe anyone could be so gullible. But the whole group smiled at the story.

Aurora and Faith proceeded to read a series of "Q updates." By then, the group was firmly entrenched in the fever dreams of QAnon. "Trump is a member of the 144,000," Faith said. "He is not affiliated in any way with pedophilia rings, the cabal, the Illuminati—which every president in recent history has been. They've just been puppets for an absolute charade. It's been a while since we've had [a president] in the light—I don't think we've had one since JFK?"

She looked around the room for insight.

"Reagan?" someone piped up.

"Reagan," Faith agreed.

"It's all coming to the surface," interjected Ryan, El Morya. On livestreams, he was often forceful—every word coming out of his mouth like a knife intended to cut. "There's no one stepping out except Mother. And that's what we're doing here."

The next day, the group was back on the carpet for another three and a half hours of conspiracies. They were back the next day, and the next day, and the next, for hours and hours and hours. Each minute of each broadcast was an opportunity to stack their conspiracy theories higher and higher, one on top of the last, building the group's Jenga tower worldview. The cabal was everywhere. They believed they would collectively ascend beyond the reach of all the lies one day— maybe very soon. They believed they had been saved by Mom. They believed what she believed: that she was the center of the universe.

This was clear during another livestream that month. As the members of the group—mostly dressed in red—concluded a prayer over bowls of food, offscreen a sliding door could be heard opening. Suddenly, the livestreamers' faces lit up and they started furiously clapping.

"God up in the house!" a man called out.

The group rose to their feet as Amy—rail thin, wearing a long floral dress—walked into the room and sat down on the carpet, at the front. "They're allowing me to give a cameo," Amy said.

She kissed her hand and blew it toward the camera, saying, "Greetings, everyone. Exciting events are unfolding." The group sat up a little straighter.

"I—um—guide you all to research what the seventh seal is, in any which way you like," she continued. "We just know directly that we are dealing with it, and the trinity energy has come together. It's a dynamic that will fuel the evolutionary process. So—"

She paused.

"LOVE HAS WONNNNNNNN!!!!" she yelled suddenly out of nowhere, thrusting two thumbs up toward the sky. Everyone clapped and cheered.

"I love you all," Mom said, standing, bowing. "In service to love everywhere present." Without offering any further insight into the seventh seal, or trinity energy, or the evolutionary process, she walked out of the shot. She was on camera for just over a minute.

"Thank you, Mother God!" her people called to her as she walked away.

PART IV
THE LOVERS

13.

The face of the woman who predicted doom beamed out from
television screens across America. She was white, middle-aged,
chestnut-brown curls cropped short. She spoke in a strange, reedy
voice—both monotone and alien. "Jesus has told me," she hummed,
"that the Kingdom of God is the consciousness of God."

"Who is Elizabeth Prophet," the news anchor Ted Koppel interjected with baritone authority, "and what does her Church Universal
and Triumphant stand for?"

It was May 17, 1990, and the focus of the news program *Nightline* was whether or not this woman was leading a cult. It was a question that people in the West had asked increasingly as she moved her
religious group from Virginia to Colorado, to California, then Montana. Their presence alone was enough to ruffle feathers; the group's
rapid-fire chants and veneration of Saint Germain, who they claimed
was Christian but that no Christian ever read about in the Bible,
made people skeptical, even nervous. Paranoia about the group grew
as Elizabeth, its leader, issued a string of predictions that implied
America would, at the very least, be the victim of some terrible

fate—nuclear, maybe. At most, the world would end. Then the nation became interested.

Whether or not the group was a cult seemed to bemuse Koppel and other television personalities. The daytime host Oprah Winfrey, too, wanted the answer. A segment that aired on her show in 1989 started with images of hundreds of dead bodies lying side by side, the more than 900 casualties of apocalyptic cult leader Jim Jones, who helmed a group called the Peoples Temple. Jones preached to his followers that before a perfect society could be established, great turmoil and violence would occur. After leading his followers to a closed community called Jonestown in Guyana, a country on the northern coast of South America, in November 1978, he forced them to drink cyanide-laced Flavor Aid: mothers and daughters, fathers and sons, brothers alongside brothers. Television footage of their dead bodies proved the power of all the end times talk. These were not just words.

Oprah told viewers about the Rajneeshees, a group led by Indian mystic Bhagwan Shree Rajneesh, who lived lavishly, even owning a fleet of Rolls-Royces. He taught his followers to believe in principles of free love, and when they purchased a large ranch in Oregon in the early 1980s, he relegated his people to living in primitive tents. Rajneesh's well-armed followers eventually attempted to manipulate local elections. Some members also discussed an assassination attempt on a U.S. attorney. Around the same time, followers unleashed salmonella in the salad bars at several restaurants in the county, which sickened and hospitalized more than 700 people. It remains the largest bioterror attack ever to occur on American soil.

Oprah wanted to know: Was Elizabeth's group any different?

"This, quite frankly, is one of those stories you save for a slow day, when not very much else is happening. And even then, you wonder whether it merits the attention," Ted Koppel intoned. "Not that the Church Universal and Triumphant isn't interesting; it is gloriously bizarre and fascinating. But it is also exceedingly strange. As one

Montana neighbor put it, 'I'm surrounded by people whose dipsticks haven't seen oil in a long time.'"

By then, Elizabeth Clare Prophet's followers called her Guru Ma, or Mother. When she greeted them in ceremonies, with one arm raised toward the sky, hand cupped upward, she also hailed Saint Germain.

"To her church members, she is the mother of the universe: the very messenger of God," a *Nightline* reporter explained. The show's cameras ducked inside underground bomb shelters and bunkers, where people had stacked canned food and guns and boxes of bullets. That was plenty to get locals talking, but one day, a radiation-proof lookout tower intruded on the pristine Montana skyline. It watched like an all-seeing eye.

But then her predicted date of cataclysm had passed. No catastrophe was revealed. The winds kept blowing, the rivers flowing, the air remained breathable.

"Disaster was averted, members believe, in part because they prayed it away," the *Nightline* reporter explained. The group believed their devotion had been fate-altering, and their prayers changed the course of time. Just like Dorothy Martin (later Sister Thedra) had told her Seekers in the 1950s, when the tragedies she had predicted had not come to pass.

Elizabeth Clare Prophet joined Koppel on the screen. She wore a baby-blue blouse, the same chestnut curls. Her smile seemed plastic, the kind that altered only the shape of her mouth, not her eyes.

"Ms. Prophet," Koppel said, "it surely cannot come as a surprise to you that your activities and the activities of your church are viewed with some skepticism, cynicism, by those of us on the outside."

She said she agreed to come on the show to correct "errors" spread about her and her church, "such as that my followers [believe] I'm the mother of the universe. This is absolutely untrue," she said. She spoke through her smile, and blinked constantly, as if a gust of wind was blowing in her face.

"You predicted that on the twenty-third of April there was going to be, what? Some nuclear attack by the Soviet Union?" Koppel asked.

"Absolutely not," she said. "I'm simply saying there's a probability of nuclear war and confrontation between the superpowers... April 23, 1990, marks the final twelve years of the ride of the four horsemen that was seen by John the Beloved, recorded in Revelation."

"Of course, it sounds much more dramatic to talk about the ride of the four horsemen of the apocalypse," Koppel said. "What is it about these twelve years in particular that's going to be so different?"

The horsemen, Elizabeth explained, were bringing karma. And evidence of that karma was everywhere: "Indeed, we are facing the greatest challenges in our nation's history," she said, "whether it be the War on Drugs, education, AIDS, cancer, the economy. And what is going to happen to nuclear weapons when they get in the hands of madmen.

"It's a nuclear age, it's common sense to have civil defense," she said. "There's Iraq, there's Libya, there's nuclear power reactors, there's accidental launches, and there is the Soviet Union."

Despite her apocalyptic predictions and all her talk of horsemen riding across stormy skies to deliver karma, she wanted viewers to know that the church was a "peace-loving people."

Her words didn't quite square with an incident that had happened the year before, which Koppel failed to ask her about. In July 1989, the church security chief had been arrested in possession of *seven* .50-caliber rifles, armor-piercing bullets, $26,000 in cash and gold coins, and documents detailing elaborate radar systems, the potential acquisition of "armored personnel carriers"—tanklike vehicles used in warfare—and, according to one report, "plans to outfit 200 people with military-style assault weapons."

If Koppel had asked about the arrests, it seemed Elizabeth would have only kept smiling.

This interview could be studied as a stunning moment in media history when a fringe leader of a conspiracist religious sect was catapulted into a national spotlight, given a platform *because* of her paranoia and strangeness. Koppel even said it—it was the sort of story that filled in on a slow news day (a relic in itself). But *Nightline* still decided to go through with it, and the entire episode felt like it was missing something. People said Elizabeth and her followers were fringe. Elizabeth said they were loving, peaceful, normal Christians. Whose version of reality would win?

Media seemed to see Elizabeth as an easy target. But the coverage showed a total lack of awareness of the hands her spiritual ideas had passed through before arriving in hers. She would build on the ideas of I AM and everyone who came before them, and create an empire for herself.

Perhaps, instead of implying that these people were the extreme fringe, *Nightline* might have redirected its cameras away from the piles of canned food, and toward the hundreds of people flocking to Elizabeth—those crowds a kind of horseman all their own. A harbinger of things to come.

Elizabeth Clare Wulf was born in a Red Bank, New Jersey, hospital to a Swiss-born mother and a German-born father on the day before Easter 1939. Her arrival into the world was heralded by the horns of the "Triumphal March" from *Aida*, an opera about a love story set in ancient Egypt, which her mother swore was playing on a nearby radio as she was being wheeled in for a caesarean section.

As a girl, Elizabeth was known as Betty Clare, and her childhood memories were marked by the panic that came with regular air-raid drills during World War II and the piercing howl of sudden sirens that could never quite be forgotten. She recalled her father being hauled away once by FBI agents, who were suspicious that any German living in the country could be a Nazi spy. He was held for six weeks at Ellis Island as they pursued an investigation. By her telling, several of his Jewish friends testified on his behalf, and when he was let go, he told his daughter to never forget this. "Be a friend to all Jews and anyone you see being persecuted," he said.

Afterward, her father descended into violent alcoholism, and directed his ire at his wife and daughter. Once, in a drunken rage, he kicked in a set of aquariums, sending forty-gallon waves of water and tropical fish flopping across the family kitchen. Betty Clare and her mother scooped the fish up with buckets, desperate to save them.

"The house was dominated by my mother's fear and my father's impending anger," she wrote. "I never knew when or for what unimaginable reason the next explosion would take place, or the next, or the next."

Once, her mother, Fridy, confided in Betty Clare that she only stayed with the violent man because she needed his financial support—that she couldn't raise a daughter alone. Later in her life, after she left for college and was supporting herself, Betty Clare pressed her mother to leave him, and Fridy finally filed for divorce. But it didn't last; her parents soon remarried.

"She did not have the integrity to stand up against a very great darkness," Betty Clare wrote. She "had been conditioned so long to abuse as the only love she knew that she would rather return to that scene than face an unknown future."

From a young age, she was deeply taken by Christian Scientist teachings and studied the faith up through her college years. This group had arisen from the waves of Spiritualism that overtook New England in the 1800s, led by a woman named Mary Baker Eddy. Eddy was a medium (who was, uncannily, not related to the Vermont mediums known as the Eddy Brothers) and developed a spiritual system that taught followers to avoid using medicine.

Betty Clare's mother, Fridy, also sought out Spiritualism throughout her life. After the deaths of several loved ones, she brought her daughter along to Spiritualist churches, where mediums delivered messages. This ideology had captivated Fridy since she read Helena Blavatsky's *The Secret Doctrine*. Later, she immersed herself in Guy Ballard's *I AM Discourses*. One night, Fridy would claim, as she read from Ballard's teachings, she drifted off to sleep, and was awoken by "a great light at the foot of my bed." She recognized it as the Mighty I AM Presence.

Under her mother's direction, Betty Clare learned that pain she experienced in life was a direct result of karma—a concept featured in Buddhism, Hinduism, and several other Eastern religions that had been adopted by American New Agers. To Betty Clare, karma was moral baggage loaded with poor choices she had made in a past life, for which she had not properly atoned. An accident that left Betty Clare with a severely injured leg was a punishment from God for some sin committed lifetimes ago. "He was making me pay for them," she wrote. "But in the process, he also forgave me."

Just before she left for college in 1957, Betty Clare pulled Fridy's copy of the *I AM Discourses* from a bookshelf in their home and stared into the glowing, familiar eyes of Saint Germain looking out from the pages. She ran to Fridy, busy in the family's kitchen. "Saint Germain!" Betty Clare exclaimed. "Why didn't you ever tell me about him?"

"I wanted you to discover him for yourself," her mother said.

In that moment, she vowed to find Saint Germain.

At Ohio's Antioch College, she had a hard time fitting in. "It was a beatnik crowd," she wrote. "I felt like I was almost the only girl on campus who had any religion and who would not participate in the immorality of campus life that was so rampant there."

Alone in her religious conviction and conservative politics, she relegated herself to "a monastic life," solitary study in the library, taking long, lonely walks. She conversed with God, who instructed her to study politics and economics. "'You have to understand what's going on in this world, because the world is heading for a very severe crisis,'" she recalled God saying. "'And until the problems of the governments and the economies are resolved…we need action in the battle and on the front line.'"

She dove further into her own studies of the *I AM Discourses* and made a habit of repeating the decrees—a series of "I AM" statements—out loud, like mantras. In the summer of 1958, she wrote a letter to Guy

Ballard—a.k.a. Godfre Ray King—confessing her devotion. She didn't know that Guy Ballard had died the year of her birth.

"Dr Mr. King," she wrote. "It is with deep gratitude that I should like you to know, you who have given your life to this Great Service, that I, too, cherish the Inner Presence and the goal of Saint Germain on this continent. I am prepared to give unreservedly of myself to this cause. My life henceforth is at the service of the Great Light."

The letter came back to her in the mail. She wrote him again and again. All were returned, envelopes unopened. Once, she spent five dollars in dimes calling every Ballard in the phone book, to no avail.

The I AM Discourses spoke of a partnering "twin flame" or a "twin ray," a "soul created with you billions of years ago, from whom you had become separated by karma." While Betty Clare was searching for Saint Germain, she was also looking for her twin flame.

During the summer of 1958, she lived in New York City and worked as a secretary at the United Nations. In her free time, she flipped through the card catalogues at the New York Public Library and disappeared into the dense stacks to research the life of Saint Germain, the real man who had once lived in France. Sometimes she could feel him nearby.

Working for the United Nations left her feeling that the organization was rotten from the inside, filled with "immense corruption and sensuality." Saint Germain, she said, "revealed to me that indeed the U.N. was not the hope of the world."

God told her to go to Boston, which she did. At Boston University, she helmed an organization of Christian Scientist students on campus and took a temp job as a secretary at the church-operated newspaper, the Christian Science Monitor. She grew frustrated that Saint Germain did not show himself to her—someone so devout. Once she ran to the top floor of her apartment building and shouted at the sky, "Saint Germain, I know you're up there! You've got to come and get me now!"

After months of dating, another Christian Scientist student proposed to Betty Clare. "You see, there is one complication," she told the boy. "I'm looking for the Master Saint Germain...The day he comes, that will be it. He's going to be the center of my life." Somehow, her boyfriend was not put off by this. As Betty Clare walked down the aisle, she said God whispered in her ear that it was only temporary. This man was not her twin flame.

By the 1960s, a number of I AM offshoot groups appeared around the country, each claiming to have contact with the Ascended Masters. One called the Lighthouse to Freedom was led by a man who claimed to be an anointed messenger of the Masters Saint Germain and El Morya. His name was Mark Prophet.

From a young age, Prophet claimed to speak with spirits and read minds. He was devoutly, even obsessively, religious; by the time he was a teenager, the young man claimed to have received the nine gifts of the Holy Spirit, including speaking in tongues. He never finished high school, but instead waded into the deep waters of esoteric spirituality, testing out Rosicrucianism and Theosophy. He attended an I AM meeting and watched as the Ballards delivered dictations straight from the Masters.

On April 22, 1961, Prophet delivered a dictation from the Masters in Boston to a small group, then led them in meditation. Betty Clare was among them. She stared at Prophet as he spoke—a married man with a blocky jaw and a gap-toothed smile, who spoke with a midwestern accent. She believed she was looking into "a pair of eyes that had met the eyes of God." When she closed her own eyes, Prophet's meditation rocketed her into another dimension entirely, where she tumbled through new planes of consciousness, saw the Masters, and experienced a "dilemma of the centuries" in "the buildup of nuclear power." When she opened her eyes again, standing with Mark Prophet was the Archangel Michael, glowing white.

Afterward, Betty Clare approached him. She confessed her belief that she was meant to be a messenger for the Masters, and that she had been searching for Saint Germain. "That very night, she asked him to train her, and he asked her to be his romantic partner," the pair's daughter Erin Prophet would later write. Mark Prophet deemed Betty Clare his twin flame.

After Prophet returned home to the Washington, D.C., area, he mailed packages of I AM class materials back to Betty Clare in Boston, which she ferreted away from her husband in a locked suitcase under her bed. One day, as she walked through a park, she believed Ascended Master El Morya appeared before her and instructed her to move to Washington to study under Prophet's direction.

After just ten months of marriage, her husband told Betty Clare it was time for her to choose: "It's either me or Saint Germain," she recalled him saying. She picked Saint Germain, and a much older married man. She dropped the name Betty Clare and began going by Elizabeth.

"This was the pivotal event of my life," she later wrote. "Everything before it was prologue."

Over the next decade, Mark and Elizabeth Clare Prophet spread the messages of Saint Germain, El Morya, and the other Ascended Masters around the United States. First they headquartered their group in Virginia, operating as the Summit Lighthouse. Then they relocated to Colorado Springs, Colorado, where they lived among a small cadre of loyal followers. Mark Prophet's earliest acolytes were initially skeptical that Elizabeth could be a messenger of the Masters; the pair waited years before she delivered a dictation onstage. Like the Ballards, onstage the pair summoned the Ascended Masters, speaking in the voices of these faraway, other-dimensional beings.

As their church grew, the pair seemed to be following in the exact footsteps of Guy and Edna Ballard, like they were deepening tracks they left in snow. And like the Ballards before them, by the 1970s they too had moved their church to Southern California.

In her book *Prophet's Daughter*, Erin Prophet wrote that with their church, her parents had "retained the bulk of 'I AM' belief and practice," adding their own spin. Mark Prophet's earliest followers were largely people from I AM. They led prayers that were recited at "high-speed" by the congregation, the words "I AM, I AM, I AM" repeated in a fast, staccato rhythm. The church members believed "we were equal before the eyes of God and needed no intermediary to speak with ascended masters."

"We believed that each of us would 'ascend' like Christ at the end of our lives (if we had been good) and go on living in bodies made of the invisible spiritual energy we called 'light,'" Erin wrote. "We were destined to become like Jesus, who was our elder brother. This was the 'true' and 'original' message of Jesus that my mother wrote about in her books."

Mark Prophet grew a spindly black mustache, and squinted more than smiled when his photo was taken. They often dressed in matching clothes. In one photo, Mark wore a pristine white suit with a magenta-pink necktie; Elizabeth stood beside him, smiling in a checkered white dress, a strip of the same pink satin belting her waist. In another photo, Mark wore a creamy brown tuxedo, and Elizabeth was next to him in a gown of the same color, a baby in one arm and a white crown atop her curls. Together, they had four children: Sean, Erin, Moira, and Tatiana. (Mark Prophet had five others from his first marriage.)

In 1972, the pair coauthored a book called *Climb the Highest Mountain: The Path of the Higher Self.* In an epigraph, they alluded that together they were God's two witnesses, which had been prophesied in the Book of Revelation. It is a nearly 600-page tome, in which Lemuria is discussed as a motherland where people sought "self-mastery," but that had ultimately fallen after they abused God's power during a "sordid period in the history of man." They call this "karmic penalties." Lemuria's final destruction came by the hand of a dark cabal, who'd sworn to create systems of "mass control" and extinguish the "Mother flame" that gave Lemuria life. The ones who escaped the destruction forgot that God was dual-gendered—both Mother and Father. The Prophets wanted to get the Mother flame back, make it burn again, and shepherd in an era when "God as both Father and Mother will provide the theme of an Ascended Master philosophy and way of life."

Though Lemuria was an idea that had already lived a long life before the Prophets, the couple pushed the story in new directions. Previously, many people told stories that Lemuria had sunk into the seas after a war with Atlantis, but with the Prophets, the destroyers became an evil cabal.

When Mark Prophet died suddenly on February 26, 1973, after having a stroke, the Ballards' story echoed once more. Elizabeth, like Edna, told her followers that their leader had ascended, and was now a Master. She revealed teachings that Mark Prophet had reincarnated several times: a high priest in Atlantis, Noah, and Bodhidharma, the founder of Zen Buddhism.

She renamed him Ascended Master Lanello, a portmanteau derived of the lives she claimed Mark had lived: Sir Lancelot from the fabled world of King Arthur, and Henry Wadsworth Longfellow, a poet who wrote about the Archangel Michael.

Initially, Prophet's death threw the organization into disarray; members of the board made attempts to curb Elizabeth's authority. The implication was that the Ascended Masters were all men; how could a woman translate their truth? In the ensuing years, Elizabeth would remove almost all of those board members from power.

For the first time, Elizabeth was alone on the stage: the one true messenger. She got to work growing Summit University and its publishing press, which would print a near-constant stream of books containing messages from the Ascended Masters. The school educated young people in months-long tuition-based retreats.

After her twin flame's death, she renamed the church. Hers would be called the Church Universal and Triumphant.

In a standard tarot deck, there are seventy-eight cards. Several are cards of death: deaths of the self, deaths of ideas, deaths of ego. When tarot cards appear in horror movies or television shows, it is almost always the Devil card or the Death card that are shown, and they are usually meant to imply literal death. The subtlety of the centuries-old card game is lost on Hollywood. Traditionally, the Death card signifies a major change: the demise of a moment, and everything that happens afterward. The Devil examines the ways temptation tests us.

The Lovers depicts another kind of death. In the seventeenth-century Tarot de Marseilles deck, the card showed a wedding: a man being passed from the arms of his mother into the arms of his lover. This is the death of the boy, and the beginning of his new life as a man.

"For me, the Lover card is a rubicon," scholar Laetitia Barbier explained in her book *Tarot and Divination Cards*, "a threshold in which one decides to step out of their comfort zone, going against the grain, toward the Self."

Over the centuries, the card evolved, the imagery changed. A sense of duality remained, but the Lovers became less about ceremony. In the Rider-Waite Smith deck, the card became a depiction of Adam and Eve. Much later, in the acclaimed Carnival at the End of the World deck by artists Nicholas Kahn and Richard Selesnick, the Lovers card features two figures whose arms are locked together in a kind of stockade.

Inside every person who comes looking to tarot cards for answers, there are undoubtedly questions of harmony and discord. Angels and demons. Feminine and masculine. The Lovers, perhaps, is an invitation to be both. To embrace the war being waged inside.

In July 1975, Elizabeth Clare Prophet called her followers from around the West to gather at Lake Siskiyou, near Mount Shasta. It was an important place; in *Climb the Highest Mountain*, she and Mark Prophet claimed it was the site of the Divine Mother consciousness.

Her followers, many of whom had begun to call her "Mother Prophet," came every year to the gathering near the mountain, where they could purchase photos of the Ascended Masters—Jesus, El Morya, Saint Germain, Mark Prophet.

"Flanked by enormous pastels of Jesus Christ and St. Germain," read reports of the event, "she welcomed her children to Shasta's cosmic breast, flowing with 'nectar from Venus.'" She spoke for hours in long, flowing paragraphs, eyes typically closed, cloaked in all white, giving voice to the Masters' messages. Sometimes, as she delivered their wisdom, she looked pained, touching her fingertips to her temples, straining.

By then, the people around Mount Shasta were used to a constant drip of New Age groups coming toward the mountain and their town. Businesses posted signs that read: "No Lemurian information." The chief of police mocked the stories of Lemurians inside the volcano. "That's where the little men live. They come in once a month and buy groceries with gold nuggets," he quipped.

Like the Ballards before her, it was no secret that the business of prophecy was a lucrative one for Elizabeth. According to the local newspaper, people joked that Elizabeth Clare Prophet should change her last name to "Profit," for how she had found a way to financially benefit from spirituality. In 1978, she laid the first bricks of a kingdom when she purchased a 218-acre property in Calabasas, California, for $5.6 million, originally built in the 1920s by the founder of the Gillette razor company.

The place was renamed Camelot—a callback to the tales of King Arthur and the fabled lost civilization of Avalon. She claimed the blueprints for *her* Camelot had come from "architects of the ancient cultures of Lemuria and Atlantis," and tasked a church architect named Gregory Mull to help design a "New Jerusalem." One article would later call Camelot the church's "Disneyland of the Spirit," where swans waddled and the staff never stopped smiling. There was an "Excalibur Square," and a Chapel for the Holy Grail on the premises.

By 1978, one church leader estimated to a California newspaper that the church membership was around 25,000; the following year, *Hustler* magazine wrote a story about Elizabeth, characterizing her as a hustler of her own kind, lambasting the roster of Masters who spoke to her as "like roll call at Marvel Comics," and opining that the church was nothing but a "sugar-coated Cult of the Self."

After Mark Prophet's death, Elizabeth had expanded the belief system, incorporating astrology into her teachings and issuing rules to followers for how to live: to eat a vegetarian diet, to practice juice fasts and undergo a steady regimen of colonics. (A tiled room at Camelot was supposedly devoted to colonics.)

Saturdays were recast as "the day of the violet flame" and "designated as a day of fasting commemorating Jesus' 40-day fast in the wilderness." Students of Summit University consumed only distilled water, herbal laxatives, or herbal enemas.

Homosexuality was forbidden. Alcohol was forbidden. Smoking was forbidden. Taking drugs "to stimulate astral experience or force the chakras" was forbidden. Clothes designed by Elizabeth could be purchased from the church—flowing dresses for women, tunics for men. Chakra colors were to be worn on designated days. Like the Ballards, Elizabeth also professed the divinity of the colors purple and white, and the evil of black, red, and orange. For those who adhered to the church's strict codes on how to live, ascension was almost a promise. Erin Prophet wrote that, in retrospect, her mother's followers were gullible and would do just about whatever she said.

The grandiose expansions brought the church a swell of media attention, as reporters tried to understand what followers actually believed, how Elizabeth had so much money, and whether she was operating a cult.

"The church is made up of little people just like you and me," one believer told the *Los Angeles Times*. "We run the whole gamut. I don't think we have any real strong liberals, but we're very into freedom."

In a sweeping series published in 1980, the *Thousand Oaks News Chronicle* laid out the breadth of the church's business enterprises. It owned a corporation that traded in gold and silver, a recording business, restaurants, food distributors. It ran tuition-based education programs from kindergarten to college level. It owned property from

California to Colorado. The church even owned a local Shell gas station. The articles seemed to touch a nerve with the church, which purchased two full pages of advertisements and designed them to look like a news article, with the headline "America in Deadly Peril."

"Most people are aware of the established fact that if a big lie is told often enough, people will finally begin to accept it as truth," it read. The church believed the newspaper's coverage had been a replication of a technique used by "Goebbels' propaganda machine in Hitler's Third Reich." The advertisement said that the press was an instrument of "the power elite" and was used to manipulate people's thoughts: "They stir up confusion and conflict, shape public opinion through managed news, destroy or reduce to impotence organized religion, demoralize and propagandize the youth, subvert the educational system, manipulate the economy, and co-opt the political leadership, thus corrupting the governmental process," it alleged.

The longer the advertisement went on, the more off topic it went, veering toward manifesto. The church railed against abortions, said people were conspiring to "destroy man's faith in God," and that the negative press coverage was a plot of "black magic or witchcraft." This hellscape could be avoided if people would see that Elizabeth was, in fact, delivering a "message of liberation." She could heal the sick, the afflicted, the addicted.

The message was clear: she should not be scrutinized.

But like Edna Ballard before her, legal troubles would only bring more bad press when Gregory Mull, the architect hired to design Camelot, took Elizabeth to court, claiming he was defrauded and harmed emotionally by the Church Universal and Triumphant. The matter started over a sum of about $30,000. Mull said it was a reimbursement by the church to cover expenses he incurred; Elizabeth claimed it was a loan that he never paid back. Around 1981, the church sued him to get it; in response, Mull countersued for a whopping $253 million.

The trial was about money, but throughout the court proceedings, a great deal about Elizabeth's beliefs and her treatment of her followers leaked out from the witness stand. Mull's attorneys claimed that their client had been brainwashed while attending Summit University. As a student, he lived in co-housing with four other roommates, adhering to a strict daily regimen. They rose as early as 5:30 a.m. and took a bus to the "Motherhouse," where the students recited decrees, ate, recited more decrees, watched videos of Elizabeth, recited even more decrees. At night they were transported back home, where they recited decrees, then stayed up until 1 or 2 a.m. doing homework, before rising again at 5:30 for...a new day of decreeing. He claimed that students were encouraged to sever any connections that they had to the outside world: parents, family, friends. According to Mull, the sleep deprivation and hours of recitation were hypnotic and made a person "very passive, very placid... You could accept almost anything. You became very pliable."

Students were required to provide something called a "clearance letter" upon acceptance into the program. "You are told that only what you confessed is what you will be forgiven of," Mull said. "And you had different things you were supposed to confess."

In the letters, students were instructed to disclose the names of everyone they'd had sex with, and when and where those relations occurred; to write down any traumatic experiences, like car accidents, and the details of when those occurred; to list anyone they considered an enemy, and where those people lived.

In a ten-page letter, Mull confessed that he had had several homosexual encounters. He believed his clearance letter would be burned immediately after Elizabeth read it, that "the confession would be known to only Elizabeth Clare Prophet and God." But Mull implied that it was later used to turn other church members against him.

His Summit training caused Mull to feel like "the world was my enemy and the only one I could rely on was the teaching committed to us by Elizabeth Clare Prophet. That she was God incarnate." Elizabeth helped select his wife, and consulted with her followers before they had children.

The attorneys argued that this case had nothing to do with religious belief, and yet religion was constantly up for discussion during the proceedings, with Elizabeth even reading decrees for the court record.

Ultimately, the jury did not favor her. When they awarded Mull $1.5 million, it was a massive loss. The paranoia that Mull insisted Prophet instilled in her followers became her own.

In a rolling landscape of clear creeks and rocky canyons that even the irreligious would understand as God's country, in 1981, Elizabeth and her church snatched up the magazine publisher Malcolm Forbes's former 12,000-acre Montana ranch for around $7 million. In the ensuing five years, her staff would continue to buy up more land around it, expanding their plot near Yellowstone National Park to 33,000 acres and making the church, according to one article in the *Los Angeles Times*, the second-largest landholder in the entire county. "In Montana, if you own a lot of land, you own a lot of power," one concerned local mused. On *Nightline* a reporter characterized this land grab as a "New Age range war" at play.

Under church ownership, the Forbes property was rebranded the Royal Teton Ranch, a reference to a Wyoming mountain retreat discussed by Guy Ballard in *Unveiled Mysteries*. At a 1982 conference, Prophet delivered a message from Saint Germain that one thousand church members needed to move to Montana to "neutralize" the dissent and anger over the group. In moving to Montana, they would be "spiritual survivalists," and begin to prep for disaster.

"They created quite a bit of panic," said Ken Toole, a former Montana state senator and the retired co-director of the Montana Human Rights Network. "Most people move to Montana because of the mountains and lakes. They're moving here to make their preparations for Armageddon."

The church acquired housing supplies from the defunct Rajneeshpuram, and those who relocated to the Montana property were given the option to purchase tracts from the church and build homes for themselves in an area it had deemed "Glastonbury." To live there meant to explicitly agree to build a fallout shelter stocked with enough caches of food and supplies "to survive any such warfare or social disruption for a period of at least one year." (Strangely, residents also had to agree not to build studios for "the recording of rock, blues or jazz music.") If they decided to sell their home, the church would take the property back for a small price.

Elizabeth had retained I AM's nationalistic style; followers sang "Hail to the Chief"—the song that plays when the president enters— from church pews. Erin Prophet said her parents were staunchly con- servative and anti–labor union. They were also political. Toole recalled members of the church running as candidates for local offices in the nearby town of Livingston, and "there was a lot of concern" that the group would turn out to be just like Rajneeshpuram.

Under Elizabeth, nationalism morphed into a kind of survivalism, which was surging in the western United States. The antigovernment Patriot movement put down roots in Montana, Idaho, and Washing- ton State, where paramilitary groups prepared to fight a mythical and ever-present New World Order. Under the New World Order's control, the government would round up American citizens' guns, and ferry people off to concentration-style camps where they could be monitored and controlled. Sometimes those elites were called Z.O.G.—short for "Zionist Occupied Government"—because they believed the govern- ment was being controlled by Jews, as the *Protocols* first noted. And perhaps locals' concerns that this was another Rajneeshpuram weren't too far off: Elizabeth's followers acquired stockpiles of guns, and enter- tained political ambitions.

According to Erin Prophet, this paranoia had always been at the heart of what her parents preached. "She and my father formed the belief that the masters were using them to fight a global Communist takeover," she wrote.

Ads for her events in the mid-1980s showed Elizabeth braiding political language with the spiritual. "Stumping for the Coming Revolution in Higher Consciousness," one flyer read. Another, for a conference called FREEDOM 1986, depicted Elizabeth, Saint Germain, the Statue of Liberty, and a range of jagged mountains all woven together into the fabric of an American flag, rippling in the wind. From a lectern, her speeches grew more fearful. "The great, Great War will come in the second half of the twentieth century. Death will reign everywhere," she predicted. "The age of ages is coming, the end of all ends if mankind will not repent and be converted."

On October 7, 1987, she revealed the first of the many doomsday prophecies that she believed would come to pass if the world did not turn toward the Ascended Masters. She dictated a message from the Master El Morya:

"Blessed hearts, the evidence is clear to us and to those who know and therefore ought to do better that the Soviet Union has never altered her position in moving toward the nuclear first strike against this nation and the devastation of Europe...Be it known to you that this nation must have the capacity to turn back any and all missiles, warheads incoming whether by intent or by accident."

As she spoke, clutching her temples, rings upon every finger, her voice sounded like a divinely appointed auctioneer:

"There are then, beloved, conditions upon which Earth and her evolutions might be saved. The areas then that which present themselves of greatest urgency is for the final binding and judgment of fallen angels, who have positioned themselves in the economies and governments of the nations, and in the banking houses, to exercise absolute control over the people. Beloved ones, for Earth to be saved, world communism with all of its supporters, agents, and tools must go down."

Erin Prophet wrote that as her mother issued more fatalistic predictions, she began adhering to an "if-then" model. "'*If* you don't return to the Lord, *then* you will be invaded.' Such prophecies were meant to be proven false," she wrote. "The idea that prophecy could be mitigated or changed based on human action was at the core of her teaching, which was opposed to predestination."

Elizabeth made a prediction that after October 2, 1989, the United States would most likely be at war, possibly deploying missiles into the sky against Russia. She knew because she had eavesdropped via "mind travel" around the halls of the Kremlin.

That got the attention of national media.

On *Oprah*, two of Prophet's daughters were guests: stony-faced Erin, then a church spokesperson, dressed in purple, and her sister Moira, with teased hair, who claimed that when she left the group, her family severed contact.

"My mother, I've seen her tyrannize and persecute people that have worked for her and given their whole lives to her for years. I've seen her break up families," Moira said, "and demand power—absolute power." She said her mother was making it so people couldn't make decisions for themselves.

Erin politely scoffed, said her sister was lying. People were free to leave, but also to disagree with her mother.

"Why do you think this group is dangerous?" Oprah asked Moira.

"I think it's dangerous because it destroys the individual and his choices. It centers around mind control. I think that the people in it, through their decrees…through believing Elizabeth Prophet is the only messenger of God—"

"—Your mother," Oprah reminded.

"—*My* mother. Their lives are completely ruled by her," she said. "The phobias, the fears that have been instilled in the members, since its inception, of the end of the world, the coming of the end, of Armageddon, are all-consuming."

Erin seemed unruffled. "We are building fallout shelters, we believe that a nuclear war is a thing everybody should prepare for," she said. The date wasn't necessarily exact, but they believed "a confrontation between the superpowers" might occur.

The television studio audience was filled with people who were either members of the church or had left it. One man named Don stood up and said he had been tasked with running military-style guns between Idaho and Montana. After a commercial break, a panel sat onstage next to the sisters. Kenneth, a former member of Elizabeth's security force, the "Cosmic Honor Guard," told Oprah he believed he was above the law. "We were trained in paramilitary tactics," he said. It was dangerous. Church members rose out of the audience to chastise him.

Steven Hassan, a cult expert, squabbled with an ordained minister speaking in support of the Church Universal and Triumphant. Current members hurled insults at former members. Moira and Erin glared at each other with daggers in their eyes. There was no conclusion, but it was quintessential American television: a spectacle.

"So, are ya brainwashed?" Oprah asked one of the men in the group, who sat next to Erin on the stage.

"'Course not," he replied.

"How would you know?" Moira called out.

"How would *you* know?" he fired back at her.

In October 1989, after the arrest of the church's chief of security, Elizabeth's third husband, Edward Francis, faced federal firearms charges, to which he pled guilty. The chief of security said that the arsenal of illegal weapons "were only intended to protect members from nuclear war." They had come to believe they were "spiritual light bearers," but, according to one account of the arrest published in *High Country News*, being light bearers "made them targets for 'the dark forces' that conspired against them: aliens from evil planets, fallen angels, capitalists and communists who plotted together."

Back in Montana, Elizabeth tried to assuage fears at public meetings. Pizza was served. The *Billings Gazette* reported that she told the room that while she felt fallout shelters were a good idea, she "feels it's unnecessary to prepare for any ground invasion by the Soviets or other hostile forces."

Word had gotten out about the elaborate construction of bomb shelters. One of the armored personnel carriers had arrived. The tall guard tower went up, elaborate fencing. On March 15, 1990, she ordered her followers into their underground shelters, where they slept overnight. When nothing happened, a third of the people exited the church. The ones who stayed believed "their prayers had mitigated the karma," her daughter wrote.

"The difficult things that happened in the church—losing a lawsuit, feeling persecuted by the government—that made her shift over into what you might call a more apocalyptic belief system," Erin said later. It was something she came to understand after she left the church, departed her position as its spokesperson, and started looking at her parents' work from an academic perspective. She scoured through her parents' writings and speeches and found that during the Cuban Missile Crisis and later, during the Watergate hearings, her parents had also ramped up this kind of panicked rhetoric. "If they started feeling persecuted, they would be more in the phase of 'we're going to be saved, and other people are going to be left to their own devices.'"

The church's public relations problems only compounded in April 1990, when several massive tanks of fuel owned by the church cracked and more than 31,000 gallons of it leaked into the groundwater. It was an environmental disaster that cost the church about a million dollars to fix.

Elizabeth for so long predicted that the world would end; instead, the one ending was her own world as the church's finances started to dramatically unravel.

By 1998 she was diagnosed with Alzheimer's disease and died of it by 2009. She hoped one of her children would take her place at the helm of the church, but all of them left it behind. Erin Prophet is now an assistant professor in the philosophy and religious studies department at East Carolina University. She moved away from her mother's teachings, but it pains her when people cast her mother in a bad light when it's so clear her ideas are infused into the wider culture.

"In a way I feel bad. My mom's dead," she said, and yet people want to "just keep stabbing her in the back."

"I think my mother was easier to attack than a man because women have often been portrayed as being deluded or hysterical. When a woman starts to say she's talking to Jesus or has had past lives, it's easier to dismiss it."

After Erin left her family's church, she theorized that the reason for all of her mother's paranoid predictions was losing the lawsuit to Gregory Mull. She had been challenged, and she lost, and in light of that loss, she made moves to keep her power. Except her war wasn't real. She created a war, and from it she derived power over a populace who believed in her predictions, and loved her, and would listen if by doing what she said they could maintain some small grip of control on their vast uncertain futures.

"Mighty I AM Presence!" Elizabeth commanded, her words from another decade now forever echoing on YouTube. Her eyes were closed, the fingertips of one delicate hand pressing against her right temple. "I AM here, O God, and I am the instrument of those sevenfold rays and archangels."

With each word, her other hand—balled into a fist—pumped the air. She wore a brilliant purple gown, and behind her, candles flickered behind glass votives, and the saints in gilded frames were haloed in explosions of bright light.

The scene cut.

Now the viewer was somewhere else—a dark ballroom, where a crowd of hundreds held their hands toward the sky, repeating the words of the man onstage.

"We are your instrument of those sevenfold rays, and all your archangels," said General Michael Flynn, the former national security advisor to President Trump and a fan of the QAnon conspiracy theory. It was nearly twelve years after Prophet's death. Flynn was speaking to the Lord of Hosts Church in Nebraska.

The video cut again, back to Elizabeth.

"And I will not retreat! I will take my stand!" she said, voice rasping from declaring these words with so much force. "I will not fear to speak!" She drew both hands to her temples. "And I will be the instrument of God's will, whatever it is."

Back to Flynn:

"We will not retreat," he said mechanically. "We will *not* retreat."

Someone from the crowd of parishioners called out, "Never!!!"

"We will stand our ground," he said.

"*Amen!*" called a voice.

"We will not fear to speak," Flynn said, droll. "We will be the instrument of your will. Whatever it is."

Back to Elizabeth.

"Here I am, so help me God, in the name of Archangel Michael and his legions! I AM! Free born!" she yelled, electrified, as if these words were shooting out of her like lightning bolts.

This was not the Elizabeth of television interviews, or public meetings. This was the Elizabeth of gods and Masters, shouting what she believed straight to the cosmos, owning it, declaring it with so much force that she seemed to be a different person entirely. This was the woman who commanded, and whom people followed.

"And I shall remain free born! And I shall not be enslaved by any foe within or without," she rasped.

Back to Flynn, a man repeating the same words, but not really saying them—not like she had. He read the words and, somehow, sucked all life from them.

"In your name, and the name of your legions, we are free born. And we shall remain free born! And we shall not be enslaved!" he said, as the people in the crowd murmured.

In any other time in history, Flynn's speech might have been overlooked. But this was the age of the internet, and a video of his words went viral among QAnon users. All his talk of "sevenfold rays" came off as . . . a little weird. Was it satanic? Had he turned against them? Gone over to the side of the cabal?

But also, because this was the age of the internet, now a new video appeared on YouTube in which a user spliced Flynn's prayer together with Elizabeth's. Now they spoke one after the other—the long-dead church leader, then the military general. It didn't look satanic, really. It looked like Flynn stole her speech.

Elizabeth professed proudly, boldly; Flynn said words. He was just one more man promising to stand his ground. A typical far-right guy proclaiming to a Second Amendment crowd that he'd never budge. A man who benefited from a presidential administration that cheered hate and violence saying he would never change, and no one in the crowd had to either.

But when Elizabeth said those words, they were infused with a kind of power that felt radical—like it hadn't been bestowed upon her by any man but existed beyond the grip of patriarchy. She was hypnotic. This was a woman yelling that *she* would take her stand. That she would be strong. That nothing could stop her in her path—whatever that was—and that every drop of her power had not been given to her but was summoned from deep inside of her.

14.

Just a few months before the world locked down in response to COVID-19, Kim Pece's ears started ringing. She thought it was an ear infection at first. But soon the ringing became the least of her concerns. She was consumed by a flood of new sensations—feelings she'd never experienced before.

Kim felt like she could read minds and anticipate what someone would say next in a conversation. Every time music was on, the beat coursed through her body like it was coming out of her bones. Her dreams were more vivid. When she was awake, she felt like she was having visions. Once, she swore she could make out the shape of a woman shimmering across the room from her, like a spirit, or a ghost.

"I would stay in my room for hours and just talk to myself because I was talking out loud to my guides, or my grandmother," she said. It was hard to know what was happening, whether it was an awakening, a mental break, both, neither.

In many ways, Kim looks the part of a yogi. She is thin with strong arms, brown hair that fades out to blond at the ends, blue eyes that gleam, a wry, knowing smile. When Kim started experiencing these symptoms, she also had trouble sleeping and ate less frequently, but did yoga more often. She wondered if what was happening was a "spontaneous kundalini awakening," which *Yoga Journal* wrote in 2021 can be triggered during rigorous yoga practices: "It is said once your kundalini awakens, life will never be the same."

In the Sanskrit language, the word means "coiled," and practitioners of kundalini yoga believe energy is stored at the base of the spine, at the root chakra, like a resting serpent. Regular kundalini practice can inspire that store of energy to flow up the body, slithering through each chakra—sacral, solar plexus, heart, throat, third eye—until it reaches the crown chakra at the top of the head, the place of enlightenment.

Kundalini awakening isn't something you plan for; typically, it is sudden, happening unexpectedly, "causing immense havoc in the body and the mind," wrote one yoga scholar. It can feel like a psychotic break. "I just thought my powers had awakened," Kim said.

Kim's husband, her two sons, and her mom were having trouble understanding what was going on. In the past, she had been diagnosed with depression, ADHD, and OCD, and had taken medication. She carried trauma from sexual abuse she'd suffered as a child. After she injured her back at work—she was working with people with mental and emotional concerns and was harmed by a client in crisis—she became addicted to the painkillers she'd been prescribed, then weaned herself off with Suboxone. Sometimes she drank, sometimes she tried stronger things. Inside of her, she had so much pain, and grasped at anything that might help her cope, like reaching for a light switch in an impenetrable darkness.

But this was something new. This time she was talking about God.

Kim had always wanted faith, but her mother wasn't religious. What little she could recall of her father, who never had much of a place in her life, included a hazy memory when he told her he was chosen by God to defeat the devil. As an adult, she was told he suffered from bipolar disorder.

Kim was fascinated nonetheless with religion. In seventh grade, she went to church with a friend's family and was in awe. "I would always cry," she said. The experience overwhelmed her with emotion and happiness. Being faithful felt beautiful and honest and essential. But it always seemed just out of her reach.

Kim was introduced to her husband, John Pece—she calls him Johnny—by the bartender at a bar called The Matrix in Ontario. He was confident, Italian, a Catholic by birth, but not the sort to put much stock in organized religion. "I shunned that out of my life as soon as I didn't have to go to church anymore," he said. "But that didn't stop me from believing in a higher power." Later, after John and Kim had their two sons, she considered enrolling them in Catholic school. "I wanted them to be able to talk about God," she said. "I grew up with nobody talking about him."

When Kim's strange symptoms began in 2019, it felt to her like something inherently spiritual was happening. She went to doctors and therapists, and they all told her she was having a psychotic episode. When she'd try to explain what was happening, people looked at her "like I was hallucinating or having a breakdown," she said. Family and friends pushed her away, unsure of how to handle what was going on. "They kind of didn't know what to do and just cut me off."

In the midst of this, in March 2020, Kim and John moved their family halfway across Canada from Ontario to a small town in New Brunswick, where she had trouble getting a new Suboxone prescription filled. Then COVID shut the world down. Kim started homeschooling her children. The stress only seemed to build.

Kim drank heavily, started using cocaine, and did yoga as much as her body could handle. She didn't sleep much and would forget to eat. One night in July, at around nine o'clock, she had fallen into an online rabbit hole, and was scrolling through posts in a Facebook group that discussed the possibility that there were other dimensional planes, specifically fifth-dimensional consciousness. One comment caught her attention—five words and a link that seemed like they were lit up by spotlights:

"This is what's really happening," it read.

She clicked. There was no thought behind the click—she just did it. A video played in which two young women were having a conversation. There was just something about them. "I was hypnotized right away. I couldn't get enough of it," she said.

As the women spoke, one of them offhandedly remarked that God was a woman. The words collided into Kim like a freight train. It was so sudden. After months of searching, it was as if a lost piece of her mind fell perfectly into place.

"I finally realized what the shadow I was seeing was—it was a woman," Kim said. She went to the website of the group hosting the livestream, and there the message was again. "It said, 'God is a woman.' It was like following the yellow brick road and my whole body lit up and was like 'YES!' So I just started reading through their material." It felt like a sign from the universe.

The next day she watched one of the group's two-hour livestreams. They called themselves Love Has Won. The hosts greeted all the new followers watching, and Kim felt a thrill, like maybe they noticed her there. "I had gone through so much and had lost so many friends and family because they didn't know how to help me," she said. "It was really traumatic. I was abandoned." But then someone finally saw her.

"And so just being recognized by these people," she said. "I just felt seen and heard and, and they were speaking about the things that I was interested in."

The women talked in conspiratorial terms about the shadowy forces at play on the planet, but that kind of talk didn't bother Kim. She liked to consider all possibilities—that maybe everything *wasn't* as it seemed.

When Love Has Won's livestream ended, Kim already knew she would be back for the next one several hours later. In the meantime, she wanted to learn everything she could, and began watching the group's backlog of videos. "Amy had done twelve years of these two-hour livestreams twice a day, so she had a lot of YouTube content," she said. Kim read the articles they posted on their website and clicked through the products in their online store: candles, crystals, artwork. "Immediately, I bought the colloidal silver."

Kim told her husband, John, about the group she had found online—she was so excited to share it with him. They had the answer she had been looking for. That vision she had seen was God, and God was a woman. And she was alive. She was in Colorado. John took one look at Amy's picture and "immediately he was like, 'This is a cult. Amy is not God,'" Kim recalled. Even if that was true, he said God wasn't this woman on the screen.

Kim brushed him off and tuned in again later that night. On the livestream, the conversation turned to how the group believed that the actor and comedian Robin Williams was their spiritual guide.

"I know it seems crazy to think that Robin Williams could be a guide for them. But pretty much anything can. You could say angels, you could say fairies. In the spiritual community . . . it's just an energy," she said.

To her, when talk turned to Robin Williams, it just felt like one more synchronicity. She was a huge fan of his movies. "They started naming off all these movies that Robin was trying to tell us things without telling us things," Kim said. "Like *Popeye*: 'I am what I am that I am that I am.'"

Viewers started typing out their favorite Robin Williams movies into the comments. Kim typed *What Dreams May Come*. "We started interacting like that," she said. As the livestream went on, the hosts and other members of Love Has Won replied to what Kim typed. "I felt like I was special, that I was chosen. That I was meant to be there. And immediately I felt contracted to be there, just like it says on their website," she said. "Like I was supposed to be doing this."

Quickly, the members of Love Has Won added Kim to a private Skype group, where she noticed that people were talking about the television host Dr. Phil, who was producing an episode devoted to Love Has Won. There was a lot of excitement that Mother God was entering the spotlight of daytime television.

"He was going to pull through and reveal that God was a woman," Kim said.

Her days filled immediately. Kim was "constantly connected" to the group. All of a sudden, she had all these new friends. There was always something to watch on the livestreams. Sometimes the hosts would pull tarot cards and interpret them, other times they would auction off art painted by Mother God. Bids filled the comments: $77, $88, $99. Watching the streams took up four hours, and the Skype chats filled in the spaces in between. Love Has Won offered healings and etheric "surgeries" over the phone, so she signed up. There were trainings. And when nothing else was happening, she had the group's never-ending radio station to listen to—always on and playing happy, feel-good music. Mother God and her followers were always on Kim's mind. Once, Kim's mother stopped by to pick Kim and her sons up to go swimming, which she loved, but she told them to go on without her. She wanted to stay connected to the group; she was serving a greater cause now, and nothing could drag her away.

During the livestreams, when trolls would come into the comments to call the group a cult, Kim started gently coming to the defense of Love Has Won. "I felt like I was helping God right away...Just right away," she said, "I was *that* vulnerable."

In a video taken in 2020, Amy Carlson sits in a soft blue armchair on a balcony overlooking the thick forest that surrounded the Salida, Colorado, cabin the group had relocated to. She wears a short pink dress covered with a print of swirling stars. Wind chimes toll in the breeze. Styx's 1983 song "Mr. Roboto" plays through speakers somewhere. As Amy speaks, she slurs. Her face is ashen, almost gray.

"You were saying?" Jason prompts Amy, who had gotten off track, her point lost.

"Yes," she says. "I commanded all my atoms to come home back into the light. In order for them to come home back into the light, they had to be fuckin' whores. *Bad.* To the bone. Rape. Pillage. Thieves."

She pauses and stares at her hands.

"Holy fucking shit. You know, I'm like eight billion egos? Yeah. I got this bitch," she says, sitting upright, running her hands through her long red-brown hair, wiggling in her seat to the music. "I got 'em, Robin!"

Jason cheers—understanding this language, this code that Amy speaks.

"Universal law!" She yells as Styx chirps *Secret, secret! I've got a secret!*

"No matter what's happened to me, I will still stand for love," she says, smiling. "You can fuckin' tear me down. You can kill me."

"Kilroy!" Jason says, singing along as the song finished.

Amy's face twists into a grotesque expression. "Kill *me!*" she yells.

"You're fuckin' done. Cabal? Over! Spiritual ego whores? Done! If you're not connected to me, you're out," Amy says, suddenly furious, ranting, though over what isn't exactly clear.

The song changes. The flying theme from the 1982 film *E.T. the Extra-Terrestrial* begins—the song that played as a child on his bike pedals past the moon with the help of his new alien friend.

"If you're not connected in, you're fucking done," Amy says.

"No E.T. go home for you, bitch-whores," Jason says.

"Fucking battle me! My own lightworkers: battle me!" Amy yells.

John Pece was getting worried.

During all their years together, Kim had "followed a lot of different spiritual groups and teachings," he said. "But, I don't know. Something seemed a little bit off about the way she was talking, the way she kept mentioning Mother God."

She'd showed him the group's Facebook page, and while he didn't see the appeal, he could understand why his wife did. "She was feeling really low," John said. "There was this group that was offering her answers and hope and praise and love."

After John brushed Love Has Won off as a cult, and said Mother God probably wasn't God, Kim was more careful about how she spoke about it. She closed inward, listening to the twice-daily livestreams on headphones, or waiting until John and her sons had gone to bed to dive back into the group's online world. At family dinners, she'd find reasons to step away, to walk outside and back online. If a livestream was happening while they ate, she'd listen with one earbud in.

Group members told her it was fine to drink alcohol—something she had struggled with. Mother God drank. "I think that attracted me. I'm like, 'I can drink again, it's organic,'" Kim said.

The group emailed Kim a copy of the Ascension Guide and she followed as much of it as she could: the garlic cleanses, the colloidal silver, the affirmations, wearing the right colors on the right days. When the group went live, she sprinkled livestream links across Facebook, in comments, on her own profile, hoping friends might watch. One day, a former neighbor messaged her.

"I watched a Love Has Won video that you posted. Can you please give me a synopsis of what they believe/stand for?" the neighbor said to Kim.

Kim was thrilled that one of her Facebook friends was interested.

"So happy you're open to feeling into God as a woman," Kim wrote back. "Mom's dream is to build a crystal school for the children to have safe and love-based learning... I'm still learning too or rather unlearning, but it feels truer to me than anything I've ever felt."

Her neighbor still didn't quite understand.

"Thank you for the explanation! I just listened to a small snippet, and it probably raised more questions than answering them," she said.

"As I'm typing out their beliefs, I'm like, 'Well how do I tell her that [Amy] was Jesus? There's no way I'm going to tell this woman that the Jesus she's always believed in is wrong,'" Kim later recalled. She tried to explain in more detail.

"Heaven is a frequency," Kim wrote back, "and our mission is to bring heaven's consciousness to Earth through Christ's consciousness."

When her neighbor asked more questions Kim couldn't answer, she just sent her the link to the group's website.

Kim spoke on the phone with members of the group that she'd met in the Skype chats. One call was with Ryan Kramer. "He couldn't believe I was already talking to angels—like, there wasn't convincing he had to do with me," she said. "And so right away, he started grooming me for going to mission." He told her, "I think you know what you need to do."

All the while, Kim's husband, John, was growing suspicious. He reached out to Kim's mother, who had also noticed a change. Kim seemed to always find a way to turn conversations toward talk about Mother God. When Kim would come by, her mother would dust off old photo albums and ask Kim to come take a look. She wanted to keep Kim from forgetting everything she was and becoming absorbed completely into the strange online world of Mother God.

No one knew how much longer the pandemic would last, how much longer the border between Canada and the United States would stay closed. But John knew he needed to make a plan to keep Kim from going to the group in Colorado.

It was clear that she was ready to leave everything behind. "I wanted to be chosen," she said. "I wanted to belong."

The world had failed Kim, but Mother God understood her.

Mother God had even left her own kids behind to serve a higher power. If Kim did that too, she was only re-creating herself in the image of her brand-new god.

In Florida, Ashley McCoy had been watching Love Has Won's livestreams for hours every day for eight months straight when she decided to go "on mission" with the group—meaning she would join them in Colorado, where the group moved to from California in 2019. Ashley had been raised as a Jehovah's Witness, but she was searching for a new spiritual path. "There really wasn't one specific route I was looking into," she said, "just more open-minded people who wanted to get together and be kind to one another."

In the summer of 2020, she left her job at Starbucks and told her husband that she was going to a spiritual retreat in Colorado, and he agreed it seemed like a good idea. Working in the service industry had made her exhausted. "I just decided I wanted to take a break from the everyday," she said. She told her manager at work she was taking something of "a sabbatical."

"I wasn't going through any kind of crisis," she said. "It just made me want to shift out of my everyday, constantly dealing with people who were angry."

Ashley took a flight from Jacksonville to Denver, then a small charter plane to Crestone. She believed she was finally meeting the good friends she'd made online. She didn't agree with them about everything they said on livestreams, like their homophobia, "but I kind of let that go because everybody is entitled to feel the way they want to feel," she said. "There's lots of religious people who don't feel homosexuality is something that should exist." And besides, it didn't seem like it was the main point of the group—they were more focused on energy and crystals, "the hippie-dippy stuff you normally see."

"They just seemed like the happiest bunch of people," she said.

The scene was idyllic when she arrived at the cabin, located off a remote road and surrounded by forestland; a group had just finished seeding the yard with grass seed, and welcomed her. But things seemed off from the time she walked inside.

"I just knew something wasn't right," she said. "I just had this feeling I got myself into something that I didn't realize I got myself into."

Ashley was given a crash course on the rules: no one at the house but Amy was allowed to drink or use drugs (marijuana, which is legal for recreational use in Colorado, was permitted). Sleeping and eating were seen as things that were driven by the ego, so both were restricted. No one was allowed to nap, and when they did sleep at night, it was for less than four hours. "We had to be on our feet all day long. If we were sitting down, we were told we were taking energy from Amy by doing so," she said. Every rule seemed to be framed around Amy and her energy. If Amy decided to stay up all night drinking, which she did often, the group was told they had to stay up too. They obeyed. If she was sleeping, it wasn't her ego taking over, but viewed as essential "etheric meetings" she was conducting with her masters.

McCoy said nearly all purchases had to be cleared through Miguel Lamboy. Personal spending, too, was seen as an extension of the ego. When they left the house, they were assigned strict tasks and made to travel in pairs. Ashley wasn't allowed to call home to her husband and son. "They try to isolate you," she said. Calling family would only be taking energy from Amy.

Amy lived in an upstairs room of the cabin with a balcony overlooking the property, and her followers could only come to see her if they were given permission. Over time, she complained of pain in her feet and her legs, which felt weak. She broke out in rashes and boils and lost a noticeable amount of weight. She explained these changes to her followers: "Fifty pounds have dropped off my body because of humanity's dysfunction," she said. As the embodiment of the planet itself, she was being tortured. To deal with the pain, she turned to things she had told the group were medicines: marijuana, alcohol, and colloidal silver.

Jason Castillo, as Father God of that time, stayed in that room with her. Followers in good standing with Amy were separated into rooms by sex. Those who weren't in good standing were relegated to sleeping outside in an RV or in what was called the "Forest Fractal"—essentially tents pitched on the property, and at a nearby house. When the weather turned cold, the people outside had heaters; on occasion those heaters would be taken away by Amy's decree.

While Father Gods in the past adjusted to Amy's rhythm of drinking and passing out, trying to ground the group back in reality when she was asleep, Jason's reign as Father God was different. He was intense, obsessively doing push-ups, walking around the house without a shirt on, barking orders, eating raw eggs. Members of the group said he was so amped up all the time, it seemed like he was using methamphetamines. When Amy was asleep, he seemed to take the opportunity to exert his own kind of control. He assumed the role of a verbally abusive father, dictating the pace of each day, quick to act as a disciplinarian. As the group filmed themselves one day, Jason assumed control of the stereo, queuing up Pantera's song "Mouth for War" from their album *Vulgar Display of Power.* "That's me," he said as it blared, several followers nodding along to the music. "Vulgar display of power."

For the most part, the group did labor. One day shortly after Ashley arrived, Jason told them to create a large garden from scratch, and they worked for days to do so. They stained the house from top to bottom. Anytime they fell out of line, Jason would scream at them. Ashley quickly learned to stay quiet, do what she was told, and try not to be noticed. But even then it was hard to know what would set the leaders off.

"I thought these people were really loving, and then when you get behind the scenes, it's very toxic," Ashley said. "There's lots of yelling. They're constantly berating people, constantly telling people that they're in this low energy and they'll send them out of the house to go in the forest."

Amy continued to preach from her bed, usually with Jason sitting next to her. She had developed a stance by then that if anyone questioned if she was God, they were out. They were ego-programmed minds. They were the cabal. They had to go. Sometimes she screamed at her followers; they interpreted this not as Amy, the kind and forgiving Mother God, but as her masters—like Robin Williams—being channeled through her, taking over her body.

After being with the group for two weeks, Ashley was given the role of cook, making house meals for everyone and delivering specially made food to Amy that adhered to specific "protocols for cooking for God." Anyone who cooked for Amy was instructed to say a prayer before preparing her food, to ensure that she had smoked weed prior to eating, to feel joy while cooking and listening to music curated by Amy, and to burn sage prior to serving the food to her.

Just as stringent as these cooking guidelines were the rules around what exactly Amy could eat. "She had a shrimp tray with a bunch of different hors d'oeuvres on it that had to be made perfectly. Her peppers needed to be chopped a certain way. We had to make her cocktail sauce from scratch," Ashley said. Each day, Ashley devised a menu, which had to be approved by Jason. She was sent on hours-long trips to find special bottles of tequila for Amy. She served Amy beer from morning until night.

Her role afforded her the ability to leave the group more frequently than others so she could buy groceries, but she could only go with a partner. They were instructed to acquire most ingredients from a local food bank. Amy "had us all tell the food bank we had three, four, five kids," she said. Ashley did what she was told. "This isn't something I'm proud of."

Eating sugar was discouraged, but Ashley kept some in the kitchen for certain recipes. "The other people would sneak in and start eating it," she said. "It's the weirdest thing—a bunch of grown people doing this." Their eating was monitored, and Ashley lost a significant amount of weight.

On one occasion, she and another member returned to the cabin after grocery shopping and realized they'd missed a few items on the list. Jason started berating her shopping partner. Ashley stayed quiet, leaning over a counter. Jason barked at her to stand up straight.

"It felt like the military all of a sudden," she recalled.

Amy ordered the group to cut down trees around the cabin, which Ashley said they did daily using hand tools because the backbreaking work would be akin to Jesus's suffering on the cross. "To be honest, looking back on it, it just seems like some evil plot to watch people be controlled, watch people do what you tell them."

As the group cut down trees, Jason looked on from the balcony, calling out orders from up above.

Back in Texas, Amy's family watched as the tone of the livestreams became more abusive and political, filled with talk of Trump and QAnon. It was hard to watch, and it felt in opposition to their upbringing. "I can tell you my mom and dad never voted. We were not a political family," Chelsea said. "We kind of just live our life and do the best that we can do for our families. That's what we're about, we're not about the political...craziness. I just don't know what else to call it."

Once, Amy called her followers to gather around a screen to watch a speech by Donald Trump. "She thought everyone was going to get disclosure," Ashley McCoy recalled, "that everything [Love Has Won was] talking about was going to come out." The anthropologist Susannah Crockford defines disclosure, in New Age circles, as "when everyone finds out the truth that aliens are real, the truth that the government has been hiding. That's disclosure."

"It was constantly about Trump," Ashley said. "He was her father in Lemuria, and was going to save everyone in the group, and somehow the group was going to be recognized."

In 2020, a Miami lawyer named Dan Agos was trying to find out where his girlfriend, Lauryn Suarez, had disappeared to two years prior.

The pair had met in law school. Him, a Jersey guy, a gregarious sports fan; her, a well-to-do South Florida gal with expensive tastes who loved to talk about astrology. They couldn't have been more opposite, but they hooked up in school, and after graduation, things got more serious.

At the University of Miami's law school, Lauryn had been the kind of student who won awards; she gained accolades during their first year for volunteering more hours than any other student. She worked for the city attorney in Sunny Isles, Florida, and had a particular passion for legal issues surrounding the foster care system. But around the time she vanished, the Florida Bar revoked her law license because of "a misstatement" or omission on her application to practice law. "I won't go into detail because, frankly, I don't know what the issue was," Dan said. "She was very stressed about the situation."

In February 2018, a nineteen-year-old man walked through the halls of her alma mater, Marjory Stoneman Douglas High School, and murdered seventeen people. "She was very upset about that," Dan said. He noticed when he touched her, it seemed like she was always trembling. "I could tell how stressed she was."

Lauryn told him she needed a break from everything, and that she was traveling to California to attend a spiritual retreat. It seemed a little odd—she wasn't all that religious. But he waved his concerns away and told her, "Do what you have to do. You are just a wound-up ball of stress right now," he recalled saying. "She was super stressed, but also super nervous, because it turns out she was lying to everyone."

Lauryn texted him when she landed in Los Angeles, and said she was boarding a train headed north. It was weird; she said she was going camping, and that really caught his attention. *You don't camp. You lie on the couch with your sunglasses on,* he remembered thinking.

The texts from Lauryn became sparser, which at first he thought might be normal; she was on a retreat and had gone to unplug. Two weeks passed. Then three. Dan and Lauryn had planned to move in together and were scheduled to go to a friend's wedding.

"Hey what's the deal here? When are you coming back?" Dan texted.

Lauryn wrote back, "When the energies allow."

Now Dan was worried.

"What the fuck does that mean?" he wrote. "I don't know where you are, I don't know what's going on." Lauryn would respond to some questions, but when she did, her messages didn't make sense. Like someone was telling her what to say.

As Dan worried about Lauryn, his phone rang. It was a friend of his, and she was in tears. "Have you seen these videos?" she asked.

She told him to go to YouTube. It was Lauryn, talking onscreen, next to another young woman. He showed it to his roommate. "We popped on the YouTube videos and saw they were just sitting around babbling about nothing and Mother God," he said. "What the hell is this?" More friends came over, and they crowded around the TV.

"Jaws literally were hitting the floor," Dan said. There was his girlfriend: not Lauryn anymore, but someone else entirely. She was "Archeia Aurora."

"It's like, 'Who are these people? What are you doing? This is not what you told us you were doing. And now you've completely cut off contact from everyone?'" Dan said. "Turns out you're all the way across the country in Mount Shasta, California?" This was something that happened to other people. Not him.

"I think there's this stereotype that a person is a loner, a kind of outcast, has a bad family life, not a lot of friends. So they go and join something like this," he said. "Lauryn couldn't have been more the opposite of that."

"She was looking for something bigger, or something more meaningful." But after he found out she was in Love Has Won, he would text her and remind her of that. "I would tell her, 'You were looking for something so much greater than you, but you found something that is so beneath you.'"

In June 2018, he emailed her. It felt like she was slipping away. He asked her about ascension—something he heard her repeatedly talking about on the livestreams. "I know you say it's hard to explain but try your absolute best in the simplest of terms," Dan wrote. "I know you feel overwhelmed by everyone reaching out to you at one time and that you are being judged because you are doing something that, to the naked eye, seems a bit crazy."

This time Lauryn replied. She said that the ascension meant "we are taking our bodies to New Earth. We are not relocating to another planet, we are staying on this one," she said. They were raising the frequency.

She told him about Mother God and the cabal. "It is a real thing. The royal family, the Rothschilds, Hollywood, Obama, Hillary, all of the elite are the cabal," she said.

She talked about the Book of Revelation, the 144,000. "I have confirmed that you are a part of the 144k, as am I. I just found out I'm Archeia Aurora, the sixth angel created, which was why I was one of the first to wake up."

She told Dan the end was coming. "We don't anticipate this going on much longer," she said. "We are at the finish line, basically."

For two more years, the world continued to not end. He saw her only once after that. He heard Love Has Won had traveled to Florida, and he made a five-hour drive north to see Lauryn. He knew he couldn't talk sense into her by then, but if she wanted to get out, he wanted to be clear he would help her.

When Dan arrived, he found her living in a tent with several other people at a campground near Yankeetown, Florida. He didn't see Amy, who was staying in an RV somewhere nearby.

"It was basically like six homeless people living in a tent," he said. Dan watched as one of them emptied a microwavable bag of broccoli onto a grill over a campfire. Lauryn was covered in bug bites. Dan asked her to come to his hotel. "I said, 'Listen, I see your living conditions right now... This is not a romantic thing. You just look like you need a warm bed and a hot shower. I'll take you back in the morning.'" She said no. It was clear to him that the other members did not want Dan to talk to her alone.

"I never went there thinking she was going to pack her bags," he said. "What I wanted to do was plant that seed in her head saying, even to all of them, there is a world outside of this."

Dan moved on, even though the details of what happened to Lauryn still mystified him. But he was weirdly not alone. He began to connect with people online. In Massachusetts, Hope's mother had started a Facebook group called Love Has Won Exposed, devoted to providing space to talk for the families of people who'd lost their loved ones to the group.

Meanwhile, more and more daily videos came from Love Has Won. The group seemed to be ratcheting up its efforts. Professionalizing. In March 2019, Miguel Lamboy received word of approval from the Internal Revenue Service that Love Has Won would receive tax-exempt status—generally afforded to religious organizations. He was listed as the principal officer.

By then, Amy hardly ever appeared on camera. She was rail thin. The pain in her legs had advanced into an overall weakness, and eventually she claimed to be paralyzed, and needed to be carried anywhere she wanted to go. The few times she still appeared on camera, she exited the frame by means of a looped arm around Jason Castillo's neck as he lifted her offscreen.

But as social media became more and more integral to Love Has Won spreading its messages, Hope and Aurora offered the perfect new image: thin young women with Instagram influencer good looks and the ability to speak for hours on end about any topic. They said they had been trained as oracles by Amy to receive "protocols" from Robin Williams and then translate them to the world. Aurora explained Amy was simply "so far ahead in consciousness, it's hard for her to be here anymore." The livestreams evolved well past the astrological forecasts of Amy's early days, when she'd speak into a headset and call anyone watching a "love being." In this new age, the group members solicited donations, argued over spiritual ideas, and occasionally broke down crying on air.

When they went live, their channel also became a kind of New Age Home Shopping Network. Hope and Aurora showed off the group's ever-growing range of "Gaia's Whole Healing Essentials" products: body butters, soaps, pyramid-shaped crystals. Gaia's "love spray," Gaia's plasma water. In one video, Hope and Aurora promised to ask the angels and guides to select a crystal to put in each customer's product order, and a special letter from Robin Williams—channeled from their master and translated through their pens.

They sold tinctures of colloidal silver, colloidal gold, colloidal palladium. They said people could drink it. They could use an eyedropper and put it in their eyes. These were all concoctions made by the group at their Colorado home. They claimed these colloidals were "one of the most ancient healing products on the planet," but that had been tamped down because of a conspiracy by the pharmaceutical industry to keep people sick.

As COVID-19 spread, the group pivoted. The tinctures were now a miracle cure for the ever-spreading virus. "Colloidal silver is the key to protecting yourself from the corona virus. It is recommended to take colloidal silver at least 3 times a day to keep your immune system functioning to its highest capacity," the group's website read. "Also, if you begin to show symptoms of the virus, up your doses to 5 times a day. In a medical system that is failing, which is being witnessed in China right now, there is no other solution to protecting yourself from the corona virus."

In April 2020, those claims were refuted by the Food and Drug Administration, which sent Miguel Lamboy and Gaia's Whole Healing Essentials a warning letter. "We request that you take immediate action to cease the sale of such unapproved and unauthorized products," it read.

15.

I n the mid-1980s, some of Hollywood's biggest celebrities claimed they found enlightenment from a small blonde woman who lived on a ranch in rural western Washington State. Her name was JZ Knight, but most of her acolytes called her "Ramtha"—the name, Knight professed, of the supposed 35,000-year-old Lemurian warrior spirit that she "channeled" through her body. Linda Evans from the soap opera *Dynasty*, Philip Michael Thomas from *Miami Vice*, and Mike Farrell from *M*A*S*H* all considered themselves Ramtha acolytes at one time. The actress Shirley MacLaine, who penned several books about her New Age spiritual beliefs, wrote in her bestselling book *Dancing in the Light* that her quest for spiritual answers led her directly to Ramtha's ranch.

"I visited accredited mediums who channeled spirit guides from the astral plane," MacLaine wrote. "But one was more profound than any of the others."

MacLaine detailed her first "session" with Ramtha, during which the petite JZ Knight channeled the being and suddenly was filled with so much physical strength, she was able to lift the actress up in her arms. "He took my hands in his and kissed them. He stroked my face. Then he gazed intently into my eyes. I could feel him pouring through JZ's face," MacLaine wrote. "As I looked into the eyes of Ramtha, I heard myself say 'were you my brother in your Atlantean incarnation?'"

"Yes, my beloved," Ramtha, this ancient warrior man, answered through JZ's mouth, tears spilling down her cheeks.

MacLaine looked to Ramtha for advice about her karma, on vitamins she should take and foods to avoid. She asked Ramtha to evaluate the scripts of the movies she was considering. She wrote that Ramtha was really into drinking wine and "several times he got drunk and JZ was left with the residue of a hangover."

During the height of nineteenth-century Spiritualism, mediums like the Fox sisters and Helena Blavatsky provided an outlet for people to communicate with the dead. But the channelers of the twentieth century were different—they actually *became* the dead: bodies occupied temporarily, and sometimes without control. Like JZ Knight with Ramtha, channelers were people who claimed that their bodies had been taken over by benevolent spirits, who then used those bodies like puppets to deliver messages. One second they were human, the next second superhuman: a body chosen by some invisible force. When MacLaine was consulting with Ramtha, she was consulting with the spirit that had taken over Knight's body.

In 1985, Knight exhibited her channeling skills on *The Merv Griffin Show*, closing her eyes, putting herself into some kind of trance, and awaking as Ramtha—speaking to Griffin in a new, deeper voice with a strange foreign accent and a Yoda-like cadence. The television host smirked as he spoke to this new guest.

Around the time of this appearance, Ramtha, too, had been speaking to audiences nationwide, often about "the dawning of a great new age. He predicted that soon a series of earthquakes and droughts would occur. In a Holiday Inn in Tampa, Florida, he encouraged people to "stockpile two years of food, just in case." Mankind would be at odds with nature, but also each other. There would be war and unrest.

Ramtha said the collapse of the World Bank was imminent, that the United States would soon become embroiled by endless wars, and that AIDS was "Earth's way of getting back at gays," according to one reporter. At an event in Phoenix, Arizona, Ramtha had supposedly told a group of gay men they would all be dead in a decade from the disease.

"One should not live in the cities . . . for in the days to come not only are the plagues to run rampant," Ramtha said by May 1986. "There will be murderers on the street who will rob your cupboards and slay you nigh for only a sliver of bread, for they are dangerous places indeed . . . It is imperative, I urge you, to move out of your cities and seek you a place that has high land."

By then, JZ Knight had purchased a fifty-acre ranch surrounded by walls and gates in the small town of Yelm, Washington, not far from Mount Rainier, a looming 14,410-foot volcano. There she ran Ramtha's School of Enlightenment—or just RSE. "In the past year," the *New York Times* reported, "scores of people, many of them middle-aged women, have left their homes around the country and in Canada and moved to the Pacific Northwest to live near a 40-year-old woman, J.Z. Knight." People were concerned she was running a cult.

In one interview, JZ explained that Ramtha teaches people to create their own reality, and "calls us gods. I mean, when was the last time someone paid you that compliment?" Local newspapers ran excerpts from Ramtha speeches, and aired concerns from Yelm residents about increased traffic as mind-controlled "urban dwellers" came there to be near the Lemurian spirit.

"I don't want people moving to live near me," Knight told the *New York Times.* "I'm not a guru. There are no such thing as Ramtha-ites. I'm not somebody's savior. This is a business."

Television cameras traveled to Yelm and JZ sat down for interviews, where she was critical of her critics. "To be other than socially acceptable is to be an outcast," she said. Reporters from *20/20* shot footage of her walking on a gray Northwest day past a garage with a Rolls-Royce, where she leaned over a fence to pet one of her Arabian horses, standing in a wide green pasture. She built a mansion on the property, complete with six fireplaces, nine bathrooms, a sauna, a spa, and a pool.

"People are entitled to say that I'm a fake, I'm a fraud, I'm the devil, I'm the antichrist," she said to *20/20.* "I'm everything but doing something good for somebody. And it's okay if they say that. The thing that I've learned is everyone is entitled to their own truth."

By the 1990s, JZ Knight had stopped giving interviews. People close to her said she was becoming more and more suspicious, scrutinizing anything that was written about her, critical of other channelers. She trademarked Ramtha and took anyone to court who claimed they could voice the words of the ancient Lemurian warrior.

When Ramtha appeared on the scene, the phenomenon of channeling had long existed in the New Age. In the 1920s, a spirit that inhabited Edgar Cayce—a southern channeler known as "the Sleeping Prophet" for the trancelike state he descended into as he channeled—spoke in great detail about life in the so-called lost civilizations of Atlantis and Lemuria and made predictions about the end of the world.

In the 1960s, a tiny-voiced poet from Elmira, New York, named Jane Roberts claimed to be the channel for an entity named "Seth," who began inhabiting her body after she experimented with a Ouija board.

Word of Jane Roberts and Seth spread far and wide, and she held more than a thousand sessions where she gave voice to Seth, who told rooms full of people that God was not a man, or a woman. As she channeled, Roberts's body seemed to physically change, her voice became commanding. She spoke in long, circular sentences in an unrecognizable accent. In the only existing video of this phenomenon, she sits in a chair leaning to one side, a hand grasping the arm of her chair, elbow pushing upward, like an emperor atop a throne. Her posture was large, confident. Seth was deeply critical of organized religion and preached a belief in the self. The spirit would dictate dozens of books through Roberts's hand. Christian leaders cautioned their followers to steer clear of the Seth books, saying that Seth was demonic and Roberts was possessed.

Channeling is one way that New Age leaders "bypass" traditional religious structures to "establish direct, personal contact with the spirit world," the anthropologist Michael F. Brown wrote in his 1997 book *The Channeling Zone: American Spirituality in an Anxious Age.* During a channeling session, a spirit essentially treats the body of the person it inhabits like a puppet it can speak through—an act that is not, according to scholars, a nefarious possession. The spirit is generally welcomed into the body of the channeler or channel.

This is different than spirit possession. In the New Testament, unwanted spirits are seen as the cause of ailments, and Jesus healed by casting those spirits out of people. This translated to spirit possession being viewed as evil by the Catholic Church and other Christian faiths. And yet still in some Pentecostal churches people believe they can be filled with the Holy Spirit, which is seen as a good thing.

By the 1980s, these chosen people delivered messages in voices different from their own from big ballroom stages and at festivals filled with audiences eager for new wisdom. This wisdom was almost never free. The business of channeling proved to be a lucrative one.

Michael Brown observed in the 1980s that the majority of channelers were women conjuring male spirits. This, he wrote, revealed "deep-seated aspects of the American character," and offered "insight into the emotional struggles of middle-class Americans as they try to survive the gender wars of our time." But a woman channeling a man was also a manifestation of generations of breakaway sects in America, like Ann Lee and the Shakers who believed in a radical conception of God that was both masculine and feminine.

"For this kind of middle-aged, middle-class-America white mom type, like JZ Knight," the anthropologist Susannah Crockford said, "it kind of gave them the ability to play other roles. Often these women have very limited roles that they can inhabit in their normal social lives."

In the mid-1940s, the eye of the American media turned toward Roswell, New Mexico, after a "flying disc" was reported to have been found on a cattle ranch. The strange metallic object discovered by a rancher was actually a high-altitude military balloon that had crashed, part of a top-secret government program to listen for Soviet nuclear tests. But people wanted to believe the planet was surrounded by alien ships.

Reports of UFOs were becoming more and more common, streaming into the FBI from the desert of New Mexico to the towns around Mount Rainier. Most, if not all of the reports, were proven to be hoaxes. A Plexiglas disc recovered in Idaho was the work of scheming teenagers. When a pair of men claimed to have discovered a UFO filled with dead aliens near the town of Aztec, New Mexico, *Variety* magazine printed the story without proof. Later it was uncovered that the men were known con artists trying to sell supposed oil-finding devices that were, they claimed, "alien technology."

In the midst of this, just after midnight on March 16, 1946, a farmworker named Helen Printes Hart gave birth to the eighth of her nine children, Judith Darlene Hampton—or just Judy—in a Roswell hospital. Helen believed she could see the future in her dreams, and read books on astrology.

Judy was one of several children Helen had with a man named Charles Hampton but that she would raise as a single mother. Helen often held several jobs to support her children, from working in cotton fields to pouring cups of coffee as a drug store waitress. Hampton was rarely around, and when he was, he was a blur of broken bottles, thrown fists, and screams. Later, Judy would write a book and claim in it that one night as her father beat her mother, one of their young daughters, a toddler, wandered outside and drowned in a creek next to the house.

Judy's summation of her early life is a catalogue of mental, physical, and sexual trauma, an index of the violence inflicted by men upon her,

her sisters, her girlfriends, and her mother. She recalled being raped by her uncle at age four, and once, Hampton tried to prostitute his own daughters. Just as meticulously as Judy detailed these painful memories, she described the demise of the men who wronged her and the women around her. This portrayal leaves an impression of her worldview: that in rage, a woman could find her power.

In Artesia, New Mexico, where her family relocated, Judy often felt pulled by expectations of what it meant to be a woman and emboldened to rebel against those strictures. At home, she ironed her brother's jeans and helped her mother around the house, and in her spare time rode her horse named Slim across the dusty desert. She was a crack shot with a .22, returning home from her rides with an armload of jackrabbit carcasses for her mother to throw in a skillet for dinner.

Judy attended Sunday school at a local church but was confused by the hypocrisies her careful study of the Bible revealed, particularly toward the women in it. In the story of Lot, in the Book of Genesis, the man's house is surrounded by a mob demanding that he produce the two male angels he has allowed to stay in his home, so that the mob might use them for their sexual pleasure.

"My brothers, do not act so wickedly," Lot said, and made them a counteroffer: "Behold, I have two daughters who have not known any man. Let me bring them out to you and do to them as you please."

When Judy questioned this story, she was told to "trust in the Word of God." To believe and have faith.

One Sunday morning, as a teenage Judy sat among her family in the pews, her older half brother and her sister-in-law walked in late, taking seats in the back of the church. The priest took notice.

"Could we please stop for a moment?" he said. The man asked Judy's sister-in-law to come forward "to the altar of forgiveness."

Every eye turned to watch as the woman walked between the pews, cheeks wet with tears. She wore lipstick—forbidden in church—and wiped it away with the back of her hand. At the altar, she knelt before the man. "Dearest child of God, it is a sin to paint your face for the evil of Satan. It is a sin to tempt the flesh. You must pray for forgiveness," the priest said, hovering over her as she sobbed.

As she watched this unfold, Judy felt her anger rising. "I looked at that poor woman on her knees, bawling and pleading for forgiveness," she wrote. "For what?"

All around her she saw hypocrites: people who accepted the Bible's contradictions. People who could see Satan in a woman wearing lipstick.

Judy stood up and shouted that God wouldn't judge someone like this. "I no longer belong here," she declared. "It is finished."

She strode out the doors of the church, and never came back.

During her senior year at Artesia High School, Judy was voted prom queen and the most beautiful girl in her class. In a photo taken for the yearbook she wore a short black dress, white-blonde hair spun into a beehive, and sat in front of a grimacing young man in a white jacket and black tie, voted the most handsome. Judy looked at the camera but didn't smile, instead cocking her head slightly to the side, wide-eyed. A look of puzzlement and obligation.

Judy would write that in high school she looked "like a calendar girl," but that the constant comments about her appearance at such a young age left her with a feeling of guilt and sadness. "I possessed a magical combination of sexy-babe, virginal tomboy looks that created quite a stir," she wrote. "To escape my pain, I spent much of my free time riding my horse. Wild and free, and alone."

Her high school experience read like a mix of the plots of *American Graffiti* and *Close Encounters of the Third Kind*: she cruised with her friends, went to dances and drive-in movies. But her teenage years also had a mystical side: in one photo from her yearbook, Judy is pictured in all-white clothing leading a cast of dancers wearing black in a "Spirit of the Light" dance that she created. Later, Judy would deem this dance "prophetic." She shared her dreams with her mother, Helen, who told her they were visions from past lifetimes, or glimpses of her future.

Once, Judy was up late listening to Bobby Darin records at a slumber party with other members of the drill team when, all of a sudden, the bedroom lit up with "an eerie red glow."

The girls ran to the window to get a look. Down the suburban street lined with houses was "a huge orange ball" hovering in the air. "It didn't make a sound; it just hung there, suspended," Judy wrote. She described it like a glowing planet covered in craters. As the girls gawked at the bizarre sight, the object emitted a series of bright flashes, sending the girls screeching for cover under stuffed animals and pillows. Judy sat still and prayed: "Oh Father, don't leave us behind, we are only children."

"The thought came to me that the world had ended," she wrote. The sight of the glowing orb reminded her of the things that she had read about in the Book of Revelation, when God unleashes fury upon the planet, and chooses only the holiest to be spared.

But then...it was over. The flashes stopped. The glowing orb was gone. The girls spoke nothing of what they saw and went to bed. Later, Judy wrote it was "a blank spot in my memory."

It would take her years to remember that it happened at all, and even then, Judy wrote that the other girls at the slumber party had no recollection of it, or simply wanted to forget.

"Something *did* happen to us that night, and something or someone made us forget it. Maybe we made our own selves forget it," she wrote. "But a part of my mind, the deep subconscious part, had held on to the experience."

Toward the end of her senior year, Judy described a feeling like her life was narrowing, and she was being forced onto a path of marriage, children, and being a content servant to a husband. Judy made an attempt to go to college in Texas but returned back to Artesia, where she reluctantly married a gas station attendant and gave birth to her first two sons in quick succession. She later wrote that her husband was controlling, unfaithful, and abusive, and her life settled into a monotony of caring for young children and ensuring there was a hot meal on the table when her husband got home from work. There were no more .22 shots echoing across the desert, no galloping horses, no strange hovering orbs.

On Christmas Eve 1970, after discovering that her husband was having an affair, Judy prayed:

"Heavenly Father, I want to make a bargain with You. I want You to make me a smart and successful woman. I don't want to be a secretary, or a cashier at Safeway. I want to be somebody *important*," she said. "I want to set an example for my little boys that a woman, their mother, can be somebody important."

She packed up her children and threw her belongings in the car. She left her husband and everything she ever knew. She left to become somebody.

The way Judy wrote about spirituality in her memoir is personal and flexible—a practice of trusting in one's own intuition. She viewed spirituality as a way of convening with the mystical, unexplained, and fantastical. Continually, she pointed out the hypocrisies of mainstream Christian churches, and the ways women have been treated as disposable by those institutions. When she wrote about her supposed psychic abilities, the words read like musings of a religiously minded second-wave feminist who dabbled in the metaphysical—which wasn't odd for someone of her era.

Her personal origin story as written in her book laid the framework for a spiritual origin story, which would later be scrutinized by people trying to figure out if she really was someone special. Judy grew up poor and female in an area of the country that, at the time, had an affinity for the fantastical; the point, it seemed, was to imply that the person she would become was fated. But to fulfill her desire to be someone, she had to leave everything she knew behind. She left the church, she left her husband, she left her home. When Judy left her life to become somebody, she was rejecting all the masculine structures that had been set to trap her. And as soon as she did that, life opened to her: she went on to lead a cable company's marketing operations in Southern California, then West Texas. In one strange scene, Judy recollects how her boss at the cable company thought she needed a different name—that "Judy" wasn't quite right for the take-charge woman he knew.

"The way you dress, the way you look," he said, "Judy doesn't fit..."

"Do you think I need a name that would look good in lights?" she asked. "You know, like they do for the stars?"

She threw out an idea: she'd once been called Zebra because of her habit of wearing black and white clothes. And that settled it: she was renamed. Judy Zebra—or preferably JZ, no periods.

"JZ it is," her boss said. "You're a powerful lady; you deserve a powerful name."

Everything before was prologue.

If her words are to be trusted, since then JZ has had men constantly throwing themselves at her, trying to control her. A Hollywood agent wined and dined her, believing she could be the next big Tinseltown star. She married several more times after her first marriage, but all ended in divorce.

Wherever she went, whatever she did, it was as if a spotlight was always tracking her, combing the face of the Earth until it illuminated her unique shape, bathing her in attention and light even when she resisted it.

This was the case one day while living in Southern California, when JZ reluctantly accompanied a friend to a reading with a local fortune-teller. At the appointment, the fortune-teller—an "old but graceful Indian woman"—emerged from behind a beaded curtain and homed in on JZ. JZ wasn't the one with the appointment, but the fortune-teller ignored that, eyes bearing down on her. "I have been waiting for you," she said.

The fortune-teller predicted that JZ would be offered two life paths, and she told her to take the one that leads to "a place with great mountains, tall pines, and lakes that shine like mirrors unto the heavens."

"If you go to the mountains and pines, you will meet The One," she told her. "If you meet The One, you will have great influence...great destiny."

JZ laughed it away. But then, weeks later, she was offered a job near Tacoma, Washington, a city south of Seattle surrounded by lush pine forests in the shadow of Mount Rainier. She thought of what the fortune-teller had told her, and she took the job.

After living and working in Tacoma for several years, JZ was hospitalized with a condition—one she never names specifically—that required her to undergo chemotherapy. This resulted in a loss of most of her long blonde hair. While JZ sparingly described her illness, she took care to describe the excruciating loss she felt when her hair fell out in chunks in the hospital shower. She shrieked and was paralyzed by the sight of her long locks swirling in the drain, wet clumps stuck to her naked body. Nurses sedated her, and afterward, lying in her hospital bed, she sank into a deep depression.

One day, a friend encouraged the ailing JZ to come to a local tent revival service. She flatly refused—"I was raised with that fire and brimstone stuff. It's crap!" But her friend begged, and JZ, defenses down, caved.

At the service, the preacher performed a ceremony for the sick, laying hands on those who needed extra blessings. JZ's friends escorted her to the front of the crowd. When the preacher put his hands on her head, a "sudden flash of blue light" came down through the ceiling like lightning, coursing through JZ's bones, knocking the preacher backward. All around her the congregation began moaning and screaming, terrified and confused by what they had witnessed.

But JZ remained where she kneeled, looking around "questioningly."

"Who are you?" the terrified preacher asked her.

"One of God's own," JZ answered matter-of-factly.

With that, she was cured.

It was the second burst of bright light that marked the timeline of her life. First the strange glowing red orb that no one else remembered but her, then this burst of blue light that inexplicably healed her. There would be one more light: a flash that would one day illuminate her kitchen and complete her cycle of transformation into a warrior, a God, a man.

Like the obsession with conspiracy theories, the Egyptomania that compelled the country in the 1830s was never far from America's collective mind. In 1963, the starlet Elizabeth Taylor donned dramatic winged eyeliner for her portrayal of Cleopatra in a lusty silver screen film, sparking renewed interest in the ancient civilization. By 1977, more than 835,000 people had attended an exhibition of artifacts found in the tomb of King Tutankhamun at the National Gallery in Washington, D.C. Hundreds of thousands more would view the exhibit in Chicago, New York, and Los Angeles.

By then, a belief in "pyramid power," or pyramidology, was all the rage in New Age circles, and writers promoted notions that anything placed underneath a pyramid shape would be magically revitalized. Food under a pyramid would be preserved, dull blades would emerge sharpened. In Salt Lake City, a group called Summum erected a massive pyramid as a temple; later, the group's founder was mummified and interred inside it.

In 1977, JZ had remarried again and stopped working, choosing to become a housewife in a handsome Tacoma suburb with her sons and then husband. One day, she came home to find the house filled with pyramids crafted out of construction paper by her husband. There were pyramids in the pantry, on top of the refrigerator, even one over the family dog's dish. The couple had recently talked about pyramidology over dinner with friends, and it seemed that her husband might have been more curious about it than she realized. JZ was initially outraged at the mess, but soon joined in on the pyramid-making. The pair lost themselves, compelled by a question of "what if?" What if the pyramids *did* work? It would be like winning the metaphysical lottery.

They made pyramids out of paper all day and all night, and delirious, JZ grabbed one of the paper structures and called out to her husband. "Attention, attention please, you are now about to witness a miracle," she said, laughing, placing the shape over her head. "In moments, gentlemen, you will witness a truly magnificent transformation."

When she lifted the pyramid, a "glimmer of bright light" shone at the other side of the kitchen. "To my utter shock and amazement, there stood a giant man," she wrote, "just standing there, aglow."

The massive man looked "like golden glitter dropped through a ray of sunlight," she said. "His shoulders came to the top of the door, and it was as if the ceiling had disappeared to make room for his head. His robe seemed to be of purple light, a dazzling display of color and crystal against this strangeness of immense human form."

A being had dropped into her home from the heavens that was both angel and Hollywood actor. She was in awe. Her husband could not see him, but he believed JZ when she said he was really there.

"You are so beautiful," JZ said. "Who are you?"

"I am Ramtha," he replied, "the Enlightened One."

In this moment she was introduced to the man who would control her like no other had. Pyramid power had brought her an ancient warrior.

Ramtha explained to a mystified JZ that he was an ancient Lemurian warrior who had come to deliver a message: he was a God, and *she* was a God too. Everyone was a God. "When mankind realizes that truth," the giant man told her, "war will cease." He said that in a past life, JZ had been his daughter and her husband had been in the Lemurian army. Ramtha's appearance was, in a sense, a reunion.

This meeting of the ancient warrior with the modern housewife played out like a slapsticky *Perfect Strangers* montage scene: for days on end, Ramtha reveled at the strangeness of modern life. He flopped onto the king-sized bed. He told her she could call him "The Ram." He flicked on the burners of the gas stove on and peered wide-eyed into the grinding garbage disposal as JZ scrubbed the floor on her hands and knees around his ancient feet.

JZ described these first days with Ramtha like he was just as annoying as every other man who'd made unwanted advances or taken something from her in the past. His arrival into her life seemed to stem from some ancient sense of entitlement.

As she cleaned and he followed at her heels, JZ quizzed him. If he was so old, why was he not a caveman? Scientists were essentially wrong about evolution, Ramtha said. She came to understand that Ramtha was not physically present; he was more like a mirage of a spirit, which he explained was because he was functioning at a higher vibration than humanity.

The longer Ramtha hung around, the more confused she felt by his presence. JZ began reaching out to churches in the phone book, explaining that an ancient warrior had teleported into her life to tell humanity about love. They all hung up on her.

One morning, JZ and her husband dropped into a local Spiritualist church, where a female pastor listened carefully to her story. The woman spoke of psychics and people who could communicate with spirits in other realms, and consoled her: JZ, she said, was simply a medium for a spirit called Ramtha.

"You aren't crazy," she said, "just gifted."

As the female pastor spoke, JZ began to transform (a process that she wrote in her memoir was only described to her, but that she could not personally recall). Her body sat up straight. Her arms flew upward, toward the ceiling. Her face stiffened, and her neck thickened, "becoming muscled and masculine." She grew taller.

"Ramtha, it's you, isn't it?" her husband asked his wife's body.

"Indeed," the warrior answered in a low voice through her mouth.

Afterward, she dove headlong into the world of channeling. She read about Helena Blavatsky and Edgar Cayce, and soon she was holding meetings of her own, summoning Ramtha into her body for small, female-centric groups who wanted his answers about human existence. But, soon enough, the constant manipulation of her body became exhausting. She felt used by Ramtha, and by the people who only wanted to see the ancient man exploiting her to spread his message. She was overwhelmed by the way people stared, eyes like prying fingers all over her.

After channeling sessions, when JZ's identity would finally come untethered from Ramtha's, she would snap back to consciousness in strange suburban living rooms, surrounded by crying people reaching out to hug her, to kiss her, to kneel at her feet. It left her feeling guilty and like an imposter. Ramtha was the Trojan horse for the thing she wanted the most. Now, finally, she was becoming someone, but it meant complete and total submission to something beyond her control.

One afternoon after a particularly draining channeling session, Ramtha appeared before JZ and commanded her to start charging money for his wisdom. "You are to ask for a tally of gold when, indeed, they come to learn," he said. It turned out the ancient Lemurian was also a capitalist; Ramtha instructed her that money was God too. God was in everything, everyone, and the least she could do would be to allow herself to live in luxury as an exchange for her body being the vessel for his messages. "I make a very good income from Ramtha," she would tell a newspaper in Olympia, Washington, "which I should, for all the work I put in it."

She became Ramtha on ballroom stages, in luxury hotels, at conferences. Her events felt like concerts. "There is a feeling of happy, excited anticipation in the air," reported the *Philadelphia Inquirer* at a two-day affair in New York City in 1983, where 250 people had come from around the country to witness JZ's transformation. Before she walked out onstage, a woman made a pitch for "a Ramtha-approved brand of 'anti-aging' pills" called Gerovital. It was a dental anesthetic that grew in popularity among Hollywood starlets in the 1950s, but was banned in 1982 "for anti-aging and associated claims" by the Food and Drug Administration—which still remains in effect.

Then the show began. From behind a velvet curtain, out walked "a youngish woman of medium height with pale blond hair and dark roots," the *Inquirer* wrote. Ramtha peppered his lectures with sentences that began with "I AM."

The crowd raised their hands with questions, pouring their hopes and fears onto Ramtha. One man worried aloud about an alien invasion; Ramtha waved it away. One reporter quoted him saying, "They could have killed us long ago if they wanted to; besides there have always been alien beings living in the center of the earth," he said, speaking in a strange European accent, much like Jane Roberts had when channeling Seth. An oilman from Waco asked Ramtha where to drill on his property. The warrior advised northeast. Ramtha advised a woman to take "that which is called Gerovital four times a day." The ancient warrior strode out into the crowd, embracing audience members. One man cried in his arms.

In June 1986, some 400 people flooded into a Holiday Inn meeting room for an "Intensive" that cost $400 per person, according to the *Tampa Tribune*. "Several of those attending the Tampa Intensive said that anyone who really wants to see Ramtha will 'manifest' the money to get there," the reporter wrote. People watched as a "masculine force" entered Knight's body, wrote the *Tribune*. "The fists clench, the face fills out and there are jowls where moments before was seen a delicate jaw line."

Ramtha's reach grew with the release of cassette tapes and videos. It's hard not to wonder if Ramtha would have made such a splash had he inhabited the body of anyone other than a former prom queen. In early mentions of Ramtha, reporters wrote with shock that people believed the spirit of a warrior could come from someone so delicate, so blonde. She "looks like a woman you might see on a jogging trail," wrote one reporter in 1986. "No red polish on the nails." She is slender. She is Bo Derek. She is a housewife. "To know her visual impact in the video tapes, you must imagine this physical woman. Then imagine a powerful, almost pulsating male inside her body."

JZ would eventually summon Ramtha on stages around the world, giving lectures in Mexico, Germany, Japan, Australia. When Ramtha spoke, crowds listened with fascination. It was as if JZ was the cup and Ramtha was the wine flowing over her brim, the thing that made the beautiful woman more intoxicating. Onstage, she was not Judy or JZ anymore. Not her. She was "him," the immortal warrior. Their names became interchangeable. Synonyms. When people said Ramtha, they meant JZ Knight, but to call JZ Knight "Ramtha" was also not wrong. There is no him without her, no her without him.

What a fascinating thing, and yet what a horrifying thing: for the world to only see you as the most famous role you ever played. Maybe Daniel Radcliffe, with his decade as Harry Potter, would understand how it feels to be Ramtha. Once you become someone great, you can never be you again.

As the 1990s closed in, JZ trademarked Ramtha. Other channelers emerged with seemingly similar routines. Near Ashland, Oregon, a woman named Penny Torres Rubin claimed to channel a 32,000-year-old "enlightened being" and member of the Brotherhood of the Light called "Mafu," and started the Foundation for Meditative Studies.

"For the serious seek-ah, Pranayama is a doorway into techniques," Mafu said, rolling every *r* just like Ramtha might. "Pranayama is doorway to a world beyond the *stahhhs.*"

"Look to thyself entities for what you truly are, which is the God I AM," she said.

JZ became more closed in even as she opened the gates of her ranch to new followers and a team of religious scholars curious to assess the veracity of her channeling claims. One scholar who visited Ramtha's School of Enlightenment believed JZ was like a hybrid of Christian Science's Mary Baker Eddy, Helena Blavatsky, and the founder of New

Thought, all rolled into one. One scientist concluded her channeling of Ramtha wasn't an act. Relieved, JZ admitted her time channeling Ramtha had been a "lonely and private journey."

There was a secrecy around RSE, and little information escaped beyond the walls of her ranch. Whispers about what really went on in there abounded. In 1992, JZ found herself trying to explain Ramtha in a court of law when she became embroiled in a contentious lawsuit stemming from her divorce from her fifth husband, Jeffrey Knight. According to one reporter, Knight claimed that JZ had used "her spiritual power over him to force him to accept an unfair divorce settlement." Knight, who had contracted HIV, testified that Ramtha urged him to avoid undergoing immediate medical treatment upon being diagnosed, and "told me that he would teach me how to heal myself, and that I should not worry about it, and that I could not die from the plague."

In an interview with a cult researcher at the time, Jeffrey Knight spoke fearfully of his ex-wife and her followers. "To me, it's not about the money, it's about standing up for myself—taking back my power and standing up to her and to this farce of a teaching that is just a money-making business for her," he said. "If I was to die tomorrow, I would know that I had done something to make some people wake up and realize that they are involved in a very dangerous, very evil, corrupt thing."

Her ex-husband's words provided the most personal look behind the curtain of RSE. It also revealed the mindset of her followers, and how difficult it could be for them to leave. By the time of his interview, Knight had left RSE, but he seemed to have a hard time shaking Ramtha, who had become integral to solving his problems. When the pair initially separated, he found himself unable to access his spiritual advisor.

"I told her when we both made the agreement to separate, that I have a lot of confusion and a lot of unanswered questions, and I really would like to have some time with the Ram by myself, and all of a sudden he was not available to me any longer," Knight said. "Usually anytime I needed to talk to him he would be there for me . . . A lot of different thoughts went through my mind, and ultimately, to where I felt like I was wrong and he was mad at me and that's why he's not talking to me."

Knight was lost without Ramtha.

In court, JZ struggled to explain her personal Lemurian to the judge. "The real target of this prolonged legal inquiry is Ramtha, the spirit from the Cro-Magnon era who Ms. Knight says has been speaking through her for the last 15 years," Timothy Egan of the *New York Times* reported from the courtroom. The marital dispute had put "the New Age movement itself on trial." When the judge asked JZ to summon Ramtha on the witness stand, she refused. The judge was "perplexed about whether Ramtha is a god, a spirit or a fake," Egan wrote. The court sided with Jeffrey Knight, awarding him a nearly $800,000 settlement. He died in 1994.

At the ranch, Ramtha was lecturing about a "New World Order" that would turn people into slaves and that could manipulate the weather. She was telling her followers to stock up on food. "You should begin tonight after this session," she said in April 1993. She told them to plant gardens. Store up water. Invest in gold. She encouraged people to build underground shelters, much like Elizabeth Clare Prophet was telling Church Universal and Triumphant followers around the same time in Montana.

These were all common talking points of far-right militias and members of the antigovernment Patriot movement, but perhaps none more so than belief in a nefarious New World Order. It had become shorthand among these far-right groups for "the idea that the nation is on the verge of relinquishing its sovereignty to a shadowy cabal of 'globalistic' and 'communistic' forces," wrote Daniel Levitas in his book *The Terrorist Next Door* about the radical right. It was a reason for those groups to "arm themselves to prevent a tyrannical government from usurping their rights."

By then, more than a thousand people had moved to the misty

towns of Yelm and Olympia to be closer to RSE. Only Ramtha and a few select people lived on the property, but followers flooded the surrounding communities, where they became known as "Ram-sters."

People brought their children with them to Yelm, many of whom attended an RSE-associated school that integrated the teachings of Ramtha into their education. David Irwin-Detrick was six years old when his mother moved him from California to Washington.

He remembered being terrified of what would happen on May 5, 1995. "Ramtha told all of the people," he remembered, "times are gonna get hard. The winds are gonna get faster. The world is gonna heat up."

Children were not shielded from Ramtha's doomsday predictions. "I was living in this community of all of this hysteria," he said. "You say these things to a twelve-year-old and what does a twelve-year-old do? Gets fucking scared."

"Then May 5, 1995, everyone huddled in their undergrounds and nothing happened," he said. He was confused. Around him word spread that "that was just practice." Ramtha's followers shifted their focus on the coming millennium instead.

As the year 2000 closed in, people around the world grew increasingly fearful of what would occur when the clock struck midnight on January 1, 2000, and whether computer systems would glitch, causing destabilizing systemic failures across society. Conspiracy theorists and fire-and-brimstone preachers who already peddled in doomsday scenarios latched on to fears over "Y2K," claiming to have the answers, and products, that would help them after most everything had ended.

16.

In Mississippi, Ben, a married Coast Guard veteran with two children, had been telling his sister, Amanda Ray, about a new group called Love Has Won that he'd been following online for a couple of months. The siblings weren't raised religious, so it was all new to her—the language, the beliefs. "We would have these really deep spiritual conversations," she said.

Ben told Amanda that Love Has Won believed a New Age was coming, and that when it arrived, they would ascend into a better place, to "this 5D earth, where there was gonna be no hate, no crime, it was just going to be all about love," she said. It was weird, but seemed harmless, and Amanda, a registered nurse and mother, didn't give it much thought.

But one day her sister-in-law, Ariane, called and said Ben was spending hours online watching the group's livestreams. He was sharing their links all over social media and had booked an "etheric surgery" with the group over the phone.

Amanda called Ben and convinced him to cancel his session. He did, but after a few weeks passed he booked another. "Once he had their spiritual surgery, he was completely committed," Amanda recalled.

Like many things in the New Age milieu, etheric, or psychic, surgeries require belief. In *Harper's Encyclopedia of Mystical and Paranormal Experience*, author Rosemary Ellen Guiley described it as a practice in which a "surgeon" uses "paranormal powers or is guided by spirit helpers." Psychic surgery involves no scalpels or other medical tools, but only a set of hands. A practitioner might put their hands onto the body of a client, then imagine operating on the body with their mind, removing whatever ails.

Etheric surgeries are different in that the imagined surgery is not being performed on a person's physical body, but their "etheric," or spirit, body. In this case, no contact is required. "While some observed surgeries remain unexplained," wrote Guiley, "many have been exposed as fraud, accomplished by sleight-of-hand tricks known to most stage magicians."

Love Has Won performed their etheric surgeries and "healing sessions" over the phone. They were one of many services the group charged money for. Lauryn Suarez's friends from Florida booked a surgery with her, having no other way to contact her, but it largely consisted of "Lauryn smoking cigarettes and talking about the ascension and Donald Trump," Dan Agos said.

In March 2020, when the news of COVID was dominating everything, Ben was alone; Ariane and their kids were out of town. His TV screen was full of panic, with videos of people clearing out grocery shelves flashing on the screen. Schools were canceled. Everything was shutting down. It seemed like what Love Has Won had been talking about all along. This was the ascension. It was really happening.

He called his sister, Amanda, from somewhere in Colorado, a couple of hours from the Denver airport. He said he was going to be with Love Has Won to serve a mission. "And I'm like, 'Okay, how long are you gonna be there? And what are you gonna actually be doing that you can't just do from here?'" Ben said he didn't know.

When he arrived at the cabin, he was clean-cut, wearing a green polo shirt and jeans, and sat tall on the livestream.

"Just got here last night. Fitting right in," Jason Castillo said.

"Yeah, hi," Ben said, introducing himself. "Eternally grateful to have found Mother."

He went on. "I know a lot of people have a lot of doubt about what's really happening out there, about what's really going on. And I'm here to say: I've dropped everything in order to be here to honor Mother," he said. "It's real. You need to feel it... Know that everything we say is the truth, and only the truth, of the highest vibrations. And we love you all, and we need you all to get here. Come to Mom, and help Mom, in all ways possible." The group cheered.

"Very well said," Jason said. "Goose bumps and tears."

But Ben would be with the group for less than two days before he was handed a drink and told to "go fight three days of darkness" in the surrounding wilderness. Later, Amanda claimed her brother was drugged.

At some point the day he disappeared, Ben called his mother to say he was walking to the airport. The family knew the airport was some three hours away, but they didn't know exactly what part of Colorado he was in. Through the phone, his mother could hear a sound like he was walking on rocks. But after that, calls went to voicemail. His family called over and over, but Ben never answered.

Online, Amanda started researching Love Has Won. She logged on to watch the livestream, wondered if she'd catch a glimpse of her brother. The family sent emails and messages to Miguel Lamboy; the group had declared nonprofit tax-exempt status, and he was listed as the group's principal officer on their application with the Internal Revenue Service. But he said he didn't know where Ben was.

Amanda created a missing persons flyer and posted it on Facebook, asking people in Colorado to share it far and wide. "I'm getting these Facebook messages, 'Hey I saw your brother sitting on the side of the road staring at the sun,'" she recalled. "It's scary because to these local people, 'Hey, look at this guy over here, this drug addict.' People are going to naturally place their judgment."

The Love Has Won website listed an address in Crestone, and Ben's family members started calling every police agency and medical facility they could find near the town. Finally, they got a lead: the police in Salida acknowledged that they'd picked up Ben after he was found naked on someone's property, and brought him to a nearby hospital—he was severely dehydrated. Refusing treatment, he signed himself out. "It was very clear to law enforcement and the hospital that saw him," Amanda said, "that he was likely under the influence of a hallucinogen."

On Facebook, a man messaged Amanda saying he had a dog that could track people. She figured why not. "I hope you're somebody that I can trust," she wrote back, and told him to start looking. The dog found Ben walking down a main road near Salida.

"This stranger stayed with my brother for six hours," she said.

The family effort to rescue him was massive—Ariane sped back to Mississippi to file a missing persons report there, Amanda and Ben's brother flew across the country to Colorado, and cars screeched south from Denver, as they all had to trust that a stranger and his dog would keep Ben safe until they got there. Amanda's brother drove Ben back home to Mississippi; they were all thankful that sometime that day he'd lost his cell phone and couldn't communicate with Love Has Won. "He thought he ascended into 5D," Amanda said. "After about a week, he was sitting on the front porch and saw bugs. And he was like, 'Why are there bugs? There aren't supposed to be bugs in 5D.'" Those bugs were the beginning of his deprogramming.

Weeks later, after they were sure Ben was safe, Ariane and Amanda dove deeper into what Love Has Won was all about. If they had let Ben wander off into the desert, who was to say they hadn't done it to other people? Amanda pulled up the group's decade-long archive of videos. What started as a group that had been devoted to peace, love, and maybe UFOs seemed to have changed over time. Become more aggressive. This group seemed to have very little to do with spiritual-ity, and more about spreading conspiratorial propaganda and getting money. Impressionable people who came to them seeking honest spiri-tual answers were mocked and cast away like pieces of trash.

"My sister-in-law said, 'I want something positive to come out of this experience,'" Amanda recalled. "'Like, we didn't just go through all of this for nothing.'"

Together, they started a website called Rising Above Love Has Won. Ben had only been physically with the group for two days, and his deprogramming afterward was extensive. It was six months before he could work again. By then, Amanda and Ariane knew there were other people like him, and they wanted to extend a hand, provide more information.

As word spread, more and more people reached out to Amanda from around the world, desperate to reach their family members who'd gone on mission in Colorado.

"They'd all had a vulnerable time in their life. For my brother it was COVID. It was like this fear of the unknown, 'What is happening, my family is out of town,'" she said. "When he went on mission, he really thought he was doing it to save his family. Like he did it from a place of love."

"From the outside looking in, you think these people are good peo-ple," Ashley McCoy, who arrived around the same day as Ben, said.

Local sheriff's deputies had by then been going to the property more and more to perform wellness checks after worried families called, frantic about their loved ones. Back in Florida, Ashley's family members had become increasingly concerned when she was gone for two months with little contact. One day, Ashley had appeared on the livestream, and mentioned the location of the cabin. An aunt had been watching, and when she heard where it was, the family sprung into action and called the police to check on her. Ashley will never forget when the officers arrived.

"The cops came over, and I don't know what it was, but that's all it took for me to find the strength to be like, 'I gotta get out. I gotta figure out a way out of here.'"

Even though Love Has Won had left her brother for dead, Amanda felt sympathy for Amy Carlson. "Amy was clearly declining," Amanda said. When she saw pictures of the woman on the livestream, her body looked emaciated. Amy was wasting away.

Amanda started reaching out to media and got the ear of a producer at *The Dr. Phil Show*. "We had gone to law enforcement, and filed through the FBI for charity fraud, and nothing was done. So we decided, okay, we're going to rely on media to bring awareness to these dangerous cults," she said. "So, we all ended up on *The Dr. Phil Show*."

17.

It was 2001, and Aaron was in sixth grade when he and his mother, Carla, moved to Washington to live closer to Ramtha's School of Enlightenment. A divorcee and mother of three, she didn't indulge Y2K worst-case scenarios, but after moving closer to the ranch, she started stockpiling food and water, just in case. Her income only afforded her so much prepping. She bought what she could. Carla's friends had introduced her to a set of Ramtha cassette tapes, and she liked what she heard.

"The concepts are more like universal truths if you're interested at all in any kind of Eastern religion," Carla said. "It's not really any different than a lot of that...I've always kind of been somebody who was interested in that kind of stuff."

She and her friends from Portland began taking trips to Yelm for a beginner weekend workshop and other events at the ranch. "You're learning a lot about this idea that you create your own reality," she said.

After a couple of years of making trips to RSE for classes and events, Carla became romantically involved with a member of JZ Knight's "Red Guard," her inner circle who act as bodyguards. When she and Aaron relocated to the area, they moved in with him. Living near the ranch made it easier to keep her membership current too; students had to continually take workshops, progressively moving up into higher levels of study, to stay current. If a membership lapsed, which meant they hadn't taken any new courses in a year, students often had to revert back to the beginner workshops and start all over again.

At RSE, Carla and Aaron went through "field work" exercises, where everyone wrote down on an index card something they wanted to see happen in their lives, or drew an image. Then they were blindfolded and walked in a large grassy field on the RSE property, ringed by a fence. Their cards were placed in Ziploc bags and clipped along the fence line.

"For hours you're walking blindfolded in this football-sized field with probably 300 other people, and you're keeping one single focus," Carla explained, "which is what's on that card. It draws you to it."

The idea is that those with the most focus will find their card. "I never found my card," she said. But Aaron did. "If you focus hard enough on the image that you drew on your card, you will manifest destiny, and hitting your card is the indicator that you've done that," Aaron said. Once, he wrote that he wanted to win the lottery, and found his card during the exercise, but "that never happened."

"Manifest destiny" was the actual term RSE used for this idea, but it is more commonly known as a nineteenth-century ideology held by early American settlers who believed God wanted them to expand America, removing and exterminating Indigenous people from their ancestral land in the process.

Kristin was also twelve years old when she started attending workshops at RSE with her parents. Her mom listened to Ramtha's tapes in the family car as she took Kristin to school: "I remember at one point being like, 'Who is this woman we are listening to?'"

Kristin's family of six frequently made the two-and-a-half-hour drive from Portland to the ranch. She remembered during one exercise on their first visit, participants sat back-to-back. Everyone stayed silent.

One participant pictured an image in their head; the other attempted to draw that image.

On one of her first trips Kristin was also introduced to an exercise called the "blue body dance." People would use a blue marker—purchased at the ranch bookstore, though it is difficult to understand its exact specialty or significance—to draw spiderweb-like shapes on parts of their body where they felt pain. Music was blasted into the room through large speakers, then everyone stood up, put on blindfolds, and danced—sometimes for three straight hours—as they tried to heal themselves by elevating their consciousness to a different frequency. The idea was "you have to break past your body in order to get to these higher levels," Kristin recalled. "You'd have to push past it."

Blindfolds were a theme at RSE. Students would do archery blindfolded, wander across the grass doing "field work" blindfolded. During an exercise called "The Tank," blindfolded participants felt their way through an indoor maze filled with obstacles. They were told that by envisioning the path, students would work their way through the labyrinth.

Mornings at RSE often began with "Consciousness & Energy" exercises (called C&E for short), where students wore blindfolds and sat on pillows cross-legged in a dark room. Staff would crank music as loud as it could go. It was Enya meets Trans-Siberian Orchestra, New Agey, with "huge drums," Aaron said.

"The lights are off, everyone's blindfolded, and then they would scream '*breathe!*' And you would force air out as quickly as you can. It makes this hissing noise," he said. "Someone would scream '*breathe!*' And you'd do it again. And what happens is you get extremely light-headed through the process."

"What I believe is that was kind of a ploy to make people feel like their body is vibrating," Aaron alleged, "they're reaching a higher frequency, a higher state."

Perhaps no other ritual was more integral to the RSE experience than the "wine ceremonies." At these occasions, hundreds of people would cram into a converted horse arena, where carpet had been laid, taking their place sitting in designated spots sectioned off with tape on the floor. For a while, the ceremonies were first come, first served. Eventually RSE started charging for spots; it cost more to sit close to the stage.

Not every trip to the ranch was guaranteed to conclude with a wine ceremony. Sometimes they were spur-of-the-moment events, and RSE would spread the word that there would be a wine ceremony that same evening. "We're two and a half hours away," Kristin said. "The moment you would hear about it, the network would go crazy. You would literally stop what you're doing and jump in the car."

Everyone knew to bring bread and multiple bottles of wine, which had to be red, and pillows to sit on (also sold at the ranch store). As everyone filed in, music blared. The aroma of past ceremonies hung heavy in the room: a persistent reek of spilled wine and stale cigarette smoke.

The crowd waited, and waited, and waited. It was like a festival. An uninhibited party. The longer the wait, the more the excitement built, higher and higher. "When is he coming down?" people would buzz throughout the crowd. And then, finally, the reason they all were there would arrive. From the chateau-like mansion, Ramtha—already inhabiting JZ Knight's body—strode across the property toward the arena. People screamed. Some would run up to and try to get close, hands outstretched for one touch from the ancient warrior, but the Red Guard would slap their arms away. This was a celebrity. A God.

Once Ramtha was on the stage, the crowd would scream and wail, and Ramtha would bask in the noise and glory he had stirred. The earpiece-wearing Red Guard surrounded the stage—a protective barrier in case people made a run for him. For most students, these occasions were the only time they would see their leader in person. From the stage, Ramtha boomed teachings. He swore. He was crass.

"I just remember my first one, looking at him being like, 'What the fuck is this?'" Carla said. "Like, trying to figure out, 'Is this all an act?'"

Ramtha looked like a woman, but commanded attention like a man—the way he sat in the chair, leaning to one side, like some powerful emperor. That strange accent. "You're just like, is this for real? What am I seeing? What is going on here?"

"If I really think about it," Carla said, "I probably would've walked away if it hadn't been that all my friends were into it. And they were *in*."

It was easy to be swept up in the party-like atmosphere. Wine grapes, Ramtha instructed, were a gift from extraterrestrials, and when the wine started to flow, it did not stop for hours.

The ceremonies stretched late into the night as Ramtha lectured and raged. Teachings about self-empowerment would blend into comments on American culture, the government, and wildly conspiratorial politics. The lectures often took on a misogynistic tone as Ramtha railed about female vanity. Sometimes the ancient warrior would single out one person in the crowd and dress them down. Kristin alleged that Ramtha confronted a female member of the Red Guard during a ceremony. "He was like, 'How many abortions have you had?'" The woman stammered, and Ramtha told the crowd the number. "He was like, 'You're not using that appropriately. You need to figure your shit out.' And it was like, 'Dude, you said that to like a thousand people.'"

People were shamed by Ramtha if they were gay. On more than one occasion, Kristin remembered Ramtha singling out a woman in a wheelchair. "Ramtha would point her out every once in a while and say, 'If you commit suicide, this is what happens to you in your next life.'"

According to Associated Press reports, during one wine ceremony in the late 1990s attended by some eight hundred people, Ramtha called a man and his common-law wife to the stage, and allegedly elicited a confession from the couple that they'd had sexual contact with a fifteen-year-old girl. But, later, when the couple was charged with ten counts of sexual misconduct with a minor, JZ Knight said she could not testify about this confession because it was Ramtha, not her, who witnessed it. The couple pled not guilty and the case was eventually dismissed; they were told not to return to the school.

Throughout the wine ceremonies, Ramtha would instruct people to fill their glasses up to the brim and hold them aloft as he gave elaborate "toasts." When he instructed, and only when he instructed, the crowd was told to down their entire glass of wine at once. No sips. Then everyone would pour themselves a refill. One reporter dubbed this a "spiritual drinking game."

"You'd fill your cup all the way up, and he would make this long, overly flowery toast to the fabric of reality. And then he'd say, 'Okay. Drink it.' And you'd literally slam the glass," Kristin said. "Sometimes you'd be two or three glasses deep in the first half hour."

Aaron and Kristin were both twelve when they attended their first wine ceremony and drank alcohol for the first time. While Washington State law prohibits alcohol consumption for people younger than twenty-one, it does allow for minors to consume it "in connection with religious services." But even then, the law is clear that "the amount consumed is the minimal amount necessary for the religious service."

But kids who attended the ceremonies drank wine alongside their family members, and smoked pipe tobacco. "The teaching was that those chemicals, especially mixed, help open connections in your brain to help you remember things better." Aaron said this idea hardly stopped at the wine ceremonies; he recalled that other RSE parents would buy liquor and cigarettes for kids regularly.

The wine ceremonies could go on all night. During the first one Kristin attended, she eventually realized she couldn't see anyone she knew. "I remember watching my parents, and my parents' best friends, literally having to crawl away because they couldn't stand to walk," she said. "I was literally sitting there by myself, this twelve-year-old filling up my own wineglass."

Ramtha would also unspool new predictions. "There will be an outbreak of a new horrible virus because certain companies need for you to take a vaccination," he predicted. "The next war will be a war of viruses and plagues, because that is the only army that has outwitted guns and lasers," Ramtha said later that year. "That is the true Armageddon."

The entire place was "very left-leaning," but also in a conspiratorial way, Carla remembered. "Like, I remember her giving this lecture that George W. Bush was like...these lizard people? Lizard people from another planet? It's just like way-out there stuff where you're going, 'Huh?'"

Carla moved back to Portland after two years. Her relationship with the man in the Red Guard fell apart—he was emotionally abusive, particularly to Aaron (who, by then, had moved in with his father), and controlling. The RSE school for children felt more like daycare than an actual education. Carla had also grown increasingly frustrated by Ramtha's incessant urging that followers stockpile food and invest thousands of dollars in building an "underground." She tried but it seemed like she could never afford enough. Finally, she just gave up. "I remember telling my friends, if the world ends, it's okay. I don't want to live underground," she said. "Honestly, when I made that decision, it was such a relief. Just so much stress was created from that fear, or this idea that you're somehow not doing something right if you're not fully participating in all of that."

By the time she left, the endless conspiracies had become exhausting. It seemed like preparing for the end of the world was at the foundation of the spiritual ideas Ramtha was preaching, but that wasn't appealing to her. "I don't believe that the government is out to kill us or create chemtrails that make us sick purposely, and all the things they talked about," Carla said.

But shaking off the ranch wasn't as easy for Aaron. He'd fallen so far behind in middle school that by the time he entered high school, he was completely lost. He never believed in what Ramtha taught, but he did continue partying like he had seen at the wine ceremonies, and used drugs. "I spiraled out of control," he said. "I think I felt like no adult had authority over me anymore."

After a few years of working a job at a tile factory, Aaron enrolled in community college, and then attended a four-year university, getting his bachelor's degree in journalism. He took jobs around the West as a reporter, and he tried not to think about Ramtha.

David Irwin-Detrick, too, was aimless after growing up around the ranch. "Some people don't hold a lot of animosity toward it. I do," he said. He also dropped out of high school. Life in the ranch instilled in him a lack of trust in any part of society. "I had no faith in anything: government, school, working for anything. If I can just manifest it, why would I work for anything?"

Both Aaron and David separately expressed how growing up at RSE—where it was preached that everyone was a God—destabilized them. It took years to try to figure out how to live in a world they'd been raised to believe was always on the verge of ending. David felt like all he needed to do was be able to survive whatever inevitable ills fell upon them.

Both, too, said they saw their mothers as victims.

"My mother," David alleged, "was taken about by this con woman who tricked people into giving them their money."

"My mom is a very loving person, and this was a massive mistake that she made. But she is a victim of this," Aaron said. "That's why cults exist, right? They get people to do things that they would never otherwise do. And I think she holds incredible guilt around it."

JZ "is a bad and evil person," he said. "They go out and find vulnerable people and prey on them and take their money and take their everything." People were living in squalor just so they could spend all their money on classes at the ranch, so they could stay current. "The juxtaposition of the school and the barn and all the people there, like a stone's throw away from her mansion, was just wild to me, even as a kid," he said. "I was just like, 'How do people not see this?'"

Kristin's parents eventually lost interest in attending workshops at the ranch, but without them, she continued making the trip alone.

Celebrities kept coming. The actress Salma Hayek joined and was seen at wine ceremonies. In 2004, a film called *What the Bleep Do We Know!?* presented RSE's teachings in a kind of quasi-documentary style, blending a New Age interpretation of quantum physics and consciousness with ideas that people can control water molecules with their thoughts if they try hard enough. Talking heads weighed in authoritatively, but unlike an actual documentary, those people were never identified. Perhaps this was because most were purveyors of pseudoscience. Among the film's "experts" were a paranormal investigator, a self-proclaimed quantum healer and chiropractor, and a theoretical physicist whose work has been characterized as "quasi-mystical" and "on the fringes of mainstream science."

Ramtha was one of the film's talking heads. "Is everyone a mystery?" he asked in his signature accent. "Is everyone an enigma?"

Kristin loved how unlike her teachers at her Catholic high school, Ramtha made everything about spirituality seem so scientific. So factual, undeniable. It inspired her. She decided she would become a physics major—believing she would enter college with a leg up on the subject after all the time she'd spent learning about it at the ranch. "Quantum physics is so *wildly* different than what the ranch was teaching," she remembered after taking a college course. "That was the first time I was like, 'Wait a second.'"

What the Bleep Do We Know!? stayed in theaters in Portland for more than four months straight and grossed more than $16 million worldwide. One of its directors, a thin man with wire-rimmed glasses and a five o'clock shadow, was named Mark Vicente.

Vicente took workshops at RSE for a decade. After leaving RSE, he would become best known as a member of the New York cult NXIVM led by Keith Raniere. NXIVM positioned itself as a company that sold a system of self-help workshops. But the business was a front and acted as a recruitment tool for a myriad of illegal and unethical practices, including some female victims being branded with Raniere's initials. In 2019, when Raniere was put on trial for sex trafficking charges, Vicente was cross-examined on the stand by Raniere's defense attorney. He confirmed to the court he was scared to speak out against the defendant because of a bad past experience with another spiritual organization when "things went south pretty badly."

The attorney pressed him to say more. "What is Ramtha?" the man asked.

"The spiritual entity that a woman JZ Knight believes that she channels," Vicente answered. He said he was a member of Ramtha's school before being drawn into NXIVM.

"Tell me if this is right," the attorney said. "JZ Knight believes she is channeling a 35,000 year old warrior?"

"That's my understanding," Vicente replied.

"It's your understanding because you were a member of the group?"

"It's my understanding because that's what she said again, and again, and again," Vicente countered.

The attorneys quibbled—how long was Ramtha going to be brought up in discussion of NXIVM, a wholly unrelated group? They conferred with the judge in a sidebar.

"I think [the jury] should know that he thinks that it's good to join a group where a 35,000 year old warrior is being channeled through a woman," Raniere's defense attorney argued. "I think that might be something that they would want to consider in whether they should trust him." The judge told him to continue.

"Did you believe that JZ Knight was channeling a 35,000 year old warrior?" the attorney asked Vicente.

"For a few years," he said.

How?

"Belief versus evidence," Vicente answered.

Vicente's belief had been particularly useful for Ramtha. In 2002, Vicente released a "rockumentary" called *Where Angels Fear to Tread* (which was produced by Linda Evans). On the cover, a Photoshopped JZ points at the viewer, like a Lemurian Uncle Sam. Filmed from 1999 to 2001 "at locations around the world," the film opens with shots of galloping horses, and JZ Knight—in flowing robes and a headband tied around her head—leading what looks to be an army of soldiers, who carry banners that read: "RSE." It was in line with how Ramtha was speaking to people at the ranch—that they had been a part of his Lemurian army in a past life, and they had reunited in this life.

The Ramtha of *Where Angels Fear to Tread* is a departure from the Ramtha of the *Merv Griffin* days. In the 1980s, that Ramtha usually appeared on stages in ceremonial garb—blazers with boxy shoulders and high necks, flowing bejeweled robes. By the 2000s, though, this older Ramtha took the stage in American Eagle and Abercrombie baseball hats and zip-up sweatshirts. For long periods, the foreign accent dropped away entirely. Kristin said that when she first came to the ranch, wine ceremonies had everything to do with Ramtha, and nothing to do with JZ. But "as time went on," she believed, "JZ started to carve out her own space."

In the film Ramtha criticized organized religion and the grip of multinational corporations and capitalism on the country. (Ex-followers speculated in online forums that the film became difficult to find after RSE ordered people to destroy or mail it back to the ranch, likely because of copyright violations over its soundtrack of bands like the Rolling Stones and Boston.) He raged that athletes were more revered in America than scientists. He told jokes, and the audience howled with laughter, even when what he said wasn't particularly funny. He said that people are like dogs: embarrassing. He criticized women: how they starve themselves, how all they care about is beauty, the perfect body, the perfect husband.

In the form of the former prom queen, who by then had clearly undergone extensive plastic surgery, he delivered monologues about not caring about one's looks. To an outsider, these words rung a little hollow.

The film features shots of JZ, or Ramtha, or JZ—it's impossible to really know who you're looking at—dancing on the stage, a bottle of wine nearby, looking like the fun lady at a suburban dive bar, out to have a good time, dancing along to everyone's karaoke song like it's her favorite too. JZ howls with laughter, opening her mouth wide and roaring. At moments Ramtha appears to be the missing link between bold Elizabeth Clare Prophet, so sure of her connection to the Masters, and brash Amy Carlson, surrounding herself with a group of people who will worship her.

Watching that film, it becomes clear that JZ Knight understands what so many of us won't admit about power in America. Money earns respect, so she built herself a palace. Beauty compels, so she has taken care to preserve her looks. A man who commands gets heard, so she became one. Warriors are heroes, so she transformed Lemuria into a battlefield.

Here was a woman with her own spiritual ideas. But it seemed her body had to be seen as taken over by a man in order to spread them. Why was being JZ Knight not enough to preach her own spiritual philosophy?

"Truthfully, I think it was probably a little ahead of its time," Kristin said. Now it's "happening on a global scale to talk about how women are second-class citizens, basically."

But even still, she had to be a man in order to push that notion. "The underpinning was that a man came into JZ Knight's body," she said, "but was still present as a woman because women need to be seen as equals."

As Ramtha, JZ is the keeper of a mystery. People continue coming to her, sitting at the foot of her stage, wanting some of that mystery.

The Fox sisters once admitted to the world they were fakes. They wanted the world to believe, and it did, and when they told them to stop, people couldn't. They wouldn't.

By 2012, an estimated 90,000 people had attended workshops at RSE. That year, during an hours-long ceremony, Ramtha unleashed a torrent of hate. According to a court filing in a lawsuit, a clip of the rant was posted on YouTube of Ramtha yelling disparaging remarks about homosexuals, Catholics, Jews, and Mexicans from the stage. When this video was leaked online by former students, JZ sued and won, and the recording is nowhere to be found.

By then Kristin had stopped going to the ranch. She liked the people she met there, and probably would have continued to go, she said, but attending just got to be too expensive. And the more time she spent away from the place, the more she questioned what she had learned there.

She sought out a therapist who specialized in treating people who had spent time in cults, if only to try to get a sense if that's what she had been a part of. "Drugs and alcohol are sometimes a cornerstone," she said. "It brings down people's inhibitions and puts them in a space of vulnerability, so that once they are intoxicated, you can start to chip away at their grasp on reality."

JZ used that power to dictate the trajectory of people's lives. People even brought their infants to the ranch for Ramtha to name.

In Thurston County, JZ Knight wielded enormous power, and in the state of Washington too, where she had contributed tens of thousands to the state Democratic Party over the years. She was long rumored to be the richest person in the county. In 2011, she single-handedly halted a 568-home subdivision from being constructed near her ranch; she sued on the basis that the new housing would infringe on locals' water rights, including her own, and the state supreme court sided with her. "Sources say she hasn't been this happy for 30,000 years," quipped a columnist in the Tacoma newspaper. The case gave her a reputation for having "good environmental ethics," according to one county commissioner.

But things changed when Donald Trump ran for president. She appeared to be all in on the candidate, who was beloved by America's fringe, but slowly found more mainstream success. RSE sent statements to media outlets that Ramtha was fully supportive of QAnon, and the school produced Q hats and Q shirts and hung a sign on the front gate of the property featuring a giant Q. Ramtha continued to issue predictions, and when COVID rippled in waves across the world, he claimed to have seen it coming all along. "COVID-19 is just a flu empowered by snake venom," he said in 2022. It destroys you from the inside out and can be used to "program you with artificial intelligence and lose your soul."

By 2023, the giant RSE compound had a tall moss-covered wall that ran along the front of the property and a chain-link fence topped with barbed wire running along the back, away from the main road. In Yelm there are several other churches; none have barbed wire around them.

On the front gate, the Q sign was gone, but new ones had been posted on all of the gates.

"DO NOT KNOCK TO TALK ABOUT THIS 'VACCINE,'" they read. "Now get off my property."

18.

A blond toddler is crying. Amy commands her people to shut him inside a closet for a "time out," and a room of adult Love Has Won followers watch as this happens. A camera captured the scene on video. No one said a word. No one asked a question about whether a child should ever be put in a dark closet.

As muffled wails continued, and the boy in the closet hiccupped and sobbed, Amy ignored him, trying to hold a conversation. "I'm in full consciousness. I'm at the 124th dimension," she said to a man who had questions about her claim that she was God. He didn't want his questions to come off like he was testing her.

"Test away!" Amy said, clearly irritated at being asked about her abilities and power. "Whatchu got?"

But the conversation was interrupted. The boy emerged from the closet when someone opened the door, and all of the adults in the room stopped what they were doing to say thank you. The mother picked up her child and handed him back to Amy, which caused the boy to start crying again immediately.

"Oh, you want to do it over again?" Amy asked. "Oh, we'll do it over again. I have no problem."

The boy yelped, struggling for breath. She handed him off. He cried, the closet door clicked shut.

Ryan Kramer handed around a party-sized bowl as the child screamed. "Mom, would you like some chips?" he asked, gentle.

Amy selected one chip and ate it.

Again, when the child emerged, Amy held him and the crying began again. Back to the closet.

All the while, Amy tried to keep talking about why she was God.

"Back to the ego thing again," she said to one of the men sitting on the floor, "that's why people don't listen. Fear of not being heard themselves, fear of being betrayed. Betrayal is the deepest feeling we have."

This wasn't the only video taken of Amy's abuse. There were dozens more. In one, Amy could be seen yanking a cat by the neck and thrusting it up and down and up and down in jerking motions in the air.

She screamed at her followers, berating them and unleashing Jason Castillo on them for punishment. John Robertson—the Father God who was demoted—was a particular target of her ire. Amy took a video as she insulted Robertson for bringing her the wrong thing for dinner. "My vision was chicken parmesan," she scolded. "I didn't say meatballs. I love meatballs. But I didn't fucking say that! *Chicken. Parmesan.*"

In another video, Amy and Jason reprimanded him together.

"Your contract is to be conscious!" Amy shrieked. "Having the unconscious is saying, 'I'm failing my contract, Mother.' Let's get it straight here."

Robertson stared.

"Say it!" Jason commanded.

"I'm failing my contract—" Robertson said, looking confused.

"What have you done?" Amy asked.

"I've been failing my contract," Robertson replied.

"Why? Tell us."

"Because my ego-programmed mind hates God," Robertson said.

"And you are?" Jason asked.

"A cockroach," Robertson responded, and Amy scoffed.

"An ego-programmed mind!" Jason exploded. He had failed the test. "I mean, how dense can you be? I basically said, 'Repeat this,' and you went to something else. You're a *whore*. You have a better insult for yourself than God does?"

By then it was clear Amy's health was declining, and her speech was more slurred in videos. Her grip on the people who sat around her bed listening, bringing her shots of tequila, seemed to be slipping. And, perhaps to feel some semblance of control, she lashed out at those around her. The ones who were unable, or unwilling, to fight back took the brunt of her rage. They were the ones who had the least to offer her.

Once, Chelsea Renninger reached her older sister and arranged to chat with her via Skype. They were excited to see each other, and they started talking just like they always had.

"She was asking about the kids—her kids—and I was telling her how they were doing, and we were taking care of them," Chelsea said. "And she was starting to get teary-eyed."

But then someone else came into Amy's room, and her eyes left the screen. "You could hear a guy in the background go, 'Who are you talking to?'" Chelsea said. "And she was like, 'It's just my sister! It's just my sister!'"

"Once she looked at him, then it was like that was it," she said.

Amy stopped being Amy. She looked back at the camera as someone else. As Mother God.

"She switched back to her stuff that I didn't understand," Chelsea said. "It was like somebody's controlling her."

And yet there was still a part of Amy that remembered the person she used to be. Archeia Hope began reaching out to Amy's eldest son, Cole, on Facebook. She sent him messages on Amy's behalf—referring to his mother as "Mom." She told him Mom wanted to get in touch with Aidan, her youngest son, who was just a toddler when she left Texas.

Hope wanted to know how they could reach him. Cole responded that he would try to get in touch with his younger brother, who didn't have a phone of his own yet.

Two weeks later, Hope wrote again. "Hey Cole!!! How are you?? Just reaching out again. Mom wants to see how you're going and we were curious if you've gotten in contact with Aidan? She loves you!!"

Cole patiently wrote back and asked for his mother's phone number, and Hope gave it to him.

A few months later, Hope wrote to him again.

Two years passed, and there was Hope again in his inbox: "Hi Cole," she wrote, "your Mom really wants to get in contact with Aidan somehow."

PART V
THE THREE OF SWORDS

19.

"Our guest today calls herself Mother God," the television host and former psychologist Dr. Phil McGraw announced as photos of Amy Carlson in various stages of Mother God flashed across the screen. Amy with her hands in prayer. Amy with glitter eye makeup. "She is the leader of an organization called Love Has Won."

It was September 2020, and in the studio with the bald, mustachioed Dr. Phil were Amy's sister Chelsea and her mother, Linda.

"Mother God, as she is known by her followers, says she has a divine plan to help humanity. But her sister Chelsea claims the group is a cult, and is concerned that Amy has become mentally ill," Dr. Phil said.

Amy had long believed she would be featured on a daytime television show. So many people with the same ideas had before her: JZ Knight on *Merv Griffin*, Elizabeth Clare Prophet's daughters on *Oprah*. Her time had simply arrived.

Amy appeared in a live feed that was projected onto a massive screen on the wall of the studio. She wore a rainbow ribbon tied at the top of her head, and a crayon-orange tank top.

"Chelsea says fourteen years ago Amy left her own family," Dr. Phil explained, "including her own children, to join a man she called Father God, and is now brainwashing members."

Aurora and Hope were there on the video screen too. Hope wore orange, Aurora a pale yellow peasant blouse covered in orange flowers. "She's gonna kick ass because all of these people are liars," Hope said, referring to Amy's critics, "and Mom's going to be sharing the whole truth."

"Let me start with you, Mom," Dr. Phil said, turning to Linda, who wore her blonde hair cropped short, and a blue blazer. She looked like being there caused her physical pain.

"Were you surprised when she abandoned her three children?"

"Yes. I was," she answered.

"Was she close to her children?"

"No, not really," Linda said. "She wasn't a very maternal mother. We had the children a lot in our family, over to our house." They hadn't spoken to Amy in a year and a half.

"And Chelsea, do you think that this is just a big con or do you think she's mentally ill? Do you think she's too far gone to come back to being your sister?" Dr. Phil asked.

"I think it's a combination. I believe that she has been brainwashed," Chelsea said.

As Amy's mother and sister spoke, both seemed profoundly sad, sitting in the studio with Dr. Phil, telling this to the world. According to Chelsea Renninger, she and her mother only participated because they wanted to get Amy help. "We didn't want to be on TV," she said. "But we had to tell the story from the truth, otherwise they were gonna just keep spreading their lies."

"I think she doesn't even know what the truth is anymore," Chelsea told Dr. Phil. But she also thought Amy was grifting money from her followers to travel and fund her lifestyle.

After a break, the show came back, and Amy was in the spotlight. Tape from a prerecorded interview rolled first, in which she answered questions asked by one of the show's producers.

"I was called onto a mission in 2006, and I just surrendered, and embraced the truth," Amy explained. "I am God. I am mother Gaia, Mother Earth. Great Spirit. Spiderwoman. White Buffalo Calf Woman. My angels told me that I had to go serve humanity, and that I had to give up everything. I did that.

"I produce miracles," she said, letting a little giggle loose. "Kind of like Jesus. I have done over 100,000 surgeries. I heal people [from] cancer over and over with the power of love."

She said it all: Robin Williams, Marilyn Monroe, Joan of Arc. Jesus.

"We're not a cult. Absolutely not. What is a cult?" she said. "A cult, like, is not transparent. Point-blank. I'm transparent."

The producer asked about former members alleging that she used sleep deprivation as a way to control people. Amy cackled, busting up into hysterics. She laughed so hard it even made the producer laugh a little. She denied it.

"Well, Amy joins us now via Skype, so welcome," Dr. Phil said.

Amy raised a hand and waved, smiling. "Hi! Love you, Dr. Phil!" She was sitting in a bed with big wooden posts, pillows propped up behind her. The room was bathed in sunlight, making her look a little purple. On the screen, a graphic read: *Amy: Says she is "Mother God."*

"So how are things?" Dr. Phil asked.

"They're very peaceful here at the moment," she said.

"Yeah? So, things are often not peaceful around you," he said, "because I've seen some of your streams, I've seen some of the videos where you seem to be upset a lot. Yelling and screaming and calling names and all. What is it that upsets you the most?"

Amy furrowed her brow.

"Well, you know a lot of those are taken out of context and not properly represented," she said. "I'm love-in-action in every moment, that is my role." But there was plenty for her to be angry about. "I've been raped several times. I've been stolen from. They burned my house down," though it wasn't clear who "they" were. "I've been come after so much. And you get a little weary."

"Well, I'm very sorry to hear that's happened to you," Dr. Phil said. "It seems like your tone is not always peaceful with your followers. Let me let you look at this and then you can comment on it."

He played the clip of Amy yelling "Kill me!" and telling "spiritual ego whores" to die while Styx played "Mr. Roboto" in the background.

"Uh, wow," Dr. Phil said, feigning surprise. "Um, that seems pretty aggressive for someone that's leading the world to love. That seems counterintuitive."

"I agree with you. It was taken in a moment where a lot of things were happening to me. And I was upset. And that's how I expressed it," Amy said.

Phil asked why she left her children in Texas.

"I did not abandon my children. I begged my angels," Amy said. "I did not want to leave. They told me I had to go on mission. If I didn't do it, then no one else would. And I had to make a jump. And I had to make a decision."

"So just a higher calling?"

"Yes, absolutely," she said. "Did my heart break every day for about a year? Yes."

Dr. Phil cued up the video of Amy repeatedly ordering the crying toddler to be shut in the closet. "Um, I'm sorry. I need you to help me with that," he said afterward.

Amy said children lack boundaries. "We started coming up with ideas on how to assist them. One of my ideas was, whatever their age is, just two minutes of time out. And if they can't get it, they go back in time out."

"Well, that's flat-out abuse to lock a child in a closet like that," Dr. Phil said. "And what really bothers me is not the poor judgment that I see on your part, but the fact that I'm looking and five or six or seven adults in the room, and not one person in the room has the backbone to stand up and say, 'This is not okay, you're not going to bully and abuse this child, and traumatize them by putting them in a closet with a closed door like this.'"

Amy tried to jump in: "What we were doing was experimenting—"

"On a child," he interjected.

"—They weren't locked in a closet. They were put in time out, Dr. Phil."

"In a closet."

After another commercial break, the camera was Hope and Aurora—who "speak for hours daily about Mother God," Dr. Phil explained. Both smiled perfect smiles.

"So, you believe that Amy is Mother God, correct?"

"Yes, we know so," Hope said. "Absolutely," Aurora said.

"So, you spend the day in the presence of the deity, of God, the creator of the universe," Dr. Phil said.

"Yes," Hope responded.

"That must be an amazing experience for you."

"It is," said Aurora.

"Are y'all aware that she says she's actually Jesus? That she's reincarnated from being Jesus?" Dr. Phil asked.

"Yes, she has the documentation," Hope said.

"Does it strike y'all as odd that she drinks so much?"

Both said no.

"I mean, you have to envision that she is the embodiment of Mother Earth. So, if you were to be Mother Earth in a physical vessel—which is Mom," Aurora explained in her matter-of-fact tone, "she is in extreme amounts of pain."

"If she's God, then wouldn't she just resolve that pain spiritually?" Phil asked.

"She can't," Hope answered. "It's based on a karmic contract with humanity."

Dr. Phil glanced to Chelsea and Linda, listening patiently, but looking even more pained.

"I don't believe any of it," Chelsea said.

"I don't either," Mother God's mother agreed.

The Dr. Phil Show devoted two episodes to Amy and Love Has Won. In the second, Ashley McCoy largely spoke about being on mission for two weeks before she actually saw Amy, and when she finally did, she was surprised by how small she was. "It was odd to see someone, a frail person, in bed in front of you," she said. She couldn't walk. She had to be carried. In bed, she drank all day.

"I have five stage level of cancer," Amy explained to Dr. Phil. "Hundred percent. Full body."

"You have stage five cancer?"

"Yes."

"What is stage five cancer?"

"That's to the bones."

Ashley told Dr. Phil she fled after two months with the group, leaving all of her belongings behind. She alleged it had been two months of sleep deprivation and mental manipulation.

Dr. Phil asked Amy if she deprived her followers of sleep.

"That is incorrect," she said as another graphic flashed on the screen: *What ever happened to the fat guy biking across America? All new Thursday.* "It's energetics and it's consciousness. A lot of beings are not utilizing their sleep properly. So, I set up boundaries."

Amanda Ray joined the show too and, alongside her sister-in-law, Ariane, told the story of her brother, Ben, wandering naked in the wilderness. She said they were concerned about the people in the group. They were concerned for Amy.

"I think she's surrounded by an entire team that's enabling her. They are profiting and exploiting her for financial gain," Amanda said. Amy listened, looking like she pitied Amanda.

"I don't like what you're doing at all to these poor people," Linda said to Amy, yelping a little as she started to cry. "I would love it if you would come home so that we can help you. You weren't raised like this. And it makes me so sad."

Rick Alan Ross, a cult expert, joined the show.

"Rick, what's your level of concern about this organization?" Dr. Phil asked.

Ross called Love Has Won "pernicious," and said they "bait and switch" people after recruiting them online. If they went "on mission" with Amy, she controlled their life. "It sounds to me like she can do nothing wrong. That no matter what Amy does or says, it's reinforced by the group as right. As Godlike," Ross said. "And in fact, to disagree with Amy is to disagree with God."

"I've never said surrender to me, I just say surrender to love and yourself," Amy responded. "And whatever your soul and your heart shares with you to do? That's what you do."

Dr. Phil seemed to be holding back his temper. "But you tell them you're God. You're actually God! You hung on the cross. You recall being crucified on the cross, and that you are God!"

"In truth we are all God," Amy said.

"That's not what you say! You say, 'I am Mother God!'"

"I am Mother God! But we are all God!" Amy pleaded.

"Yeah, but Amy, in the livestreams," Ross said, "they talk about the importance of *your* work. Focusing on *you*. Subordinating themselves to *you*. So, if you're not encouraging them to completely surrender to you—and to obey you, and to be submissive to you, and submit to your orders, your ideas, et cetera—then why are they repeatedly saying this in the livestreams?"

"I encourage them to follow their own heart and to serve love," Amy said.

"Hope? Aurora? You would like to respond?" Phil asked her followers.

Hope was defiant. "This group of people sits there and trashes Mom with lies and things that are not true that we address every day on our livestreams with the whole truth. And they still choose not to listen." Amy's mother, Linda, was stoic.

Aurora spoke up. "And I just wanted to address everything that you guys are showing about Mom is out of context."

"Please, put it in context," Dr. Phil said.

"I would love to," she said. "There is a history: Years ago, decades ago...parents would physically discipline their children. And that was okay."

"That does not justify putting a child in a closet and closing the door. And it wasn't okay to beat children years ago," he said. "So, you're setting up a paper tiger, tearing it down, and trying to justify abusing a child by terrorizing them, putting them in a dark closet."

"Well, I disagree. But I'll move on because time outs are time outs," Aurora said.

"No. That's not true," Phil pushed back. "Time outs are not locking a child in a dark closet."

"We'll move on because we all have different perspectives—"

He cut her off. "We'll move on because you don't know what you're talking about."

"Okay, love," said Aurora—the woman who, as Lauryn, once fought for foster children. "I have been with Mom for two and a half years, and I will tell you she is the absolute most brilliant, kindest, sweetest being...She has taken me from a highly dysfunctional place and made me highly as brilliant as she is."

Hope swooped in.

"I would not be the person, the feminine you see on the livestream every day in front of thousands of people, if it wasn't for what she has done," she said. "She is my best friend. She is a companion. She has shown me so many beautiful aspects of this planet that have been forgotten. And that is love. And why the people you see are going against her is 'cause they can't feel love."

Hope talked in a rhythm, a cadence, a drumbeat, words said but without feeling, lifeless, monotonous, constant. "There are so many grander things on the horizon for this planet for everybody to see. And it starts with Mom. She is the way."

With this speech, Hope was now livestreaming on Dr. Phil's

platform, Aurora smiling next to her as usual. "I owe everything to her. No matter what anybody says. No matter what her family believes."

She talked. Explained. Decreed. Repeated. She had said all of these words before.

"What she did to her children? It's all been higher-guided. It's love-based. Mom didn't want to leave her children. She did it for all of us—"

Phil cut her off and offered the last word to Rick Alan Ross.

"Well, Dr. Phil," he said, "I think what you just saw is a beautiful example, or a disturbing example, of cognitive dissonance."

And that was it. "It just ended very abruptly," Amanda Ray said of the episode. "We were like, 'Is that the show?' . . . It really did feel like all he did was exploit Amy."

It was clear that Amy needed help. It felt like the perfect group to help her: a cult expert, her followers, an ex-follower, her mother and sister. Like maybe all together something positive could have come out from it.

But Linda felt duped by the entire experience. "The producers presented it to us in a completely different way," she said. They told her that Dr. Phil could help her daughter, speak to her, bring her back to reality. "It was not at all what we expected." And it felt like the last opportunity to reach her.

Afterward, Amy mocked the show.

"I WILL SAY I WAS JUST IN FRONT OF A WHOLE BUNCH OF LIARS . . . USING A L9T OF MY VIDEOS OF CALLING HUMANITY OUT FOR BEING DUMB ON BALD MAN SHOW," she wrote on Love Has Won's chat room. "IM SO BAD . . . OH I'M A CULT EVERYONE PLZ RESEARCH A CULT . . . JESUS CHRIST, GOD COMES ALL HELL BREAKS LOSE."

The group's appearance was one of the only times when Amy, as

Mother God, had been forced to answer questions about her belief system, and her abusive behavior. But, even still, years after that show aired, a question about Love Has Won still lingered, one that never was fully answered on *Dr. Phil*. Was a group a cult if it mostly existed online? Few people had come to join Amy on mission in Colorado. But people like Kim Pece seemed so taken in by the idea of Amy as Mother God, and were ready to follow her, even from afar.

"This is the way that cults are now," Rick Alan Ross said. "Everyone is online, everyone uses social media platforms." Money is exchanged through PayPal, Venmo. The people who came to Colorado were simply her inner circle: the workers she depended on to care for her, who would withstand her abuse and dote on her. But the online following was her cash cow: a bank account she could always tap into.

"This is the future," he said. "Why would any cult leader neglect that when it's so ripe for exploitation?"

20.

n his garage in Eastern Canada, John Pece slammed down his phone as the credits at the end of *The Dr. Phil Show* rolled and ran into the house, where Kim was sleeping. He woke her up: "It's a cult," he insisted. He seemed angry, but also a little scared of what he had seen about Love Has Won.

Kim, groggy from sleep, recoiled. The pair got into a huge argument. John thought Kim was being sucked into something, that she was too involved to see it clearly. And Kim felt hurt that John, this man she'd loved for so long, couldn't see that Love Has Won was the only help she could find. When her family and doctors were telling her she needed medication, they were the only people who understood her and accepted her as she was.

"She was dead set on it being the truth," John said. "I kept trying to tell her, 'Listen, you're being brainwashed.' But I couldn't get through."

The disagreement kept up for weeks, and their conversations seemed to go in circles. "It was taking us down a really dark road," he said. John started researching cults online, reading about thought reform and how to talk to someone who might be falling into a cult. It felt like Kim was dissolving. "I was gonna do whatever it took to stick it out with her and hope and pray that things would turn around."

John formed an idea, a plan he could rely on if things got bad enough. He took his eldest son aside and told him that things might start to feel a little weird around the house. It might not make sense at first, but he told his son to trust him. To go with it—everything would be okay. The boy said he understood. John called Kim's mom, then her sister. He told them all the same thing: he had a last-ditch plan.

One evening, after another argument, Kim said she'd had it. She didn't want to be with John anymore. She was ready to end everything for Love Has Won. Furious, John left the house and slept in his truck.

That night he realized if she pulled any further away from him, she'd be gone forever. Lost to the Matrix. And so the next morning, he walked in the front door and said the words he never thought he would have to say. He said them because he loved his wife.

"I believe," he told Kim. "I woke up to God. Mother came to me."

Kim was overjoyed.

Kim eagerly let her friends in Love Has Won know that her husband had finally come to accept Amy as God. She logged on to Skype. "Johnny woke up to Mom!" she announced.

People in the group said they were happy for her, but Kim got the feeling that they actually weren't. They cautioned her: people who go on mission together don't tend to stay together.

Even so, John started to blend into Love Has Won, going to all the online spaces Kim was in. He made sure to keep their radio station on all day, and at work—he managed a hydroponic store at the time—he would listen to the livestreams, knowing Kim was back home soaking up every word. He was blown away by the number of groups they facilitated on Skype; being in Love Has Won was like having another full-time job, with all the streams and chats and notifications going off all day. Each morning, Kim and John woke up and sent Amy messages: "Good morning, Mom!"

One day while at work, John scrolled back into the Skype chat history to understand what Kim had been saying and found messages about him. Kim had told the group that he liked to edit photos and videos, and people chattered that he might be useful to have around. Maybe he could make a documentary about them.

"Every corner I looked in there was just another form of manipulation," John said. But in a way, he thought it was no different than what any company does online: collecting information, using it to curate advertising that might get people to spend money. "You collect data on your users and then you use that to hook them further, because the more hooked they are, the more money they're going to send you," he said. "Bottom line is it was all about pulling more money."

He found the livestreams excruciating. The twice-per-day broadcasts ran three hours each, and so for six hours each day he sifted through the words trying to understand all the ways they'd pulled Kim in. At home, Kim wasn't hiding anymore; sometimes the couple would sit side by side watching on their separate devices so they could individually comment on the streams.

All the while, John felt a horrible guilt building. "She was so happy that I joined with her," he said. "I mean, as much as they were manipulating her, I was manipulating them into believing that I believed their beliefs. At the same time, I was manipulating Kim as well. On one facet, that didn't feel great. On the other, though, I knew it was a necessary evil for me to at least keep that connection."

He would do anything to keep her from running. To keep her from becoming just like Mother God, this woman he saw before him, withering on the screen.

"You really have no other recourse besides that. You cannot kidnap a person and get it outta their head. You cannot take everything away from them—that will just drive them deeper into it," he said. "All you can do is support and love them."

One night, after Kim had a few drinks, John started to notice Kim was talking different than she usually did, like some part of her was doubting the story of Mother God. It felt like a window. When Kim went to bed, John rushed to her laptop and pulled up a few tabs in her browser. "I put in Google searches." He typed "How to tell if I'm in a cult?" and left the page open.

"I had left up really good information," he said, "crucial things that would possibly help further trigger critical thinking."

The next morning, Kim woke up a little hungover from the night before. John was having a smoke outside, looking out over their wide green property, when she came out to see him.

"Something's not right," she said.

"What do you mean?" John asked.

Kim didn't mention the tabs left open on her computer. But that morning, in one of the private Skype chats, she noticed a photograph of Mother God's altar. It caught her attention. In the photo, underneath the altar, "there were all these bottles of Febreze," Kim said. It seemed so absurd. Mother God was the keeper of all things, the pinnacle of all beauty and goodness, but she needed...Febreze? For what? "And I was like, 'What the fuck? You're the planet?' This doesn't work for me," Kim said. "It's filled with chemicals."

On the porch, John broke down when his wife told him she was done.

He was expecting a delivery that day. He'd ordered some books on thought reform and deprogramming from cults but figured it would be months before he could give them to Kim.

"That's when I told her, 'Okay, I've been undercover, and I'm sorry,'" John said.

Kim was shocked.

"I can't believe you lied to me too," she said.

21.

Because they loved Mother God so much, because everything she did was sacred, because maybe they were forced to say it: Aurora and Hope went live to share a story.

On this particular day, Amy had been in bed and desperately needed to go to the bathroom. She called out for someone to help, but no one was around.

Amy had dragged herself out of bed and onto the floor, not wanting to pee in the bed. "Somehow, some way," Hope said, "Mom managed to get there."

Amy pulled her body into the bathroom and peed on the tiled floor, before dragging herself back again into the bedroom, where she lay next to the bed until someone found her. "She was begging Robin and the Galactics, somebody to help her," Hope continued. All the while, Aurora stared at the camera, placid and half smiling.

While relaying this story, Hope and Aurora played voice notes Amy recorded on her phone. She yelled, sounding hammered, saying something about drinking two Mai Tais, mentioning Robin Williams, but it was mostly incoherent.

Hope wiped tears away from her eyes.

"I'm by myself, and some*how* I managed to take myself to the bathroom," Amy yelled. "Why? *Why* am I sitting here by myself? Without no one? Nobody fucking cares a shit about their fucking mother, or I wouldn't be in this moment, in this space. I'm left alone. All alone."

Aurora and Hope kept listening.

"Humanity," Amy slurred, like the words were molasses dribbling out the corners of her mouth. "What have you done? Fuck you."

The week before *The Dr. Phil Show* aired, news outlets in Kauai, Hawaii, reported that a "bizarre Colorado organization" called Love Has Won had settled into a luxury rental house with a view of the ocean, surrounded by sandy beaches and palm trees. The group said that they had come there because Amy was actually the Hawaiian goddess of volcanoes fire, Pele, and that there would be a portal to Lemuria in Hawaii.

"Mom says, 'Hey, I'm Pele, let's go,'" Ryan Kramer said one day during a livestream, his words sharp. "Pele, the goddess, has said she would return. Here she is. Okay everyone? Let that sink in to everyone on this island."

The trip was Jason's idea, one that Amy supposedly did not want to take, but that he forced her into, believing it would heal her. In videos, he carries her to the beach, where she sits on the sand, smiling out at the ocean. She is frail—bones under taut purpling skin. In one, she sits at the shoreline, water flowing over her feet, a stereo playing Counting Crows. She points to a leaf floating in the surf. Jason picks it up, hands it to her. "Wow. This is from Lemuria," Amy said, turning it over in her hands. "Straight from the inner Earth... That's where they're gonna take me. Whenever."

From the house, Amy would log on to Facebook and try to go live. But, for whatever reason, few people tuned in to watch her videos. "I only got like seven people," she said during one livestream. "Why? Why does everyone hate me? And I'm the most loving of all!"

She believed she was dying, and the reason was that the world was killing her. On one livestream, Hope chastised viewers. Amy was on a "death mission," she said, because people weren't waking up to the message that she was God.

Meanwhile, concerned loved ones of people in the group continued to contact authorities. Online, vitriol surged toward Love Has Won after several articles were published. Trolls said Amy should die for victimizing so many people, duping them into believing.

As the news of the group's arrival in Kauai spread, locals became concerned. "We've been through a lot together and take great pride in protecting the sacredness, safety and health of our community," one nearby resident said. People took issue with a white woman claiming she was Pele, saying she was the God they should be worshipping. On one livestream, Amy yelled, "Hawaii, fuck you! I'm Pele! Fuck off, bitch."

"That was highly offensive to the whole Hawaii kingdom," one woman told the *Denver Post*. "That was almost like a threat to us."

On September 4, 2020, a group of sixty-some protesters gathered outside the Love Has Won house and joined hands for a *pule*, a Hawaiian word for blessing or prayer. And then for three days, the protesters chanted and sang. They held signs that read "Cult Not Welcome Here," "U R NOT PELE," and "Get Cult Out." One person shouted, "Why would you abandon your children and make other people follow you as a fake mother?"

The longer the protests went on, the more intense they became. Eggs and rocks were thrown at the house, the windows of a blue SUV in the driveway smashed, fires lit. "They were telling us that we were invading them," Aurora said to a local TV news station. Hope sat beside her, nodding. "And that we were somehow trying to destroy their culture, when we weren't." She told a newspaper, "They clearly don't like anyone from the mainland."

The mayor arrived at the house to calm people down, and soon the police announced they would be escorting Amy and the group to the airport. As they sped away people battered the car with rocks. "Never come back!" they yelled.

"Bye, Amy!" called another. "You're a rotten mother!"

After the debacle in Hawaii, the group returned to Colorado, where Amy's health continued to deteriorate. Aurora, Hope, and Faith continued to dutifully attend to every need of their queen. The livestreams continued uninterrupted. The chats went on all day. Orders of colloidal silver kept being shipped out to waiting customers around the world who had woken up to the truth that God was a woman who was once named Amy Carlson. Some people who'd come on mission decided it was time to leave. They couldn't see God anymore in Amy, only a dying woman who needed a hospital but was surrounded by people who refused to bring her to one.

Amy's fragile condition was something the group talked about on their daily broadcasts. On one particular livestream, Aurora and Hope answered viewer questions about whether Amy would in fact seek medical care. "Yeah, there's no way that Mom would go to a 3D doctor," Aurora said. "There's been moments where Mom has asked us to take her to a 3D hospital, and we're like 'nope.' Because there's no way. We know exactly how a hijacking works. And you can bet your fucking ass that someone in that hospital . . . would go straight for Mom and do who knows what."

Other times, Hope would explain that the Galactics were the ones instructing Amy to stay away from doctors. In all her pain, Amy would sometimes question if this was all crazy. If she was really Mother God or not. Aurora and Hope explained this was just her "spinning out." Of course she was God, they told her. This was the divine plan. Even as Amy—the game master who'd created the rules of this game they were all playing—faltered in her belief, the players she had so meticulously indoctrinated ensured she stayed in character. The game had turned into a prison cell by then, and her wardens would not be letting her out. "She had already agreed to this process. She had agreed for her vessel to do all of this," Faith would say. "And that was the biggest gift."

Hope had long sat next to Amy's bed, scribbling meticulous

notations of everything Amy ate and said, believing that each precious word was an utterance of the divine. These notes would one day be considered a Bible.

As her savior withered before her, Hope compulsively documented her declining weight. In 2004, when Amy was pulled over for drunk driving in Texas, her five-foot-four frame weighed 135 pounds; in 2021, Amy weighed less than 100. The people around her began to believe her ascension to 5D was imminent. Getting to 5D was something they would do in their earthly bodies—they didn't have to die to get to that dimension. But they began to think that starships would be coming to "evacuate" Amy, and she needed to be light enough for them to pick up. "[One hundred and three], 104 was the ideal weight for ascension," Hope wrote. "When the Ascension happens, the next phase of the mission will commence."

Instead of taking her to see a doctor, Amy's followers treated her based on messages from Robin Williams and the Galactics. They gave her potent cannabis oils, Xanax, muscle relaxers, gabapentin. Sometimes Amy would consume more than 10,000 milligrams of the colloidal silver tinctures they made themselves, which they said could cure COVID and cancer. Sometimes they served it to her ice cold in shot glasses. Other times they brought Amy a liter-sized container of colloidal silver, and she tipped it back, drinking straight from the bottle.

Decades back, as the world amassed Y2K horror scenarios, a new economy surged offering preparations in case doomsday came to pass. Frantic, frenzied, paranoid people prepared for a hellscape of atomic fallout, readying themselves to subsist on a diet of freeze-dried beef stroganoff and to live behind gas masks.

At "preparedness expos," vendors hawked everything one might need to weather the apocalypse: buckets of potato powder with a shelf life of twenty-five years, water purifiers. Demonstrations showed people how to hook silver wires up to batteries, and then charge those wires in glasses of distilled water to create a substance called "colloidal silver." These people believed pharmacies likely would not survive the nuclear apocalypse and so this concoction was marketed as a make-it-yourself cure-all.

An ad for the substance in *Alternative Medicine Digest* professed that colloidal silver could cure everything from food poisoning to pinkeye to meningitis. "Silver is a powerful, natural antibiotic and prophylactic yet has no side effects," one Wisconsin "health center" claimed.

At one particular preparedness expo, a libertarian man from Montana named Stan Jones watched a vendor's how-to on making colloidal silver. It seemed easy enough. The world hadn't ended yet, but back at home, he started having a glass of this homemade brew every day. Later, he ran several unsuccessful bids for Montana governor and the Senate on a platform that Ronald Reagan was too liberal, and that a "one world communist government" was lying in wait, readying for a chance to overthrow the country.

Even though Jones never had a chance at getting elected, the press lavished him with attention. It was hard not to, because after several years of drinking a glass of colloidal silver a day, his skin had turned blue. Not Smurf blue, but a kind of gray-blue, like stormy ocean waves. He stood at lecterns in a suit and tie and gave speeches about making abortion illegal, and his skin was blue. Jones told reporters people often asked him if he was dead.

He had an irreversible condition called argyria, caused by silver exposure and buildup. Before people decided silver was something they wanted to drink, this condition was seen in miners and factory workers who processed it. In the 1920s, a story off the Associated Press wire read, "Blue Skinned Man, Side Show Freak, Dies at New York." When doctors performed his autopsy, they found "all his organs and tissues, including brain, heart and muscles, were of the same brilliant color."

In the 1990s, as the blue-skin-causing colloidal silver surged in popularity, the Food and Drug Administration sent a barrage of letters of warning to companies selling the product and making false claims about its healing properties. The agency proposed a ban on silver being sold in over-the-counter products. It threatened injunctions, penalties. But it was like playing a game of Whac-A-Mole, with new sellers always popping up, claiming it was a magical cure-all the pharmaceutical industry was conspiring with the government to keep hidden.

Colloidal silver's popularity only seemed to grow. Gwyneth Paltrow went on *The Dr. Oz Show* to say she sprayed the stuff under her tongue and in her throat to keep away viruses. During COVID-19, the televangelist Jim Bakker hosted guests who claimed colloidal silver was a cure. The conspiracy-addled host of *InfoWars*, Alex Jones, sold silver toothpaste and silver wound gels and a silver solution that his listeners could gargle around in their throats.

Once, a reporter from *Inside Edition* did a series of interviews with a man named Paul Karason who drank so much colloidal silver that his skin turned a hue that Sherwin-Williams paint might deem "favorite jeans" blue.

"When did you first realize you were blue?" the reporter inquired.

"A friend . . . came by and asked me what I'd done to myself," Paul said, admitting that he also rubbed colloidal silver on his skin.

"Do you feel that you've been treated differently because you're blue?"

"Oftentimes."

"If you could change back to the way you were, would you do it?"

"I'm not sure."

Paul continued to drink the silver. He developed prostate cancer. He lost his job. He lost his fiancée. He lost his house.

"People were rather reluctant to hire blue people," he said in a follow-up interview with *Inside Edition*. He moved back to his hometown of Bellingham, Washington, where he slept in a homeless shelter. He reconnected with a girl he knew when he was in school, before he turned blue.

"Blue man has a girlfriend!" *Inside Edition* cheered.

"He's quite the guy despite the fact that he's blue," the woman said. *Inside Edition* did one more update when Paul died after having a heart attack and a stroke. He'd never stopped drinking the silver.

It was clear that Amy did not have much time left. Jason had long carried her wherever she needed to go, but by March 2021 she could not hold him around his neck. Her arms were limp. Her skin was a deep purplish blue.

One day, Jason announced that he had received a message from the Galactics to take Amy from Colorado to Mount Shasta, and that the group needed to split. He and Faith would take a group to California with Amy while Aurora and Hope would stay behind in Colorado, where they would continue the business of livestreaming all day, asking people to make donations to fund "the ascension."

In Colorado, Hope and Aurora would lean even further into conspiracy theories, antisemitism, bigotry. "Hitler's intentions was to serve the light," Aurora said. "[Jews] wanted everyone else to do the work and they would take the money...The idea behind the concentration camps was to teach them to work."

At Mount Shasta, her people would help their God into an inflatable tub filled with water, where Faith would blow bubbles into Amy's dazed and smiling face as photos were taken. Her collarbones stuck out from her body like razors. Faith clipped yellow and orange hair extensions to her head, and Jason carried her to a lawn chair outside, where they pushed her upright to feed her cocktails through straws and colloidal silver from the bottle. Faith continued Hope's work of documenting the remedies dictated by Robin Williams to administer to Amy. She wrote "colloidal silver, Xanax, vape pen" in looping letters.

"Mom's ascending," Aurora said back in Colorado, smiling widely on the livestream. "I'm so excited."

"I'm fuckin' excited," Hope said. "Get her on the fuckin' Air Force One. Trumpy-Trump, pick her up. Germain, Robin: scoop her. Whatever it fuckin' takes, we fuckin' ready!"

Aurora cracked up laughing. "Let's go!"

But in early April, Amy told her keepers that the Galactics informed her she would ascend from Oregon, and not Mount Shasta. And so the group sped the two hours north to Ashland, a New Age hotbed where Amy had spent time shortly after she left her life in Texas behind. There, Jason pushed Amy in a wheelchair into a room at Callahan's Mountain Lodge—a log-cabin-style hotel with Jacuzzi tubs in many of the rooms. She was barefoot, draped in blankets, head nodding backward and mouth dropping open, eyes fluttering.

In the room's Jacuzzi, Amy lay on her side, motionless, bones jutting from the water like a ship run aground. Her people covered her with a blanket in the water. They moved her to the shower, where she lay on the floor as someone sprayed her. It was too much for even Faith to witness. One of Amy's most loyal deputies, who'd done so much recruiting in her name, left the hotel.

Aurora and Hope, upon hearing that Amy had been moved and her ascent was imminent, flew to Oregon, where they curled around her as her body died, as her jaw went slack and hung open. They combed her hair and put jewelry around her neck and petted her blue skin. They surrounded her in crystal pyramids and paintings of saints, of portals, of pyramids, of Mount Shasta, of Q. They strung Christmas lights.

After she was dead, they continued to observe the corpse, waiting for movement, a message. "Mom is breathing," they wrote. "Resurrection?" They poured water and colloidal silver into the dead body's mouth, held an electromagnetic field reader up to her, testing for some kind of frequency. They claimed her body stayed warm. They bent her arms and legs and said she never went stiff. They said they smelled her breath.

Eventually, they wrapped her body in a sleeping bag and drove to a campsite in the woods, where they stayed for days having campfires and eating buttermilk pancakes, and Jason slept next to Amy's dead body in a tent. Some members of the group came from Colorado to join them: Ryan Kramer, John Robertson. They waited for a sign for what to do next. Would the starships not be taking her body? Should they float her down a river? They had spent so much time talking about ascension, but appeared to have little detail on what would occur.

After they waited for days for the Galactics to take action, Jason told Ryan and John to help him load the body into the car.

They were taking Mother back to Colorado.

It was a Wednesday. April 28, 2021.

The house at 4 Alcedo Court was cluttered, but not messy, and when the Saguache County deputies walked inside, it was quiet. All the lights were on. John Robertson and several other members of the group casually looked up from their work untangling strands of twinkle lights under the watch of a Mother God tapestry hanging on the wall. They seemed unperturbed by the sudden arrival of a cadre of law enforcement in the middle of the night.

One by one, the police handcuffed and escorted them outside. None said a word. When Ryan was asked by an officer if he had any weapons or objects in his pockets that could poke someone, he said no in a small voice, and the officer emptied out a lighter and a wallet. The others had crystals in their pockets.

With the house cleared and the occupants handcuffed and sitting in the idling patrol cars, the officers gathered in the back bedroom of the house. Twinkle lights strobed wildly; the ceiling, the windows, the room's edges all were adorned with lights. Lights also glittered in a pile on top of the bed.

Despite all the aggressive flickering, the room was dim, but bright enough to make out the statements on the walls: "Jesus is a Woman," "The Event is Here." There were stuffed animals and a vase of flowers, candles, and salt lamps.

One by one, the deputies stepped toward the bed, shining flashlights toward a lump underneath the pile of twinkling lights. The lump was so small, it was easy to miss.

Amy's body had been tightly tucked into the bed, swaddled in an REI sleeping bag. When lit up by their flashlight beams, the skin of the corpse sparkled: a silvery, almost blue hue. The closed eyelids were coated in a layer of green and blue glitter.

Mother God had been mummified.

The officers were standing in a shrine. The discovery seemed to hit each of them slightly differently. One laughed nervously. The lone female officer stood in the room for minutes and just stared at the corpse, blue and glittering.

"Starting to get a little funky," Sheriff Dan Warwick said as he walked out the bedroom door and back through the house. The others followed him, gathering in the living room.

"Weird shit, dude," an officer wearing a Colorado flag balaclava over his mouth said. "How long has this lady been missing . . . or dead?"

"She wasn't missing," the female officer answered. "She's the leader of Love Has Won."

Sheriff Warwick pointed to the tapestry over the couch. "That's her, actually."

The others looked at the photo, then back toward the bedroom, trying to make sense of it.

"These girls aren't nothin' like I'm used to seeing here. Usually, the girls in this place are drop-dead good-lookin' girls," Warwick went on, "and it's like what the . . . ?"

"What the hell are you doing here?" another said, finishing his sentence.

"Well, we know what they were doing here," Warwick said. "Smokin' dope."

Warwick told stories about times he'd come to the house after various calls from concerned family members. Once, a Love Has Won follower told the sheriff he had a warrant out for his arrest, and that he wanted to turn his life around. They all laughed at that.

A balding officer walked into the conversation from the back bedroom and started listening.

"You liked it how he said Mother was sleeping?" Warwick asked, referring to the way Jason had greeted them at the door, saying, "Mother is in rest. She has rested."

"I'm like, 'Yeah, she's here in the house dead, you son of a bitch,'" Warwick said.

"Where?" the bald officer asked, and the others told him he'd walked right past the body.

Warwick took him back into the bedroom and again shined his flashlight on Amy's face, laughing at the other man's reaction.

"Oh shit," the bald one said. "They painted her."

In the living room, Colorado balaclava was still confused.

"So they all worship *her*?" he asked. "All the people we just took outside?"

The officers pointed to the art on the walls. The tapestry. Amy's head Photoshopped onto Jesus's body. Above it, someone had painted a word in bright graffitied letters:

"AIDAN," it read.

When Amy Carlson died, she weighed seventy-five pounds. One Saguache County coroner guessed she had been dead for a while. "Must be a couple weeks or more," he told the *Denver Post*.

An El Paso county coroner ruled that she died after her body declined from alcohol abuse, anorexia, and "chronic colloidal silver ingestion." She did not have cancer of any stage.

Silver was in her liver. It had turned her blue. Her body had begun to mummify, and, the coroner reported, when it was found, she was wearing a headband adorned with blue and green gemstones. It looked like a crown.

22.

In the days after the body of Amy Carlson was discovered, the seven members of Love Has Won who had been living in the house were arrested on charges of abuse of a corpse and misdemeanor child abuse. In interviews with the police, they said Miguel Lamboy had pulled all the group's money out of the bank, leaving the group with nothing. Before Amy's body had even been discovered by the police, Miguel submitted paperwork to register a new nonprofit—Gaia's Crystal Schools—with the IRS.

Mother God was dead and Father God was in the county jail, but the group's livestreams never stopped. If anything, they got bigger and more global, with members from the Netherlands and South Africa hosting broadcasts, and others delivering the message of Mother God in Spanish. The day after Amy was found two men went live from Australia with the title "Where We Go 1 We Go All," a QAnon slogan.

On May 2, a woman named Bobby went live for Love Has Won. "Well, good morning, everyone!" she said. "So, a lot's going on. And the most beautiful thing of all is that Mother God has ascended." She clapped her hands and cheered.

"She's not in any more pain. And that's all that matters. She has ascended. She is in full power again. And we celebrate because she fulfilled her contract. She did everything she came here to do, which is wake people up, and she passed the torch to us, and now we hold the light for her," she explained. After twenty minutes of talking about ascension, she strayed to other topics: twin flames, disdain for President Joe Biden.

Aurora and Hope lay low until May 15, when they finally did a livestream from Vermont, also announcing Mother God's ascension. They registered a nonprofit of their own, one they called "5D Full Disclosure."

Around that time, news broke that the people who had been arrested would face more serious consequences. A deputy district attorney announced that the charges would be amended to "tampering with a deceased human body," which carried a maximum sentence of more than a decade in prison.

By then, investigators understood that Amy had died in Oregon on or around April 16—nearly two weeks before her body was discovered by the police—and her corpse had been transported in the back of a Nissan Rogue for more than 1,200 miles.

As the news spread that Amy's body had been found, family members of people in the group and former Love Has Won followers began to panic about what could happen next. Amanda Ray said, "It was very, very scary." Everyone's minds went to Heaven's Gate—the group in California that committed an act of mass suicide, believing they were leaving their bodies behind so their souls could ascend into passing UFOs.

But after enough time passed, it seemed that the group would simply go on without Amy. There was too much money to be made.

Aurora authored a book that told the story of Mother God and her beliefs, and also adapted it into a children's book. With Hope, she launched a new website for 5D Full Disclosure filled with original content. There were instructional videos. A twenty-four-hour "high vibe" radio station. A podcast. A daily livestream. A blog. It was exactly what Amy had done years before with the Galactic Free Press, the First Contact Ground Crew Team, and 5D News.

But Aurora and Hope appeared to have ideas of their own, creating school curricula for preschool-to-high-school-age children to learn the story of Mother God, and plans for a "New Earth Transitory Government," with a new version of the Constitution. On the group's Telegram channel, people chatted day and night, posting conspiracy theories and pictures of the 144,000. There was Helena Blavatsky. Prince. Bob Marley. Michael Jackson. Trump. Putin. Hitler. And everywhere, there was Amy. They sold new products under the name New Earth Healing: colloidal silver eyedrops for children, adults, and pets. Gaia's nasal spray, containing colloidal silver, plasma copper elixir, plasma gold elixir. They said these products could treat tuberculosis, bubonic plague, malaria, AIDS. In 2022, the FDA sent Aurora, Hope, and New Earth Healing Essentials a warning letter, just like with Love Has Won.

But by 2023, they were simply selling bottles of colloidal silver and colloidal gold for as much as $333 under a new name: Sacred Spirit Apothecary.

Even as a kid, Amy wanted to be onstage. Maybe, in the end, that was what all this was. She was admired and revered; not an actress, or a singer, but a goddess.

"She got her stage show. They did put her on a pedestal. She wanted to be loved," Chelsea said. "She wanted to be that star, and they were giving her that to an extent."

Soon after Amy's death, the story of the mummified cult leader with blue skin created a media frenzy, and the family was inundated with attention from reporters. There were TV specials, podcasts, phone calls from random numbers, trolls on social media, friend requests on Facebook from the followers of Mother God around the world, who used images of Amy as their profile pictures.

"The hardest part is she's still our sister, a daughter, and people act like she was just this crazy weirdo that didn't come from this nice family, and that we shouldn't be grieving her," Chelsea said. "Like, I've had lots of people say she deserved to die for what she'd done. It's just like, you gotta understand, this is still my sister. She didn't seem like my sister, but she was still my sister, you know?"

Ultimately, the charges levied against Amy's followers in Colorado were dropped. When news broke that no one would see consequences for how they handled Amy's dead body, Chelsea was shocked. "It was just sickening," she said, "but there's nothing I can do. I mean, she's gone." The judge sealed off the case files from the public.

"It was terrible," Linda, Amy's mother, said afterward. "Nobody deserved to die like that." Later, a documentary would be released by HBO that captured footage of the group during Amy's last days, and the ways they seemed to be worshipping her body. But it disgusted her family, especially the way Jason—this man who said he loved Amy so much—acted. "Somebody said, 'Well, he must have really loved her,'" Linda said. "But did he really? Is that love? Letting her die like that? I don't think that was love."

Linda watched the footage of the people around Amy, tipping silver to her purple lips, documenting the things they were giving her. It looked like they were slowly killing her. Linda felt fresh anger after the series' release that no one was held accountable for what had unfolded. People who watched the docuseries popped up online to criticize Linda for being a bad mother, for not trying harder to bring her home.

"People think it was so easy to get Amy to come home. It was not that easy. She had to be deprogrammed," Linda said. "She needed big-time help. We didn't know how to do that."

Linda will never be at peace with any of it: The night Amy walked out on her family. The way she left her children behind. The wild theories she spouted online. The way she called herself God and people believed her, then those very people ushered her toward death. "I probably never will be," Linda said. "Because there's doubt in my mind that she wasn't killed."

"They're still advertising. They're still making shirts with Amy's name on it. They're still putting things out there, and I'm like, 'Really?'" she said. "Sometimes I wanna call and talk to them about it, but then I'm like, 'That's not gonna do me any good. They're not gonna listen to me.'"

She learned that lesson from being Amy's mother; a process of living with sorrow and betrayal and continual strife—like the Three of Swords card, where a set of blades pierce through a beating heart.

After his release from jail, Jason Castillo left Colorado, and for a time tried to start a new group called Joy Rains in Mexico. But by the spring of 2023, he was in a Wisconsin jail, arrested on unrelated charges.

When Ryan Kramer walked free in Colorado, he answered the questions of a local news reporter curtly. "God is a woman," he said, words needling and sharp.

"And that's Amy?" the reporter clarified.

"That is correct. Let everyone know that's all I have to say. God is a woman and this whole planet will know," he said. "You will all know."

PART VI

THE ACE OF CUPS

23.

Mother God was found dead by police on Kim Pece's birthday. After her husband John's revelation that he had been faking his belief in Mother God, Kim quit the group entirely—deleting her posts about them, blocking their accounts. She quit and tried to forget it ever happened.

She sent a message to her old neighbor, the one who'd taken the time to ask her about Love Has Won and everything they believed. To the end of a string of messages in which Kim talked reverently of Mother God, she added another.

"Love Has Won is a cult," Kim wrote, "a dangerous organization that has collected God's vulnerable children seeking answers...The mind control is intense and almost got me...It had me for a moment."

But not having Love Has Won left Kim with a huge void in her life. She was back where she'd started, back before she found Mother God. She'd feel angry toward John for betraying her trust but then gratitude that he lied to her. Her mental health plummeted, and she drank wine to numb herself, to cope, to escape. One winter night, in a haze of tequila, she battered herself in the head with her fists and, when John went to put the boys to bed, walked outside to the shed, tied a long scarf around her neck, and pulled tight. It was a cry for help.

"I was just embarrassed and started to think I couldn't trust myself. My kids couldn't trust me. What did I do to them?" she said. "It was the only way I felt that I could get the help that I needed." An ambulance came and she went to the hospital.

After that she tried going to Alcoholics Anonymous, but it wasn't for her. The way people adored the group's founder, and the language they used—it felt like another kind of cult.

She signed up for a mental health treatment program, but because the pandemic was still raging, "they put me in a group scenario online. I tried to log on into a group setting and I couldn't." When she missed two sessions, she was dropped from the program. "They took me off the list and didn't call or check in," Kim said. "Why would you put somebody in an online group setting when I just told you I was deceived and went through like hell on an online group setting?"

On her birthday, after having a spa day with her mom, she heard the news about Amy's body being found in a house in Colorado. It felt like a sign from the universe that she had to keep trying to heal. She said, "Now I can't avoid it."

Kim had heard the term "spiritual emergence," and wondered if, all this time, that was what happened to her. "Spiritual emergence" or "spiritual emergency" was something studied at length by Stanislav and Christina Grof, a psychiatrist and psychotherapist respectively. They defined it as "episodes of nonordinary states of consciousness accompanied by various emotional, perceptual and psychosomatic manifestations." The Grofs argued that spiritual emergencies are "an evolutionary crisis rather than suffering from a mental disease."

"Individuals in this type of crisis experience themselves as being in the middle of the world process, or being the center of all things," the Grofs wrote. People become preoccupied with death and the afterlife and a "return to the beginnings of the world, to creation, the original paradisean state, or the first ancestor."

Oftentimes, people undergoing spiritual emergencies "focus on some cataclysmic clash," they wrote. "Capitalists and communists, Americans and Russians, the white and yellow races, or secret societies against the rest of the world... The process culminates in an apotheosis, in experience of being raised to a highly exalted status, either above all humans, or above the human condition altogether—becoming a world savior or messiah, a king, a president, emperor of the world or even lord of the universe."

Online, Kim encountered a group called Spiritual Emergence Anonymous. She decided she would give an online setting one more try.

Marie Grace B. was raised in what she thinks of as a "scientific family." She was taught to use logic, facts, that "reality is three-dimensional," she explained over a video call from her home in California. In her late sixties, she wore her hair in long gray waves, and wind chimes tolled in a slow breeze around her.

In 1979, Marie Grace was a college student when she started experiencing "just plain altered states of consciousness," she said. She had taken up a regular meditation practice, and each morning sat for a half hour in the stillness of her mind. At first, it helped her.

"Things started really changing inside my consciousness," she recalled. It was like the clarity that meditation gave her deepened: she felt blissful and separate from the stresses of regular life. "But then I started to experience things I kind of didn't believe in," she said. She thought she could read minds. She heard voices. She believed she could sense ghosts around her. She thought she was becoming clairvoyant. At first, she kind of enjoyed what was happening, but then when it didn't stop, she got scared.

"What was fascinating and wonderful at first suddenly felt like I was on a really wild ride," she said. "I suddenly was like, 'I wonder if this is like what people experienced who were going crazy?'"

Things escalated. Not only was her sense of newfound wonder

distracting, but it became clear that people thought she was strange. One day, during a biology class, her professor was explaining DNA replication, and she kept raising her hand to interrupt his lecture with questions.

"And finally, this guy got really irritated at me." Afterward, in the bathroom, she noticed the way other students were looking at her. "I was not fitting in, and I was afraid if I ended up talking to a doctor or a therapist, they'd lock me up in a mental institute."

Eventually she dropped out of college and sequestered herself in a cabin in the Rocky Mountains outside Boulder, Colorado. "I said, 'I think I just need twelve months to chill.' I just moved into this cabin, and I'd go down to this town, down in the valley, and I'd go to the library, and I'd get spiritual literature," she said. "I'll just chill. I'll just figure it out."

For a year she ate rice and beans and read about the mystical side of world religions. "If you look at the Christian saints, they go through these intense periods of suffering and it's like they're misunderstood by their counterparts," she said. "They often go through physical suffering, illnesses, near-death experiences, or jail."

She studied Buddhism, and the lives of yogis, and devoured the *Tao-te Ching*—a foundational Taoist text. "I *got* that book," she said. "I got it in my bones."

But after a year, she was running low on money. Studying had given her a better sense of what might be happening to her, but she still had no idea how she could function in the world. "I kind of made it my goal that I had to survive in society," she said.

She knows how her story sounds—like she took too many drugs and permanently altered her brain. But Marie Grace insists that what happened to her was not triggered by drugs, and if anything, the intense feelings that stuck with her make substances of any kind—drugs, alcohol, caffeine, sugar—seem repulsive. "That's the last thing I need."

This seismic shift never really went away, not entirely. She now thinks she's experienced multiple spiritual awakenings during her life.

"The first was at age twenty-five. I had one at thirty-eight, I had one when I was forty-two and one when I was fifty-seven. And each time, whatever was going on in my life, [my] lifestyle dissolved, and I had to start over again," she said.

One day, she got a "divine message" to enroll in a twelve-step recovery program, but she wasn't an alcoholic. Even so she began attending Al-Anon meetings, a group catering to the loved ones of addicts that has a twelve-step recovery process with steps like "Came to believe that a Power greater than ourselves could restore us to sanity," and "A decision to turn our will and our lives over to the care of God *as we understood Him.*" Marie Grace was particularly interested in the group's twelfth step, which acknowledged that "Having had a spiritual awakening as the result of these steps, we tried to carry this message to others, and to practice these principles in all our affairs."

"I worked the twelve steps," Marie Grace said. "I began over the years to feel like that was really the most spiritual thing I'd ever done. I'd worked with the yogis, and I worked with teachers and enlightened people and churches. I didn't have any prejudice against anything unless they were dubious—a cult, or not ethical. But I felt like that twelve-step program was really inspiring and it really kind of hit the core of what real spirituality is."

The program had been so helpful and fulfilling for her that in 2016, she wondered if it was possible to create something similar for people who had undergone spiritual emergencies. She envisioned a program that could help people ground themselves and integrate into society. One that would have helped her when she came out of the mountains.

Over the years, she'd met other people who had undergone spiritual emergences like she had, and they often described their experiences in terms that felt familiar. Suddenly, they felt raw, like they had no skin; that their thoughts came at such a rapid clip, they couldn't grasp on to any of them; that their consciousness expanded more quickly than they could handle.

"When we were hitting the peak of this spiritual emergence, we didn't care about money. So there were a lot of us living in cars, and vans," she said, "before we can kind of stabilize and get our job and get anchored in society. I thought you know what needs to happen is there needs to be a support system."

Marie Grace asked a friend who'd had a similar spiritual experience if she'd help her formulate a twelve-step program. By 2017, they assembled a pilot group and began to implement it. They called it Spiritual Emergence Anonymous, or SEA.

"Usually, twelve steps ends with a spiritual awakening. So we *started* with the spiritual awakening, and we ended with spiritual transformation," she explained. And they dropped the word "God" from their steps. Instead "we call it the power of goodness."

When SEA opened their virtual doors for public meetings in 2018, they had a strict code not to advertise. "We figured God would send people if we're supposed to do this. And God sent people."

In SEA meetings, everyone only uses their first name. No one shares titles or what they do for work. There's a rule about not dispensing advice. The meetings are free. Word spread. A group formed that spoke only French. Another spoke only Slovakian. SEA remained committed to not blending into the world of spiritual commercialism that seemed to be everywhere on the internet. Marie Grace was not SEA's leader, but just one member of a "service board" committed to aiding the group.

"People are selling themselves as therapists or coaches, they're selling their programs like, 'This is how I can help you,'" she said. "I'm not putting down helping people, but there's a lot of money to be made... there's a lot of money that starts to pass a lot of hands."

By charging money, she said it gives people a sense that they can purchase enlightenment. She calls that "spiritual bypass."

"It's when we use spiritual practices and spiritual ideas to believe that we're farther along a spiritual path than we are, and we bypass or avoid the inner psychological work that it takes to heal ourselves from within," she said. "If it's true spirituality, it's coming spontaneously from inside... It's coming from within. And so you don't make money off of that."

At SEA meetings, people arrive to support and be supported; to listen and be heard; to feel emotionally refilled—like the Ace of Cups. Some are undergoing a spiritual emergence. Some have family members in crisis. Spiritual emergence "has a really strong aspect of loneliness. You want to be with other people," Marie Grace said.

"And that's why it is so appealing to join these movements, these cults."

On a winter day in 2022, the members of the Spiritual Emergence service board popped into the Zoom window one by one from around the United States and Canada. They were all women. Marie Grace called in from California. Kim Pece logged on from New Brunswick.

Teresa, in Calgary, spoke about how she grew up with an awareness of God, and had taken some religious studies classes in college, but wouldn't have considered herself overly religious when she experienced a spiritual emergency in 2003. "I was just basically having a lot of trouble, and having a lot of confusion," she said. She was hospitalized four times, and on each occasion, she was overcome with a surge of religious imagery. "It was like that was the language I was speaking, but I didn't have the community or the rituals to ground it."

Jessica, from Maryland, grew up in the Mormon Church, and then spent time during her young adulthood as a Catholic. In 2021, she was involuntarily hospitalized. "They were thinking I had schizophrenia or bipolar," she said. "But I knew it wasn't. I believe what I had was a spiritual emergency or a spontaneous kundalini awakening."

"It was like an explosion of everything coming at me. It felt like this full download of knowing everything about how the universe works."

Each person discussed how when they described what was happening to them to others, they were treated like they were crazy. Or some were told by people within the New Age community to be grateful for their sudden enlightenment.

"When I went to someone and told them what was going on...

They said, 'Do you realize how many people are trying really hard to get where you are?'" Marie Grace said, smiling.

Kim nodded and laughed. Jessica put her hands over her face—a yoga teacher said something just like that to her. "He was like, 'Oh, you're so blessed,'" she said. "I'm like, 'I feel like I'm dying!'"

"You think you're Jesus," Teresa explained.

"Yes!" Jessica said. "*I was Jesus!*"

"I remember being out on my deck and saying over and over, 'I am not the Messiah. I am not the Messiah.' It was like this faucet was on, and I wanted to turn it off." No one wants to be a God. Not really.

Kim chimed in. She said when she was having her spiritual emergency, all she could do was go online and search for answers. "And that's when I found the New Age cage," she said, laughing, referring to Love Has Won. "The thing with being online is the indoctrination is constant."

Kim talked about Amy, and the members of the service board listened. After some time passed, she came to believe that Amy had also had a spiritual emergency. That maybe they were more alike than she realized, more equal. Not a God and a follower anymore, but two spiritual women in crisis who needed help. This notion helped her forgive, and finally start to heal. "[Amy] was surrounded by people who wouldn't let her out of it," Kim continued. "It just kind of got away. It snowballed...She didn't have anybody around her that supported her in a healthy way. You get taken advantage of when you're vulnerable like that."

The women nodded.

When asked if any sort of traumatic experience had sent them spiraling, Marie Grace pushed back. "I mean, trauma's really popular right now. It's a little highly suspect. A lot of people making a lot of money off creating this department called trauma," she said.

"Well, yeah," Jessica said. "It's like, life is trauma. Like we're all born. That's very traumatic...Trauma is born out of the ills of our culture that's very sick and stressed and cruel to one another."

Kim interjected. "It's more about pain and what are we taught when we feel pain? Or what are we taught to do? What does the dentist do? They numb the pain . . . Numbing has been something I've done my entire life."

"It's learning to be uncomfortable," she said. "And you can't really do that when you're surrounded by people who want to fix the pain."

24.

The speakers for the 2023 Conscious Life Expo came to the Hilton Hotel near the Los Angeles International Airport from around the world. The roster read like a who's who of the modern-day New Age movement: there were channelers, mediums, crystal healers, astrologers, authors of books about near-death experiences, a "holistic hypnotist." There were YouTubers, Instagram influencers who talk about alignment as well as theories of a secret race of reptilians. The leader of an antivaccination group was there, a raw foodist who sells colloidal silver and believes the Earth is flat, an influencer who said the COVID vaccine would implant a chip for "the Beast" to take control of anyone who got it. There was a journalist who investigates aliens, a lawyer who represents alien believers, authors of books on aliens. Many of the speakers had been frequent guests on George Noory's *Coast to Coast AM*; Noory was also a keynote at the expo.

And there was a couple who had started a new group in Ashland, Oregon, where they rebranded themselves as gurus that went by Mother and Father. They claimed they had been mentored by Saint Germain. In Hawaii, and near Mount Shasta, they led retreats about

Lemuria. The pair moved to a $2.6 million ranch in Ashland and, for a time, operated a store that sold golden "elixirs" they claimed were created by monks in the Himalayas for $222 a bottle.

At one session, a pair of residents of the Lemurian Fellowship, located two and a half hours south in Ramona, California, stood at a lectern in a drab conference room, wearing matching tan shirts, and gave a lecture about "Lemuria's Blue Messengers." Their names were Sally Funk and Bob Kappel. Both were seventy-two years old.

"It wasn't that long ago when we would talk to others about Lemuria, hoping it was the first time they had heard about this highly advanced ancient civilization," Bob said to the audience. "This afternoon, you'll hear for the first time about Lemuria's blue messengers."

Next to Bob and Sally was a simple map of Lemuria: black lines on white paper, an outline of the place that they believed used to take up most of the Pacific Ocean, its borders stretching from the western coast of Australia to southern Alaska, where it ran down the coastline of North America all the way to Baja California. The map was the work of a Chicago osteopath named Robert Stelle—or "Dr. Bob"—and an author named Howard Zitko, who believed they were reincarnated Lemurians, and founded the Lemurian Fellowship in 1936. Stelle's writings on Lemuria, which he claimed were from the Akashic Record and were delivered to him by a Master, form the backbone of the group's beliefs and classes.

"First of all," Bob said into the microphone, "how many of you have strong connections to Lemuria or maybe you feel you lived there?"

A few hands went up.

"Well, that's about ten people out of fifty. That's very good," he said. "We can assure you, you likely did. And the reason for that is that many Lemurians are reincarnating today to help re-create the highly advanced civilization that existed on that continent. If you feel a connection to Lemuria, it may very well be a longing in your soul to return to the way of life you once knew. For those of you who are here out of curiosity and don't feel a connection—that might be the rest of you— and that's okay too!"

Bob called for another show of hands: "How many of you believe there is intelligent life existing outside of Earth? Anyone?" The entire room of people raised their hands. "Oh my goodness! Well, this is great being at the expo, it's a terrific audience.

"When I first learned that those who came to Earth to help humanity were angels, I immediately believed them. It was like an inner knowing," Bob said. "The truth is that there are wiser beings than ourselves like God and Christ, who guide us in how we can live in harmony and fulfill our purpose."

He painted a picture of what life was like in the ancient lost continent, which he called "Mu" for short. "The reason why this history is so important for humanity today, because at this point in time, all things are recapitulating," he said. Before it was destroyed, he said Lemuria was a 50,000-year-old civilization that was watched over by angels, who wanted to help humanity, to "enable us to create happiness in life, live closer to God." It was a tranquil place filled with purpose, where honesty and integrity were societal values shared by all. Bob said reports of theft on Lemuria were rare. "Unemployment and poverty? These were unknown," he said. "A workman was considered the equal of an executive." Every person was equal. Everyone was given an education, which started at home, where women cared for children and instructed them on Lemuria's values. But women wanted to be there—caregiving was seen as prestigious and noble.

"If you close your eyes a moment and think of living that way, you can almost feel your shoulders beginning to relax, and the tightness in your chest, your gut, and your back easing just a little bit," Bob said. "It's a nice feeling to have, isn't it?"

According to him, while Mu was an advanced civilization, it had no system of writing, and communications had to be memorized and delivered by messengers, who were highly respected. The messengers traveled the wild, rugged country by foot at night, and "they began to dye their bodies blue with certain berries and herbs," Bob explained. "Even when the moon was out, they could almost melt into the shadows."

The distinguished messenger profession was carried through generations of Lemurians. "After several generations, there was a peculiar change in these children. The skins of both these boys and girls developed a bluish tint, and eventually they were born blue and kept the color all their lives," Bob said.

In the version of Lemuria his fellowship tells, it's a fantasy where everything was once good and equal. They believe we were good eons ago. And for eons, too, that goodness has been absent—vaporized by our collective bad karma. It's a most hopeful version of Lemuria, believing that what was once possible could again be ours.

And yet it was surprising that in that story of good, there's an element of racial hierarchy. That even there in a place of all good things, in Lemuria, one's skin color came with status and privilege. And that didn't feel different at all.

Later, in a Zoom interview, Bob and Sally peered into the camera—both wearing glasses, Bob in a blue Hawaiian-style shirt and Sally in a pastel pink T-shirt. Behind them on an easel was the map of Lemuria that they brought to the expo, the right shoulder of the fabled place running along the West Coast.

Before 2007, when Bob moved to the sixty-acre property of sprawling meadows and flower gardens that houses the Lemurian Fellowship, he was an attorney in Manhattan. He grew up Jewish, and in his twenties he became interested in New Age books and magazines. He read *Atlantis: The Antediluvian World*, by Ignatius Donnelly, the long-dead representative from Minnesota, which mentioned Lemuria. But he wanted more. Something about it felt so familiar to him.

"I was very open about religion," he said. He had heard about the Lemurian Fellowship, and sent away for their reading materials. "For some reason, I read this, it all made sense to me. I didn't have any resistance to it."

Sally, on the other hand, has lived at the Lemurian Fellowship for over fifty years—she moved there from her home state of Virginia when she was 22. "You have to realize that we were both products of the '60s, which was a time of tremendous change. The war of Vietnam, just a time of upheaval when people our age were really wanting to make the world a better place," she said. "I knew that I wanted to do something to help the world, but I just didn't know what it was."

"I was searching," she said. "To me, searching meant you go from the Episcopal Church, to the Lutheran Church."

Before she left for college, her mother gave her a book called *Many Mansions: The Edgar Cayce Story on Reincarnation*, about the prominent channeler. "I thought it was kind of weird, but the more I got into it, the more sense it made to me." Her mother also gave Sally a book from the Lemurian Fellowship. "It resonated so deeply with me. It was exactly what I wanted. Because in it were tools for living, not just living my life as a better person, but the whole purpose of the philosophy is to bring back this better civilization—this purposeful kind and positive civilization that existed on the continent of Lemuria."

They explain that their belief in Lemuria doesn't supplant religion. "It's a spiritual way of life," Bob said. They have people from myriad religions who come to the fellowship. You can be any religion, or no religion, and live the Lemurian way.

They believe in Masters too. Conrad Funk, Sally's husband, who is eighty-six, said, "We usually work with Masters that are right here on Earth. They are human beings—highly advanced human beings. They don't make themselves physically known to us. So we often speak of them as working behind the scenes." They contact them through meditations.

They do not consider themselves Theosophists. They didn't know who Guy Ballard was, or the I AM Activity, had never heard of Ramtha. Mount Shasta holds no special significance for their group.

The property where some members live is called "The Gateway," Sally explained. "It's meant to be the gateway to the new order. And you know there are these names now—the new order, the brotherhood—and they've taken on these awful meanings now. Actually, the new order is meant to be the new world civilization or the new civilization on Earth, which is meant to be a happier civilization."

They don't believe in the New World Order. They laugh when asked about a cabal—that's not their thing either. "We're trying to create a better world. And that includes all people, all races, all creeds, everything," she said.

When asked what life was like in Lemuria, Bob explained that women were equal to men. "In Lemuria," he said, "if you had the ability, the opportunity was there for you to do whatever you wanted to do. So it was a very fair society in that fashion. People weren't held back. If a person didn't get ahead in society, it was because they either didn't have the ability and they needed more training or they just didn't have the inclination to move ahead. It was all up to the individual, but the opportunities were there."

"It isn't the same competitive anxiety that there is now to get ahead," Sally said. "There was more contentment with life and oneself, and one's value through living spiritually and caring for other people."

When questioned if life is like that at the Lemurian Fellowship, they laughed.

"Not yet," Sally said. "We wish." But it does feel like a safe place. "You can leave your cell phone out, you can leave your car keys out and you know nobody is going to take them."

They feel like they're working toward something. Along the way, they have disagreements and conflicts, but work them out. They eat together. They all chip in to make things work: "small things that you don't see on the outside," Sally explained. "Sometimes people will leave things to other people to do. That doesn't happen here. Somebody will come into the community building and empty the dishwasher instead of leaving it for somebody else."

And yet duties seem to fall along the lines of traditional gender roles: Women share cooking duties. Men mow the lawns. They share cleaning and garden work.

They study. They read. They teach classes. They think people are more aware now of Lemuria than ever before. Unlike Love Has Won, the Lemuria Fellowship believes Lemuria was destroyed because people "didn't really follow universal law successfully," Sally said. It wasn't because of some great war with Atlantis. In their teachings, "when the continent of Lemuria sank, Atlantis rose."

"And unfortunately, it went the way of Lemuria. Again, we destroyed ourselves because we're just too stupid to live sometimes. We just can't seem to get it right," Sally said.

"I think these are trying times," Bob continued. "I think the Lemurian masters have a plan. Somehow this is all gonna work out... The masters have assured us that the continent of Mu has already begun to rise."

"Now whatever that means, we don't know," he said. "We certainly don't know the future."

Lemuria is a well-known concept among New Age believers, but seems to be entirely foreign to people who study and work with lemurs—the subject of Philip Lutley Sclater's original 1864 theory.

On a rare sunny early spring morning in Oregon, the ring-tailed lemurs that live at the Oregon Zoo came to settle side by side on a gnarled log. Each turned to face in the same direction, toward the sun. In a long line, they sit like they are in a yoga class: butts perched on logs, legs in front, hands resting on knees.

"They like to warm their bellies," Kate Gilmore, the zoo's curator of primates, said as the last lemur dropped into the line on the other side of a large window, turning her soft white underside toward the light. These animals, sitting here looking like they are worshipping the sun, are the world's oldest primate species.

"They are so far removed from apes and monkeys, it's ridiculous," she said. "Like seventy million years ago, they split off from a common ancestor." Around the corner from the ring-tailed lemurs, past a rocky outcropping, a pair of burlier red-ruffed lemurs keep to themselves.

To understand lemurs, Gilmore prefaced that one must know a little about human evolution—that it's a misperception to think one primate begat a new primate, and then, somewhere along the line—*ta-da!*—there were humans. Evolution is not linear. It's more like a tree, where branches sprout from a trunk, and from those branches, new branches form. "Things just shoot off and become their own thing," Gilmore said.

There are two kinds of primates: simians and prosimians. Humans evolved from simians; so did apes and monkeys.

Lemurs are *pro*simians. There are about a hundred different kinds of lemurs. The tiny mouse lemur weighs around 30 grams—as much as a lightbulb. There's the orange-eyed ring-tailed lemur, the one everyone knows: cute and translatable to plush toys and animated movies. There's the dwarf lemur, which hibernates; there's the pure white sifakas. The strange, bat-eared aye-ayes have long, spindly middle fingers with a ball-and-socket joint, which aid in it eating grubs (but also, as scientists have found, are used for picking its nose). All of them can only be found on the island of Madagascar.

Madagascar itself is a fascinating place, isolated from the rest of the world. It was the last place on Earth to see diverse groups of megafauna go extinct, and "one of the last large habitable regions to be colonized by humans," according to the guidebook *Lemurs of Madagascar.* Madagascar was home to tiny hippos, massive jumping rats. There was *Crocodiles robustus,* a massive crocodile that looked like it had horns, and the "elephant bird," a ten-foot-tall flightless bird that weighed more than a thousand pounds. And there were massive lemurs, too, some as large as gorillas.

The most accepted theory of how lemurs came to live on Madagascar, and only Madagascar, is almost as fantastical as Sclater's continent dissolving into the waters of the ocean.

After the breakup of the supercontinent Gondwana, 200 million years ago, distant ancestors of today's lemurs inadvertently traveled from Africa to Madagascar on large masses of floating vegetation that broke off from the mainland, perhaps in a storm. This is called a "rafting event," or more technically, "oceanic dispersal." And long after Gondwana broke apart and Madagascar became separated from Africa, it stayed joined together with India for another 70 million years.

The idea of animals inadvertently "rafting" to remote islands is not unheard of. In the scientific community, it has explained the existence of several species of reptiles, birds, and primates in places far from their indigenous lands. After hurricanes blasted the Caribbean in 1995, on the coast of the island of Anguilla, fishermen watched a haphazard tangle of trees—a natural raft—float in the water, then collide with the shoreline. Scientists found that several green iguanas that were native to Guadeloupe, an island some 200 miles away, had been on the trees. Within three years, the iguanas had bred a colony in their new Anguilla home.

In 2011, one tectonic plate subducted underneath another, triggering a massive earthquake that sent a 130-foot tsunami into the Tohoku coast of Japan. Months later along the western coast of the United States and Canada scientists discovered some 289 species of mostly invertebrates (like mollusks and worms) within a floating mass of debris, which had inadvertently made a thousands-mile-long oceanic journey.

Once lemurs arrived on Madagascar, they were able to thrive and proliferate relatively free of predation. They could be, according to Gilmore, kind of precious.

"They do *not* like getting wet," Gilmore said. "A lot of them don't like getting their hands sticky. They were allowed to evolve to just be higher maintenance. They were able to afford that luxury."

Which is pretty much the opposite of the apes and monkeys that remained on the mainland of Africa, which "had to be pretty hardcore and just deal, and adapt, and move on," Gilmore said. "These guys could just sit and sun their bellies." It was like when the lemurs arrived on Madagascar, they found utopia.

"A lot of animals that end up on an island kind of become weird and wacky," Gilmore explained. "I mean, if [lemurs] were on an island with monkeys, they would've been wiped out. Monkeys are *way* more aggressive, way more territorial."

Gilmore can understand why Sclater floated his lost continent theory back when he did, long before the concepts of continental drift were accepted science and any rafting event had been documented. "To be fair, the idea of an ancestral primate floating on a raft of grasses to an island also seemed a little strange," she said.

The Mozambique Channel is some 300 miles wide and separates mainland Africa from the island of Madagascar. People didn't think it could have been possible. But then geologists proved that if the waves were moving just right, a rafting event was absolutely feasible. "But of course, it's a freak chance," Gilmore said.

Sclater simply took a swing at a scientific theory and missed. Gilmore pointed out that despite Darwin being so irked over lost continent theories, many people thought his theories were also absurd. "A lot of scientists didn't love Darwin," she said. "It wasn't like he was applauded for these theories, because it took a big hit at religion and creationism."

Lemurs' survival on Madagascar is fascinating in its own right, but it's also the only non-human primate species that is a matriarchy. In the lemur world, one female helms an entire troop of up to thirty individuals, and that leader's daughters and their female progeny outrank all of the males. For the most part, this means that females get preferential access to food and sleeping spots. "We think feeding priority is because females are responsible for carrying babies," Sara Sorraia at Duke University's Lemur Center explained. That takes energy, and their young are carried for months by mothers. Breeding season for ring-tailed lemurs lasts forty-eight hours. "Males have one job two days a year," she said.

Some female leaders are more dominant than others. Some are benevolent. Lemur society is less violent than other primate societies, and when there is violence, it's less extreme. Males and females are generally the same size—no one can really throw their weight around. Lemurs mark their territory with scent, and when irked, they might shake their tails. If a male is eating something a female wants, she might cuff him on the ear and take it. But overall, things stay calm.

Sorraia said that it was only in the 1960s that primate researcher Alison Jolly upended popular notions in primatology by discovering that ring-tailed lemurs' society was matriarchal. "Out of the more than a hundred species of lemurs in Madagascar today, all but just a couple of species are female dominant," Sorraia said. And the ones that aren't female dominant are *co*-dominant. "There is no male-dominant species." For this discovery, Jolly was like a Darwin of her day.

When Jolly died in 2014, the lemur expert Patricia Wright recounted to the *New York Times* just how earth-shattering this research had been. "This was a real surprise to people in the '60s," Wright said. "Female leaders were still so rare. And here comes a woman presenting a model of primates where the females are leaders—effective leaders."

And yet lemur habitats remain some of the most threatened in the world. Forests where lemurs live have been decimated by extractive industries. Much of the land, already extremely infertile, has become "a moonscape of baked red earth" because of slash-and-burn farming practices. Lemur populations are threatened by poachers and subsistence hunters, and in some villages, the presence of an aye-aye is feared, seen as an omen of death and destruction.

There is an irony to this: far away, in America, the New Age movement created Lemuria, a neverworld where females once reigned, where they were queens and seers and high priestesses. And in the real world, one female-dominated primate society exists. It is real. It is threatened. The extraordinary facts of this story have been overlooked entirely.

25.

adison Stroud was seven years old when her mother, Amy Carlson, left without a word. Amy and her father had gotten divorced when Madison was four, and for most of that time, Madison had lived with her paternal grandmother. But she always looked forward to seeing Amy. She was fun. And then, one day, she was gone. "I was just confused that I couldn't see Mommy anymore. I didn't understand why," she said. "Before I found out all of these things she was doing, I idolized her. I mean, that was my mom. I didn't know why she left. I thought she was lost, and I had to go find her."

As a little girl, long before Amy left, Madison wasn't quite sure how to think of her. "I knew that she was my mom," she said, "but I knew she didn't take care of me. I knew I was in this weird situation as a kid, but I didn't understand it."

Amy had always been like a real-life Disney princess, a beautiful woman with a big laugh and a gorgeous singing voice. "I used to love princesses, and I have a memory with my mom in this Aurora dress," she said, referring to the character from *Sleeping Beauty*. Someone took a picture of Amy in the dress, posing with her little girl, and that photograph became Madison's memory.

But that memory often gets clouded out by the others she has of Amy, few of which are good. Years later Madison was twenty-one years old, living in Corsicana, Texas, with her fiancé, working as an adult caregiver in an assisted living facility. Madison gave the sense that finding things to say about Amy was difficult. Most of what she can recall of her mother is an absence—an empty space where there could have been a person.

"I have a memory of her waking up in the morning, and just kind of like darting out of the door. I was trying to get her attention, and she wasn't coming back. I think that became a core memory because she actually did leave later on," she said.

Madison doesn't remember that she had left before; people have told her that when Madison was a baby, Amy left her in a crib all day alone at home. Later that day, her grandmother came over and found Madison. "I had been there all day by myself. All day. Not fed, not changed, not anything. I've been in my crib all day screaming. That's what she had walked into," she said. "She took me and didn't bring me back for a long time."

After Amy left to become Mother God, for long periods of time Madison forgot about her completely. Once, her older brother Cole told her to pull up the Love Has Won channel on YouTube. He said, "'Sis, our mom is a cult leader.' He blatantly just said it like that," she remembered. "I didn't believe him at first... He's my older brother, he messes with me all the time...

"He showed me her YouTube, and I was like, 'You're kidding.'" She sat staring at the screen, watching the woman who was supposed to be their mother refer to herself as Mother God.

"It was so weird. It was so random. Like I just didn't follow it. You didn't know what she was talking about because she sounded so wacko," Madison said. "I didn't understand what she was praising."

Years later, in 2016, Madison was on a school bus coming back from a choir trip when her cell phone rang. It was Amy. "I kind of went along with the conversation. Everything she was saying, I didn't understand. It kind of sounded like she was on drugs." Amy asked if Madison wanted to come stay with her in Florida. "I was like, 'Okay, I'll definitely talk to my grandma about it.'" She knew she wasn't really going to ask. "I just didn't want her to feel sad or anything. Because I knew in my mind, I was like, 'No, I'm not going.'"

It was just a normal day when she learned her mother had died. Nineteen-year-old Madison had just pulled into a gas station to fill up the tank in her car when her aunt Chelsea called.

"She says, 'Hey, before this gets out in the news, I wanted to let you know that Amy died.' And I thought she was kidding. I was like, 'Excuse me? What? Like no, she can't be. That doesn't even make sense,'" she said. They said goodbye, and Madison went on with her day. "It didn't set in for like a week, and then I was in my car, and I had a total meltdown about it 'cause I felt like I could have done something. I felt like I could have done something to help her. But I couldn't. There was no possible way . . . I think we kind of all blamed ourselves for some of it. Like it really shouldn't have happened to her."

Looking at photographs of Amy at the end of her life—blue skin, bony arms—Madison had a hard time even recognizing her. "There was nothing about her that was the same that I had remembered," she remembers. What could she even say?

Mostly, Madison thinks about what parts of Amy might be inside her, lying dormant, waiting to wake up.

"I get very worried about going down the path my mom did," she said. "And all these different drugs going around, and psychedelics, like I'm super afraid to try anything not natural because I don't want to get stuck in a trip, because that seems like kind of what my mom did, was get stuck in a trip."

She and her fiancé, who works as a tow truck driver, are saving up to move out of Texas. They want to move to Colorado—to set up a new life in a new place.

I asked Madison if she noticed the conspiracy theories that her mother talked about becoming more popular. She said yes; it's a confusing time to be alive. "There's just so much these days to think about. People's brains are expanding. People are finding out different things. People are actually going back and looking at this history stuff that actually happened, and not listening to everything our teachers say."

Recently, she'd been getting into a few conspiracy theories of her own. "I've been really into this Antarctic theory that Antarctica is actually like a wall all the way around us, and outside of that wall is actually what they call outer space," she said. "My fiancé can tell you all about it. He got me into it."

"And then the flat Earth theory, he got me into that," she said. "There's a lot of things in it that makes a lot of sense. Like flying a plane, they would have to go down every few thousand feet in order to stay on the Earth, and not go into outer space." But, later, she did more research and decided she didn't believe that.

"It's something different to think about," Madison said of these theories. "You know when you hear something like that, you're like, 'No.' But then you start thinking about it and you're like, 'Well, maybe?'"

Cole Carlson is the only one of Amy's children who really remembers her. That's what he calls her—Amy. It never really felt right to call her Mom.

As a kid, Cole lived with Amy, but they were less like family and more like roommates. She microwaved him Chef Boyardee or Kid Cuisine meals, or brought home bags of McDonald's from work, put it in front of him, and left. "Most of the time I was left alone to just entertain myself. She would mostly sit in the garage drinking a beer, smoking cigarettes," he said. She seemed sad. She cried a lot. "She would go off to karaoke bars and I would be at home." Their neighbor would come over to check on Cole and make sure he went to bed.

He has some memories of Amy being motherly. She used to sing lullabies to him when he was little, and even now, if he hears "You Are My Sunshine," he'll tear up.

But mostly Amy was "stressful." He was a scientifically inclined kid, and it didn't seem like she understood how to talk to him. She would become unpredictably furious with him, and when Cole got in trouble, she resorted to physical punishment. She never shut him in a closet. "She hit me. She spanked me," he said. "And she would put soap in my mouth, but not bar soap, liquid soap, so I always ended up getting sick." Sometimes he would wake up in the morning, and Amy had brought home men she'd met at karaoke; once he recalled walking into the kitchen to find her holding a knife up to a man he'd never seen before. She told Cole to call 911.

His childhood was severed, in a way, when his parents separated. "I had one childhood with a very, very loving and attentive father. He always said if I'm happy, he's happy," he said. "Amy was the polar opposite…if Amy was happy, I should be happy, was her philosophy. My dad would eat dinner with me, would watch TV with me, would play with me. Amy would not."

Sometimes Cole would go long periods of time without seeing Amy. He hadn't seen her in several months once, when he was eight or nine, when she picked him up and brought him to a run-down church near Dallas. Amy told Cole he couldn't come to the service and needed to sit in the basement.

"It really sucked because there was nothing to do. I was the only kid down there. So I was just alone. And there were coloring books, but they were all colored in," he said. "And that's what we did that day."

As he got older, it seemed like the gaps between when he saw Amy got longer and longer. He can't remember ever seeing her on his birthday, which is also Christmas. For his tenth birthday, he planned to see Amy and meet his little brother Aidan. But Amy suddenly disappeared; she left town to meet a man she met online. It didn't last. She came home with stories of abuse, that she'd been locked in a closet and had to flee.

Not long after, Amy picked up Cole and brought him to a Barnes & Noble bookstore one day. There was a book she desperately wanted him to see, and they sat at a table in the store reading a Christian story about two angels. Afterward, sitting in the car in the parking lot, Amy looked at her son with wide eyes.

"She told me I was a crystal-eyed child, and that Maddie was also a crystal-eyed child, and Aidan was a diamond-eyed child or something like that," he said. "Me and Maddie would basically help her get humanity to the New Earth, and Aidan would help her establish the kingdom, and rule it, or something."

Cole had no idea what to say to this.

"I thought she was batshit," he said. "I immediately knew that is not what normal adults tell children. It stuck out to me. It's still one of those things in my head where I look back and I'm like, 'Yes, absolutely. She was already gone at that point.' That was basically the appetizer for what was to come, so to speak."

It wasn't long before Amy would disappear again, and completely. "We had Thanksgiving dinner, and either the next day, or one of the few days after that, she was gone again," he said. Her car was gone. Some of her things were gone. She was "in the wind," Cole said. She didn't say goodbye.

"I was very angry for a really long time," he remembered. "I was just straight-up abandoned by my mother."

Years later, around 2012, Cole started to hear conspiracy theories that the Mayan calendar had predicted that the world would end on December 12—two weeks before his seventeenth birthday. It sounded like something Amy would believe. He tracked her down online, and, sure enough, she was talking like the world was about to end. After watching her on a video, he typed a comment in the chat box, and she sent him her phone number.

"I talked to her on the phone," he said. "And I poured my heart out to her, sobbing, telling her how much it hurts, what she did, and how much it hurt to see the pain that she caused everybody else in my family."

He told Amy how he remembered her own mother, Linda Hay-thorne, collapsing onto the floor shortly after she disappeared, and Cole had to comfort her. "That's not something I could forgive her for. I just asked her, 'How could you say you love me and our family and then do this?'"

The sound of him sobbing through the phone seemed not to affect Amy at all. "She basically said, 'Cole, you're holding on to the past too much. You need to get over it.'"

In a way, that phone call helped dissipate Cole's anger—not because she told him to get over it, but because on the call it felt like he was talking to a different person entirely. "She sounded mentally younger," he said. "She came off like she was oscillating between being an excited child and adult-ish, mentally speaking. . . To this day I can't really come to terms with how much of Amy was in her control. Like, how much of how awful she was because she was legitimately kind of shit, and how much of it was mental illness, untreated, coupled with alcoholism, drug abuse, and childhood abuse that she suffered? I couldn't separate these things. I couldn't really be mad at her anymore."

Over the years, a morbid curiosity would sometimes lead him to her website. He saw she called herself Mother God. "I always thought it was very ironic," he said, "this paradox of this woman who claims to be everybody's mother, but she couldn't even be a mother to three of her own children."

Cole was in college the next time he saw Amy. It was 2017, and he was attending Portland Community College, and she reached out to let him know she was staying at a nearby Airbnb with the Father God of that moment, Andrew. He didn't look much older than Cole. She asked if they could all go to dinner. "I said, you know what? Why not?"

Cole arrived at Amy and Andrew's Airbnb with his partner at that time. But when they got there, Amy was teeming with anxiety and said she couldn't leave. "She was convinced she was under surveillance, and they were trying to kill her. Again, I don't know who *they* are. Some-body was trying to kill her," he said. They got take-out instead from a nearby Indian restaurant. "She talked to me and my then-partner for a while, told us random stupid shit . . . then we left. And that was the last time I saw her."

Every now and then, he would hear from one of her followers on Facebook Messenger. They reached out on behalf of "Mom." Mostly, they told him Amy wanted to get in touch with Cole's little brother, Aidan, who had no interest in speaking with her—a person he had absolutely no recollection of. "She was trying everything that she could think of to form some kind of bond or connection with Aidan," he said. "I don't know how much of that was because she really thoroughly wanted to because she missed out on someone's life, or if, again, it was connected to the fact that he was a 'diamond-eyed child' who was very important for setting up the new kingdom on Earth."

Eventually Cole moved to Germany, where he received his master's degree in microbiology. In 2021, Amy died.

"It was hard to mourn because it's not like I had great feeling for her. You know? I had always kind of hoped maybe one day down the line something would happen and she would either admit herself or get admitted to a hospital for an extended—*extended*—treatment, and I could actually have a conversation with her where she understands the consequences of her actions and showed proper remorse and growth as a human being. I always kind of hoped that. Obviously, she was never going to be normal. But maybe would live to a nice old age and slowly become part of our family again. That didn't happen. She died."

After her death, sometimes Cole would meet people all the way in Germany who already knew that his mother was the cult leader found mummified in a shrine in Colorado. It's happened "more often than I'd like." Sometimes he tried to make a joke of what happened—"How many people can say their mummy was a mummy?"—and other times, he became inexplicably sad, mourning the loss of a person who intentionally lost him.

Cole said Amy wasn't a monster, then relented. "She kind of was. But the truth is reality isn't so simple." Calling her a monster doesn't get at the problem: that she hid underneath a veil of religiosity to scam other people, and that she was hardly the first person, or the hundredth, to do that in America. A whole lineage of people came before her, claiming to be a female God, claiming wisdom from Masters, claiming contact with UFOs, claiming beliefs as facts and facts as lies. None of her ideas were her own, and likely they were so ubiquitous by the time they reached her, she had no idea where they came from. And that will continue. It already has. Her own followers were doing recruiting of their own.

"There's still members of this cult doing activities. There are still people at risk of being scammed—not just by those people, but people like them," he said.

In a way, Cole sees what happened to Amy as the result of a failure of multiple systems, and the way America puts people on a pedestal.

"I think we live in an age where it's generally more acceptable to go see a therapist, but it's still not acceptable to be 'crazy' and need to go to a hospital for an extended period of time because you have a severe disorder. That is still very heavily stigmatized," Cole said. Amy had to process what was happening in her brain in a brutal society—a society that discards anything and anyone that is broken, that prizes beauty and fame and God and money and little else.

"Her life was not as glamorous as she wanted it to be. I think part of that is the messaging in our culture. You're supposed to be a big shot... She was not good enough to be a singer."

Instead, she ended up a manager at McDonald's, a single mother of three children. "I think that in her mind these were not things befitting of Amy Carlson. They were not important enough, big enough. You don't really have a choice in our system. You settle. I think a lot of people have to settle on something that's not their dream because they need to eat. They need to pay for the roof over their head."

Her life was not a fantasy. So she made up stories where the stars and starlets were her Gods. Without fame or money, religion was the only thing that could bring an everyday person the promise of a mystical life.

Cole sometimes thinks about that time she left him in the basement of that church. What were they doing upstairs that she didn't want him to see? By then he was well versed in the ways of the God-fearing. With his father's side of the family, he understood the words and gestures of the Southern Baptist faith. "This might be slightly controversial," he said. "In my head I really don't see that huge of a difference between the megachurch I used to have to go to and Amy's cult. It's just a matter of magnitude, acceptance, and success."

His pastor wore stylish suits. Amy took her followers' donations and bought a car, an ATV, a vacation to Hawaii. "I think there's sort of this foundation laid out for people to use to manipulate and control people," he said.

"Those people who are unscrupulous are the ones that make it to the big, big leagues. Because they step on everybody below them." In a culture where religion is so revered, religious people can get away with just about anything. "You see it with the evangelical Trumpers, the QAnon people. When I listen to some of that kind of stuff, I hear old fire-and-brimstone pastor speak," Cole said. "They're just repurposing this language that's already there. They're using the tools that have already been developed for them."

After the HBO documentary about Amy and her group was released, the director of the film gave an interview to *W Magazine* in which she discussed that Love Has Won could only become popular because the American health care system had failed so many people. It was a generous criticism, but even she seemed to have been duped by the conspiracies at the heart of Love Has Won. "The system is no longer working for anybody," Aurora said in the film. American society is a "constructed reality based on belief systems that are illusionary... You have to exit the Matrix."

The director's assertion seemed to miss the lie at the heart of the group's elaborate performance. It overlooked that Love Has Won was based on a legacy of belief in America, and thrived from a structure in this country that allows people to lie if they say it's in the name of their God. Love Has Won thrived on hate and spread it as far as they could across the internet. Whether or not God being a woman is provable, Amy sold herself as one and got people to sit at her feet while she called drunken rants and conspiracies prophecy. She surrounded herself with those who desperately wanted to believe, and those people fed her, and clothed her, and cared for her needs like she was royalty. She got them to concoct substances that can poison people. Eventually they fed her own poison back to her.

Love Has Won duped people by exploiting the mythology that America loves to recite: that you can *be* somebody if you want it enough. That's what makes this country so free. The freedom to create your own destiny. The freedom to believe in what you want, and who you want. Amy wanted to be worshipped. She found believers willing to do that.

And she benefited from the protections all religions in America get, where all you have to do is sincerely believe in something for it to become sacrosanct. It was what Helena Blavatsky did, what Edna Ballard did, what Elizabeth Clare Prophet did, and what JZ Knight continues to do. They left their old lives to some extent to re-create themselves as the spiritual beings they wanted to be, beyond the reaches of masculine structures. They became enlightened on their own terms, then they offered that enlightenment as a product.

When Amy Carlson's body died in April 2021, she left her followers in the way she had left her family so long ago. But the conspiracies she tapped and stirred stay alive. The very name of her most loyal followers' new venture—5D Full Disclosure—centers on the idea that the truth behind conspiracy theories will be revealed, proving that they were right all along.

Amy might be gone, but she is preserved online, forever young and ready for a new audience to hear her say "Greetings, love beings" every time humanity begins a new cycle of fear and chaos.

"Why wouldn't you buy into it?" Cole said. "Somebody comes along and says, 'Hey, this world sucks, right?...But you know what? I'm gonna build a new world. Come follow me. The aliens are coming. The Earth is ending. The aliens will take us to a new planet, and we can build a new society. How awesome does that sound?' That sounds amazing. Sign me up."

EPILOGUE

A NOTE ON SEEKING

One spring afternoon just before summer solstice, during a week when I was researching this book and the warm days in the Northwest were just beginning, I had been watching videos about Lemuria all day when I decided it was time to take a break and walk outside. I was staying in a beach lodge at the southwesternmost corner of Washington State, where the wind and storms are treacherous and constant. I bought a large, sweet coffee and took a walk on the hard sand. Coming upon a piece of driftwood, I sat and stared at the roiling mass of gray before me, keeping my distance. The day was bright and warm, kept reasonable by the near-constant wind.

My mind was deep into Lemuria, but also on the news that five wealthy aspiring explorers were lost somewhere in the Atlantic Ocean in a deepwater submarine. They'd paid $250,000 apiece to get up close to the ruins of the *Titanic*. It was such a strange story to break through the news cycle of politics, and murder, and war.

The *Titanic* still held a grip on people more than a century after it sank: this out-of-reach temple to human opulence, broken and resting in another realm. The ship had transformed into a watery crypt of poor, third-class passengers and crew members. It was odd to think that the wealthy now pay to get close to it. One man who had previously made the expedition told the *New York Times* that "you just drop like a stone for two and a half hours." It was hard for me to conceive of that kind of depth.

The connections felt almost too on-the-nose. For more than a hundred years, the *Titanic*'s fate had been subject to endless conspiracy theories, including one floated by QAnon that the ship was deliberately wrecked by the Rothschilds—a nineteenth-century Jewish family who built a banking empire in Europe—in their plot to take over the world. The family has remained at the center of antisemitic conspiracy theories ever since.

But then I wondered if I had been steeped in the New Age too long and was starting to search the horizon for connections and correspondences to make this story apply to my own work, to give it purpose and value, and ultimately to make this all about me. It was a circuitous knot of thought.

The lost men had only forty hours of air left, and searchers from around the world were frantically scouring an area twice the size of Connecticut to find them. With Lemuria, I had been thinking so much about James Cameron's *Avatar*, and the blue-skinned humanoids living on another planet, whose existence is threatened by humans' desire to mine their home for resources. With this lost submersible, my frame of reference became another James Cameron film: *The Abyss*. Even the *New York Times* wrote that the story of the lost men was like two James Cameron films—*The Abyss* and *Titanic*—rolled into one.

The Abyss isn't just about being lost in the depths, it's about breathing—about having enough air to make it. In the film, a specialized team of underwater SEALs are sent to recover a missile that has been lost by a submarine that was paralyzed by NTIs—non-terrestrial intelligence. Aliens. But as the team got close, they too became trapped. To save everyone, Bud, the rogue hero played by Ed Harris, donned a suit filled with experimental amniotic fluid, a liquid he must allow to fill his lungs in order to breathe, like an embryo in the womb. He must drown himself to live. At the end, the technology works, and he travels to the NTIs' strange city of color and light, where the universal truth of everything—love—is revealed.

Just south of where I sat, the Pacific Ocean melded with the Columbia River, a deep waterway that splits Washington and Oregon from each other. That spot is called "the Graveyard of the Pacific" because of the way the waves and wind and water create a cyclone of disaster for ships; an estimated 2,000 vessels have met their end there. In fact, it was where the Wilkes Expedition's ship—the *Peacock*—ran aground and caused the men to venture south on foot toward Mount Shasta. People call God all-encompassing, and yet again and again massive oceans test our ability to grasp our planet's size and depth. We see this vastness, but we don't ever seem to truly understand actual power until we try to tangle with it, and by then it's too late.

When I spoke to Duke history professor Sumathi Ramaswamy, she told me that the strange story of Lemuria came across her desk because of something cultural, not religious. Shortly after Philip Lutley Sclater floated his theory about Lemuria, people embraced the idea in the Tamil Nadu region of India. There, Lemuria was "recast as the birthplace of the Tamil people, their ancestral homeland lost catastrophically to the ocean." When the Lemuria theory came to them, their world glittered with a new kind of sheen. They saw themselves as the only living remnant of a lost place. And this belief wasn't something held on to by the fringe; in the 1980s, the head of the government in Tamil Nadu helped create a "documentary" that retold the story of the Tamil people with Lemuria—renamed as Kumari Kandam, or "the virgin continent"—as its origin.

"The story of Lemuria," Ramaswamy said, "is told in schools of a particular kind, that cater to the poor and the already undereducated. It produces a split citizenry where you have certain citizens who are educated in normal history, science, and so on. And then there are people who are the subordinates who are getting this kind of history."

Ramaswamy told me that those beliefs about Lemuria are still held with incredible conviction, and interest in the lost place surges from time to time. In 2004, a tsunami devastated Sumatra, Indonesia, Sri Lanka, Thailand, and India, killing an estimated 228,000 people; the event was triggered when one of the Earth's gigantic tectonic plates in the Indian Ocean slipped underneath another, causing a massive earthquake.

Just before a literal wall of water hit the coast of India, the ocean receded. It was a curious sight. "There were all manner of underwater structures that revealed themselves," Ramaswamy explained.

People claimed they saw temples. "I don't think that was true at all," she said. "But there was all this new fantasy." In the aftermath of the tsunami, another Indian head of state said the truth of Lemuria had been finally revealed. The ocean—"that malignant force that destroyed our culture and our civilization"—had created another reason for the story to start all over again.

She anticipates that this will keep happening: with climate change pressing down on the planet, as ocean levels rise and coastal floods crush and tsunamis obliterate, the unbelievable force of the water and the Earth will only cause more destruction. Where there is destruction, or fear of it, there come new myths.

The paleontologist Renee Love spoke about how evidence of the Earth's face constantly changing is "absolutely everywhere." You just have to know what you're looking at.

When you understand how the Earth operates and get an appreciation for the slow burn of geologic time, everything changes. This place is always moving. We are always moving. All of this is inevitable.

Perhaps then Lemuria can be whatever you want it to be. At its most optimistic, it's the place described by the Lemurian Fellowship where there is no poverty, no war, no gender divides, no class. No lack, no wanting. But every utopia falls apart. The depths of human imagination are endless but unrealistic.

The ocean, on the other hand, is deep, but not infinite. From the beach, it looks like chaos. It crushes and takes and ruins and does it all without remorse. I respect a thing that does not feel. It is both sad and good at the same time. An ultimate kind of power. It is the closest thing to God I can conceive of, and so I try not to stand too close. I sit and revel from a distance, and as I do, it feels ridiculous to think too far into the vast uncertain future. That would seem to miss the point entirely.

ACKNOWLEDGMENTS AND NOTES ON SOURCES

My understanding of the Love Has Won belief system came over a long period of investigation in which I read documents, books, and blogs authored by Amy Carlson and members of her group, and watched Carlson's own videos and hours of her group's livestreams. Interviews with her family—her mother, Linda Haythorne, sister Chelsea Renninger, and children Madison Stroud and Cole Carlson—helped me understand her life through their eyes.

Carlson's ex-partner and one of the first Father Gods, Andrew Profaci, gave me deep insight into the Mother God portion of Carlson's life. The descriptions included in chapters 2 and 21 came from my analysis of police reports and body camera footage obtained through public records requests to Colorado law enforcement agencies, as well as Carlson's autopsy report. My interviews with Kim Pece, Ashley McCoy, and Walter "Riccey" Paschal, each of whom considered themselves followers during various points of Love Has Won's existence, illuminated the inner workings of the group and Carlson's changes over time. Family and friends of members, particularly John Pece, Dan Agos, and Amanda Ray, whose brother's name has been changed, shared their experiences of having loved ones disappear into the group. Multiple interview requests sent to Lauryn Suarez and Ashley Peluso, through their latest venture, went unanswered; Miguel Lamboy also did not return requests for comment.

This is a book grounded in science. My writings about continental drift and plate tectonics were aided by readings throughout history on the topic—from before and after the process was accepted as scientific fact. Renee Love, a paleontologist at the University of Idaho, was indispensable to my understanding of how the Earth's land masses move. The vast array of interpretations of the Lemuria story came from speaking with Duke University history professor Sumathi Ramaswamy, and from her book *The Lost Land of Lemuria: Fabulous Geographies, Catastrophic Histories*. Additionally, I analyzed differing views on the idea—from journalistic coverage throughout history documenting people's belief in Lemuria to New Age writings on lost worlds that present such phenomena as indisputable fact.

The published journalism on the New Age milieu as a whole, and especially the figures discussed in this book, is thin. I conducted interviews with people from across the spectrum: religious studies scholars, believers, seekers, people very much within the movement and people very much trying to flee it. I also consulted a host of books on the topic both from people who believe in the ideas and those who study them from a distance. The following list of sources is not exhaustive: *Women of the Golden Dawn: Rebels and Priestesses* by Mary Greer; writings by Edgar Cayce; *The Channeling Zone: American Spirituality in an Anxious Age* by Michael F. Brown; *A Republic of Mind and Spirit: A Cultural History of American Metaphysical Religion* by Catherine L. Albanese; *Occult America: White House Séances, Ouija Circles, Masons, and the Secret Mystic History of Our Nation* by Mitch Horowitz; *The Burned-over District: The Social and Intellectual History of Enthusiastic Religion in Western New York, 1800–1850* by Whitney R. Cross; *Harper's Encyclopedia of Mystical and Paranormal Experience* by Rosemary Ellen Guiley; *Radical Spirits: Spiritualism and Women's Rights in Nineteenth-Century America* by Ann Braude; *Ripples of the Universe: Spirituality in Sedona, Arizona* by Susannah Crockford, as well as her piece in *The Handbook of UFO Religions*. I also consulted writings by Mary Farrell Bednarowski, Robert Ellwood, Catherine Wessinger, and Nicholas Goodrick-Clarke.

The Fox sisters were controversial figures. I derived my knowledge of the pair from archival newspaper coverage of when they were young girls and their supposed gifts emerged, of their events and séances, and of their eventual demise. I found Barbara Weisberg's *Talking to the Dead: Kate and Maggie Fox and the Rise of Spiritualism*, which reports deeply on the sisters, to be fascinating, and I've quoted it throughout.

Helena Blavatsky was even more controversial than the Fox sisters. My understanding of her was also informed by how reporters portrayed her during her time in New York. I consulted Vsevolod Solovyoff's *A Modern Priestess of Isis* and Richard Hodgson's 1884 report on her for the Society for Psychical Research. I conducted interviews with religion scholars about Blavatsky's influence, and with members of the Theosophical Society based in Portland, Oregon. Additionally, my reading of the biographies *Madame Blavatsky: The Mother of Modern Spirituality* by Gary Lachman and *Madame Blavatsky's Baboon: A History of the Mystics, Mediums, and Misfits Who Brought Spiritualism to America* by Peter Washington helped bring her to life.

For a large portion of my career as a journalist, I have specialized in writing about political and religious extremism in the western United States. As a consequence, my work has often led to an understanding of the staying power of antisemitic conspiracies and hate spread by Henry Ford, a mainstream figure, and William Dudley Pelley, a fringe figure. University of Rio Grande history professor Scott Beekman was generous with his time as I interviewed him about his book *William Dudley Pelley: A Life in Extremism and the Occult*. I conducted research at the University of Washington's Special Collections, which contains an archive of Pelley's work and helped me understand his influence, as well as referencing the files that the FBI kept on Pelley, which demonstrate how law enforcement perceived his activities.

I conducted research and interviews in and around Mount Shasta, California, with a variety of people, from shop owners and workers to vortex tour guides. During one trip, I sat in a supposed vortex and was led in guided meditation to the Lemurian city of Telos, which some believe is inside the mountain. My skepticism, I suppose, was a barrier to my admittance into the fabled place.

James Wilcox and Jude Baldwin, librarians at the College of the Siskiyous in Weed, California, gave me access to their archives on New Age groups, which proved to be a critical repository of information on the I AM Activity, Guy and Edna Ballard, and a host of groups that have chosen to live and worship in Dunsmuir and Mount Shasta. I read analysis of *United States v. Ballard* and the family's cases in the lower courts, as well as FBI files kept on I AM. Additionally, the following books helped me better understand the impact and appeal of the group: *Sincerely Held: American Secularism and Its Believers* by Charles McCrary; *Love Cults and Faith Healers: The Story of America's False Religious Prophets* by Arthur Orrmont; and *Psychic Dictatorship in America* by Gerald B. Bryan. While the Saint Germain Foundation declined to answer my questions, they did provide links to several "I AM" Come! Pageants and mailed me literature.

Elizabeth Clare Prophet existed in the modern age, and I was able to watch many of her speeches and sermons, as well as review coverage in newspapers in California and Montana and the national media. Court transcripts of *Church Universal & Triumphant, Inc. v. Gregory Mull* were a valuable source of information about one man's experience in her orbit. Elizabeth Clare Prophet's daughter Erin was generous to speak to me about her mother. Additionally, Erin's writings as a religious studies scholar and her book *Prophet's Daughter: My Life with Elizabeth Clare Prophet Inside the Church Universal and Triumphant* offered indispensable insight into her mother's life from the perspective of a family member. I also consulted Elizabeth's own memoir, *In My Own Words: Memoirs of a Twentieth-Century Mystic*, to understand her early life.

I have David Irwin-Detrick to thank for introducing himself in a Missoula, Montana, bar and sparking my interest in Ramtha's teachings. Irwin-Detrick, as well as Carla, Aaron, and Kristin (all of whose names have been changed) generously shared their experiences with me during hours of interviews. A spokesperson at Ramtha's School of Enlightenment said, "JZ, Ramtha, and RSE are not 'New Age,' although many people classify us that way. So it is not important to us to be represented in your book." My interview requests were declined. Details of Knight's early life were drawn from her 2004 memoir, *A State of Mind: My Story*. Throughout the 1980s and 1990s, as Knight channeled Ramtha on stages around the world, newspaper coverage of her events increased and television programs gave context on her impact.

Interviews with Marie Grace B. and six other participants in Spiritual Emergence Anonymous helped me understand one path out of traumatic spiritual experiences for some people. Additionally, Sally Funk and Bob Kappel were generous with their time in explaining to me what life is like at the Lemurian Fellowship, where the tale of Lemuria is believed in but conspiracy theories are not entertained.

The staff at the Oregon Zoo was kind to show me around the lemur facility; I give credit to Kelsey Wallace and Hova Najarian for understanding that this project, while about spirituality, also had a tie-in to lemurs. Kate Gilmore and Jason Delibero have much better things to do with their time than speak to a reporter writing about Lemuria, but they did so with enthusiasm. The same thanks goes to Matt Borths, curator of fossils at the Duke Lemur Center, and Sara Sorraia, who turned me toward the writings of Dr. Alison Jolly.

Tarot cards are used throughout as a thematic tool to organize the narrative and tap into archetypal meanings. If readers view this as a spread of cards to interpret, it is up to them to derive their own conclusions. Tarot and divination cards were my entry to the world of the New Age; they were also a discernment tool used by Love Has Won. I had early conversations about this book with the poet, artist, and scholar Coleman Stevenson, whose highly intellectual classes on divination, tarot, creativity, and writing were my light in the dark through the pandemic. I thank her for giving me ideas for research and for being a sounding board.

The writers Sheri Boggs and Kris Dinnison gave me careful direction on early drafts that helped me steer a narrative of such size. Later, Heidi Groover and B. Toastie Oaster, two of the finest reporters in the Pacific Northwest, offered me their sharp eyes and keen journalistic senses, which improved the project by leaps and bounds. My friend Justin Foley, my sister-in-law, Karen Sottile, and my mother, Sue Sottile, all weighed in with critical feedback. I'm grateful to my friend, the poet and musician Steve Von Till, for giving me his blessing to use a line from a song by his band, Neurosis, as the title of this book. Lastly, my long friendship with Chuck Canfield, and a mutual interest in all things strange, was early inspiration for this work.

This project was written across the western United States at any place I could find where someone would let me stay awhile and write undisturbed. Two of those places happened to be the homes of long-passed western writers I admire. I wrote my book proposal inside the 1894 miner's cottage long owned by Edwin Dobbs, which sits on a hill above Butte, Montana, as a snowstorm raged outside. I have Christy Hays and the Dear Butte program to thank for bringing me into the fold. I spent much time researching and writing in the quiet rammed-earth house of the author Clyde Rice, on the banks of Oregon's Clackamas River. And I was generously afforded multiple artist residencies at Sou'wester Historic Lodge in Seaview, Washington, where the bulk of this text took shape.

I owe much thanks to the librarians and booksellers who have championed my work over the years, and to the loyal subscribers of my newsletter who have kept me funded and fed during lean times.

It is a strange time to be publishing books and making journalism. I'm lucky to have my agent, Joe Veltre, and all the good people at Gersh, in my corner of the ring.

Matt Giles fact-checked this book and more than a dozen other projects I've written before this one. I consider him a trusted partner in my process and could not have done any of it without him.

Writing a book on New Age ideas for such a prolonged period

means some of those ideas soak in. At times it felt fated that this manuscript ended up in the hands of my editor, Maddie Caldwell, who was meant to work on this project, and provided me brilliant guidance and encouragement along the way. I thank the staff at Hachette and Grand Central Publishing for giving so much support.

This book is dedicated to my husband, Joe Preston: my first editor, first reader, the person who helps me nurture ideas and who, when it's time to take a break, takes me out into the trees. A long time ago, I told him that, one day, I would like to write books. He has never once wavered in helping me achieve that goal.

ABOUT THE AUTHOR

Leah Sottile is the author of *When the Moon Turns to Blood: Lori Vallow, Chad Daybell, and a Story of Murder, Wild Faith, and End Times.* Her investigations, features, and essays have been published by the *New York Times Magazine*, the *Washington Post*, *Playboy*, *Rolling Stone*, *The Atlantic*, and *High Country News*. She is the host of the investigative podcasts *Hush*, *Burn Wild*, *Two Minutes Past Nine*, and *Bundyville*. She lives in Oregon.